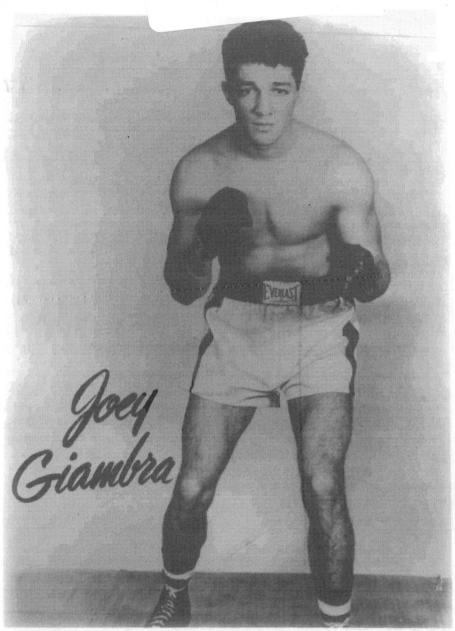

THE UNCROWNED CHAMPION

Boxing and the Mafia in the Golden Era

Joey Giambra, Gina Giambra, and Joey Giambra Jr.

authorHOUSE®

AuthorHouse™
1663 Liberty Drive
Bloomington, IN 47403
www.authorhouse.com
Phone: 1-800-839-8640

First published by AuthorHouse 3/12/2010

ISBN: 978-1-4490-5072-6 (e)
ISBN: 978-1-4490-5071-9 (sc)
ISBN: 978-1-4490-5070-2 (hc)

Library of Congress Control Number: 2009912139

Printed in the United States of America
Bloomington, Indiana

This book is printed on acid-free paper.

Contents

Places, Times, and Names have not been changed. This is a true TELL ALL of actual events and times. Reader discretion is advised

Chapter One

It was 1965, and a blizzardy day in Beckett, MA. The driver of a brand new Chevy Caprice lost control and hit a mountainside. The front wheels of the car straddled over a deep drainage ditch while the rear wheels rested on the highway. The drivers' head went   through the windshield in whiteout conditions.

The handsome face was torn and bleeding. The shirt was blood soaked and sagged terribly over the chest. The curly black hair was wet with snow and matted with blood. It seemed to form a crown of thorns on the small pillow under the seemingly crushed head. The priest had taken one look at the young man being taken from the station wagon and then began running to him.

"Who is he?" the priest asked the attendant as he ran along beside the stretcher.

"Joe Giambra, the middleweight contender," the attendant replied. "Don't you follow boxing?" he muttered.

Joey could barely hear the attendant's reply, but he could see the hospital corridor, and he could hear the priest speaking in Latin. On the verge of shock, Joey suddenly rasped barely intelligible words. "Hey! What's that? What are those words?"

The priest, queasy with his own inexperience, heard the fear in Joey's voice. "It's all right, my son," he panted, trying to keep up with the running attendants. "I'm just speaking Latin."

"Hell, I know that. I been going to church all of my life," Joey mumbled. "Just don't remember those words."

The priest gulped, "I am giving you … the last rights," he replied.

"What? Last rights?" Joey said.

"You have a nasty head wound … and you lost a lot of blood. You have a fractured rib … You might slip into a coma and …"

"But am I that bad? I can't be. I'm going to be champion, and I can't die!" Joey tried to sit up on the stretcher yelling.

And the priest said, "It is in the hands of *God*," as he switched back into Latin and continued.

Joey could feel the newfound awareness ebbing and had only one thought: he was going to die and no one would even know. His eyes suddenly filled with tears. *I am all alone,* he thought. In front of the stretcher, Joey saw doors swinging open and realized he was entering the operating room. He clenched his jaw in spite of the pain, trying to stem the flow of tears. Suddenly, the lights above him were very bright, and he could hear the snipping of scissors cutting scar tissue from his forehead and feel them stitch him back up after someone began cutting off his clothing. He closed his eyes against the glaring whiteness of the lights and felt his consciousness ebbing. Joey felt tears run down his face as he remembered hearing how people's lives passed before them as they were dying. *That's what's happening,* he realized. *The priest was right; I am dying.*

A sharp head pain caused him to grimace, and in that bright darkness, he felt his body levitate against the surgical lights. He looked down at the team of panicked doctors reacting to the loudly beeping heart monitor nearly flat lining as the trauma doctor screamed, "More plasma! More plasma!"

As Joey heard all of this, he floated down, reentering his body. He opened his eyes, looked at the surgical lights, and shot through them like a rocket to space. As he went through the layers of the universe, he felt a quick shot of heat to his head. It felt as if it was the sun. And when he opened his eyes again, he was climbing up a small hill in his hospital gown, and he felt the air hitting the opening as he climbed. Suddenly, just before he reached the top, he heard children's laughter from beyond the small hill. He started for the top and then stood there. He saw women and men laughing and in conversation, holding goblets of nectar, some chasing each other. There were also young children playing with small white rabbits, young deer, and birds all around. It was like euphoria, the Garden of Eden, maybe even heaven. Joey wanted so badly to join them, but as he tried to take his first step, he realized his feet were stuck to the earth. Just then, he heard a thundering voice loudly saying, "Go back! You are not ready yet!"

He shouted to where the voice came from, "Who are you? Where am I?"

Again, the thundering voice loudly said, "Go back! You're not ready for us yet!"

Just then, a big gust of wind pushed him back, and he began tumbling backward in a ball. At the end of the roll, he bumped his head on a rock, and suddenly, he became a three-year-old boy, bumping his head as he crawled, screaming and crying, under a bed. (His entire life from when he was three-year-old boy, all the way to when he was a thirty-three-year-old man, his whole life in between this time frame happened as he ebbed in and out of consciousness.) So here it goes …

The Beginning (Ages 3–15) 1934–46

Joey, who was about three years of age, was playing by the potbelly stove, and his mother was cooking. His father came in after drinking most of the afternoon. It took only a few words from the quiet, pregnant Rosina for that rage of his father's to escape, and he looked at her and slapped her away from the stove. He said, *"Strashanad, butane, disgracia"* (tramp, whore, disgrace that you are). He claimed that the baby she was carrying wasn't his, but rather the baby of his father's best friend, Mr. Mike Fulletta, who was also the accused father of Rosina's last baby. He would visit Joey's mother when Joey's father wasn't at the house so he assumed that Mr. Fulletta was his mother's lover and had gotten her pregnant. So as he was angling her toward the bed, which was right off the kitchen (the bedroom was the only bedroom in the place; the rest of them slept on the floor), Joey crawled really quickly under the bed and bumped his forehead, eerily, right on the spot where he went through the windshield of the crashed car, which we mentioned earlier.

Now as his father pulled Rosina's hair back, he grabbed a coffeepot from the four-burner potbelly stove and raised his arm to the scared Rosina. She screamed, "Mikelle, Michael, what you do this to me? Why you hit me?"

And in Italian, they were yelling to each other.

"The baby is not mine! It's Mr. Fulletta's. You think I'ma stupid!" he yelled.

And she kept saying, "No! No! The baby is yours! I don't do that with anybody. You the fatha."

When Joey had gotten under there just securely enough to look out where all he could see and hear were the feet going back and forth and the screaming, all of a sudden, his mother was pushed onto the bed, and the spring came down on his head because it was really low. And It hit Joey again on the forehead. He was crying, and then he heard his mother cry as well. She was crying too, because she had just been hit with the coffeepot on the head by his father. He didn't know how many times his father struck her because he couldn't see. And just as his father was ready to finish the job, his brother, Angelo, who happened to be on his way home, heard there was a lot of trouble in the apartment. So summoned from the street, he ran up the three flights of stairs to the apartment. The door was open, and when Angelo saw his father ready to give a final blow with the coffeepot to his mother's head, he grabbed his father by the shirt collar, pulled him off of her, and pushed him on the floor. Angelo was short; his father was about five feet eight and a half inches tall. Angelo was about five feet seven, but he was a good street fighter. He dragged him to the door and threw him down at least one flight of stairs saying, "If you ever come back, I'll kill ya!"

Their father responded with, "*Disgraciata!* You motha, she's a bumb … she's a tramp." He was making remarks to his brother, Angelo. He didn't know any better why his father would try to kill his mother.

In the meantime, the managers of the building had called the police. And then when his father got down to the first floor, the police were there waiting for him. They brought him back upstairs with handcuffs, and they asked his brother, "What happened over here?"

Angelo said, "My father had a fight with my mother." But he didn't know himself what had caused it or why their father would do all that. It came out that he thought that his mother's pregnancy was not by him but by his friend and that was why he hit her. Then Angelo was told that they were taking their father to jail. After everything had calmed down, a few months later—Joey's father was in jail the whole time awaiting trial—they went to court for their father's trial. The judge found him guilty. His mother had a bandage on her head. They were all sitting next to each other. Joey's sister Connie was there and of course his brother Angelo, but the rest of the eleven kids were at the house.

When they found his father guilty, the judge said, "Do you have anything to say before I find you guilty?"

He tried to explain to the judge that he believed that his wife had had an affair with his best friend and that was why she was pregnant and that it wasn't his baby.

The judge said, "It doesn't make any difference why. I am going to put you away in jail."

Just then, his mother jumped up and said, "Pleasa, Judge, my husband's a gooda man. He just a have a no job. He so bad cause he's unhappy. I don't blame him, and he is the father."

And that was it, and as his mother spoke up for his father, he said, "I don't want to go back to you."

The judge said, "Well, you're going to leave Buffalo, New York. We'll give you bus fare, but you are not going come back and bother your wife anymore. Now I'm going to release you from custody, and the police will take you to your house to get some clothes, and then they will take you to the bus terminal."

Afterward, Joey's father, Mike, moved to Chicago and worked for a friend of his brother, who owned a restaurant. Joey's father was said to be an amazing chef. Later, Mike would buy this restaurant. It was the only restaurant in the stockyard and would later be worth a gold mine. A Jewish organization tried to buy the restaurant, and when he wouldn't sell, they bombed his place in 1941. They eventually talked Mike into selling. Soon after, Mike moved in with his brother

Bill (whom Joey was originally named after). He was the manager of the Ford Motor Company in Detroit.

Moving forward, Joey was six years old when he started escorting his mother to and from the market. They always walked quickly, for in the Italian ghetto, anything could happen and often did. One afternoon, they were walking quickly past an alley, when two "toughs" grabbed Rosina and dragged her into the alley. One held her arms and covered her mouth while the other ripped off her dress. Joey yelled and screamed as he flailed away at the one pulling off his mother's dress but was easily shrugged off. He ran to the street and began yelling for help as he watched the two men pull his mother deeper into the alley. Out of nowhere, Angelo appeared. He charged down the alley without asking what was wrong as Joey continued yelling for help. But Angelo didn't need help. After only a few seconds, the two men had run away, and Angelo was trying to cover his mother. Rosina was badly bruised but hadn't been raped. The incident, however, caused changes in all of their lives. Angelo quit school and went to work as mechanic, later earning enough money to move the entire family out of the tenement on Terrace Avenue to a better neighborhood. Two of the girls also quit school and went to work. Finally, the years of being on welfare ended for the Giambra family. The next few years found Joey and his mother moving every few months, living like Gypsies, off welfare but still unable to pay rent. Between moves, they would survive by staying in an old wooden shed behind the house of a friend. The floor and blanket became a communal bed. Rain or snow, hot or cold, the weather outside was the weather inside.

They had moved in and were living at his Brother Angelo's house temporarily until they found another place. Angelo was married, but there were thirteen of them, so they took up all the bedrooms with the other kids. One day, after Joey turned seven, while celebrating his first Communion, they were all on Angelo's porch when Joey saw his father get out of the car with his uncle Bill. Joey got really uptight, because the last time he had seen his father, he had tried to kill his mother with a coffeepot and he was scared. So he hung on his mother's arm.

His father was looking up, saying, "Guillermo! Guillermo!" In Italian, it meant Billy—William, which was Joey. Joey had been named after his uncle Bill who had just showed up with his father. He said, "Guillermo, Guillermo, come to your father," with a slight Italian accent. But see, in his father's mind, Joey was the last baby he had had. He was his son. He knew Joey was his kid, he said, and wanted to take Joey back to Italy with him. Now Mary, his kid sister, the baby Rosina had been carrying, was born after Joey, when Joey was two going on three. She was also the last born to Rosina and Mike. So he called Joey down to him, "Come down and kiss your father."

But Joey just held his mother tightly and wouldn't move. He didn't want to go down to him. His mother said, "Go to your father."

Joey said sadly, almost crying, "No! No! He's not my father; he tried to kill you!"

And Mike wouldn't come up to the step where the young Joey's mother was standing either. There were stairs and a porch-like area where Angelo and the rest of the family were standing. So Joey's uncle Bill came up the steps. He picked Joey up and put him in his arms, while saying, "You made your first Communion and all that." He reached into his pocket and took out his wallet. He took out a five-dollar bill and handed it to him.

Joey looked at it and said, "What's this, Uncle? What's this?"

He said, "This is five dollaz. Don't spend it all in one place," with a slight Italian accent as he put Joey down. He went back to his mother. His father wanted to hug him and kiss him good-bye because he was going back to his home place. The rest of the family didn't know that.

So then, his uncle said, "Uh, well, itsa gooda this way. He's a not a going to be here no more. He's going to Italia."

So then they jumped in the car. They all said good-bye, and then he left. He never got a chance to pay attention to the hurt and love left in Rosina's eyes. He still wouldn't give in. His father was still adamant. "No, that's not my baby. That little girl's not my baby," he said in an Italian accent; it was a little girl, his sister Mary.

He wasn't there when she was born, and Joey never saw his father again.

Now between ages seven and twelve, Joey sold newspapers, sang in saloons and on the street corners, shined shoes, and did everything he could to earn pennies, all of which he gave to his mother. By the time Joey was a few weeks from thirteen, he was left with no choice but to join one of the many gangs around. The gangs would fight each other but would team up and fight any individual who did not belong to a gang. You couldn't survive without a gang's protection. But although Joey could fight, he was always the first to run from a fight and the last one to get into a fight. One evening as Joey was on the way home with his pennies earned that day, two older boys began to chase him. Though he ran through alleys, they caught him and hit him a few times, but somehow, he got away. As they chased him again, he climbed a tree in his terror. They laughed as they looked up at the trembling Joey crouched in the tree. One began to climb up after him. Suddenly, Joey felt like one of his comic book heroes: Batman. He stood up in the tree, paused dramatically with his arms outstretched, and jumped, convinced he could fly to the roof and get a way from the boys. Much later, he was discovered on the concrete lying on his back. For a long time, as he lay in the hospital, Joey didn't know who he was or even who his mother was. It was two days before the amnesia left him, and two weeks before he left the hospital. No bones had been broken, but he did have an injury to the lower spine that would force him to develop his body or suffer back trouble the rest of his life. After the doctor told him this, Joey thought about the gang fights that would never stop and the "toughs" who were always chasing him, and he thought about how professional fighters were always exercising and training.

Joey was shining shoes at the neighborhood bars and restaurants. It was 1943, and he was twelve years old. He shined the shoes of Vito Domiano (aka Buck Jones). Domiano was the Mob underboss of Western New York (Buffalo). He gave Joey his first ten-dollar bill; he kind of liked Joey. Also, Joey gave him his best shoe shine. Joey would run into him twice a week, and Domiano would always give him a ten-dollar bill. Joey never knew at the time that Domiano would become a key person in his life.

The thoughts blended so naturally that Joey suddenly knew he must learn to fight. He had been out of the hospital only a few days when he went to a boys' club in the neighborhood. He told them he wanted to learn to fight. The attendant sent him to a brute of a man they called "the Boss." The Boss was older and at least twenty pounds heavier. He grinned sadistically when Joey repeated his desire to him. "Put some gloves on, kid!" He yelled. He reached for a pair himself and began lacing them on. "We gotta see if you have any natural ability first, kid." He looked down at Joey, who was trembling so they had to hold his hands to lace up the gloves.

When they rang a makeshift bell, he put up his hands and began running away from the smirking Boss. As Joey was forced against the ropes, he saw a roundhouse punch coming at his head. He instinctively ducked and countered with a right cross thrown upwards and caught the Boss right on the button, flooring him. Joey knew he had hurt his opponent and was afraid of the rage which he knew would result in him being beaten severely. But when the Boss got up, in place of the smirk was a genuine smile. "I'll be damned," he said while rubbing his jaw. "Nobody ever did that before."

By the time he was thirteen, he had learned all that the boys' club could teach him about boxing. He decided to join Mickey's Gym, a place more dedicated to boxing, and found himself with about forty other young fighters. He was still shining shoes and still taking the money to his mother every day after working out at the gym. Once, on the way home from the gym, he dropped into a bar, which was owned by Ralph Martin, thinking he could make a few bucks shining shoes. Everyone seemed to be extremely happy inside, and it was infectious. Within minutes, Joey was singing while he was shining boots and was being thoroughly enjoyed by everyone inside. There was a woman who was especially kind to him. She insisted that the men who were having their boots shined tip him. As Joey dropped by the bar each night, they got to be good friends. One night, when there weren't too many people in the bar, she told him about herself. He was amazed to find out that the bar was for lesbians and homosexuals; the owner himself was bisexual and would wear makeup. Joey was told all of this by Georgia. Then Georgia gave Joey his first bit of education in sex, explaining that she was a lesbian. She had been straight before she left her husband after her son was killed by a speeding car. Soon after, she moved in with her girlfriend who was very attentive, sympathetic, and understanding. She kept feeding Georgia booze and was so gentle that Georgia simply floated in a semiconscious state through the first night of lovemaking. The experience and the subsequent ones proved to be so much more satisfying than what she had previously known that it became her way of life. After a couple of years, however, the affair ended, and Georgia was now a bachelor lady.

Joey still didn't understand about lesbians until one night when he began to dance to a Jimmy Dorsey record. He was joined by a little blonde who came out of a back booth, just walked over, and started moving in on him. Soon, the crowd was applauding and yelling at the dancing. Joey felt eyes on him, and it felt great. For once, other people in a group were noticing him. He began to try a few intricate moves, when suddenly, he was grabbed from behind and slammed to the floor. He felt a solid kick to the ribs and then saw a switchblade at his throat. A mean bull dyke was ready to cut him, not withstanding his plea that he was only dancing. She just kept yelling, "Stay away from my woman, you punk!" She would have probably cut him, if it wasn't for Georgia, who walked over and kicked the bull dyke in the face. Joey listened as Georgia explained to never mess with any woman in the club because they were all taken or were waiting for a lesbian lover. He didn't say anything, but when he left that night, he knew he would never be back.

Joey was thirteen when he had his first fight. When he was ready to learn how to fight and protect himself, he went to Mickey's Gym and started training himself. After about two weeks, Joey was asked by Mickey McInerny, the gym's owner, if he "wanted to go up to Canada and fight one of the fights."

Joey told him he had never fought before.

Mickey told him that didn't matter and that he looked good in there. So Joey said, "Okay. Where is it?"

Mickey told him it was in Oshua, Ontario, Canada.

Joey asked, "How far away is that from Buffalo?"

And Mickey said, "About a hundred and fifty miles."

Joey had never been that far away from the house. He was to take on the champion of Canada. Joey didn't know. He had never fought before. He was thirteen at this time. So when they got to the fight—they had eight classes of fighters in those days—Joey was in the featherweight class. There was flyweight, bantamweight, featherweight, lightweight, welterweight, middleweight, and heavyweight. Joey took the featherweight champion fight. The featherweight guy weighed more than Joey who weighed in at one hundred and twenty. The maximum weight was one hundred twenty-six pounds, and Joey's Canadian opponent weighed one hundred thirty-five. They cheated a lot on the weight then. All he had to wear for boxing attire was sneakers, bathing trunks, and a towel for a robe. He was a poor kid. He couldn't afford gear. They put a Canadian guy in his corner as a second. (The first is the manager, and the second is the trainer assisting the manager.) When Joey's opponent came in the ring, he got a standing ovation. He had all this beautiful stuff on, nice shoes and all that kind of stuff. He had a two-day growth of beard. And he was the featherweight champion of Canada. But Joey didn't know because he was only thirteen (he was supposedly sixteen). They didn't check his weight or his age.

The Canadian guy working in his corner said, "Are you scared?" This guy looked mean to young Joey. He had a badly healed broken nose.

Joey said, "Yeah. He's going to kill me."

The guy said, "Try to land the first punch. See, then you have a chance, but if you miss ... you better run like hell," which was funny.

So when the bell rang and he came out of the corner, real mean-like, Joey just put his hands up to his face to protect himself. When his opponent threw the two punches, Joey threw his right hand right in the middle and knocked him out. He went down, and they started counting, "One … two, three … Go back to your corner," the referee told young Joey. Joey was scrambling around the ring trying to find his neutral corner. Then, the referee started over, at that point everyone knew what was going on. "One … two … three … one … two … three …"

Finally, the people got disgusted and started booing the referee and saying, "The guy's out. He's just laying there. The American won the fight."

Finally, he raised Joey's hand. Joey went back to his dressing room. He was the only fighter that night to win the championship out of the group from Buffalo. Joey's brother Sammy was fighting the main event middleweight championship under a fictitious name, Jimmy Di Jumpatista, a Polish name belonging to the fighter who was supposed to fight but had gotten sick. His brother Sammy became Jimmy Di Jumpatista. Joey took his shower really fast so he didn't miss his brother's fight. There were no seats; it was a sold-out arena.

One guy by the apron said, "Hey, Joey, come here. I want to talk to you. You are a good fighter."

Joey didn't know who he was but went to sit down. It was right next to the ring, you know. Sammy and the opponent came out, and Sammy looked scared. His opponent was an Olympic boxer. That's how good this guy was. So when the bell rang, the guy threw a punch at Sammy, and Sammy went down. The guy never even hit Sammy. He faked the knockout.

Joey said, "Sammy, what are you doing? Get up! He didn't even hit you."

Sammy said, "Get the hell outta here!" as he peeked at Joey after faking the fall.

Joey couldn't believe what had just happened. So they got back to the dressing room, and Sammy said, "What, are you crazy? They might not pay me the money!"

They were to get thirty-five dollars and any meal on the menu if they won or five dollars and a hamburger sandwich if they lost. Either way, it was a lot of money.

Sammy said, "I'm not using my real name. Why should I take a beating for this guy?"

So they sat there and ate hamburger sandwiches. Joey asked his big brother Sammy if he felt bad for going down. He said he was a Giambra.

Sammy said, "You punk, you got lucky."

So they went back to Buffalo. And when they both arrived at their mamma's house, she was waiting up for them because it was about 3:00 AM and they never came home late. They knocked on the door, and Rosina answered. She said in an Italian accent, "Who are you? What do you want?"

Joey said, "No, it's us, Billy and Sammy."

She said, "Where you been all night?"

Joey put his hand in his pocket, pulled out the thirty-five dollars, and said, "Look, Mom, I was working."

Thirty-five dollars in those days was like a thousand bucks, and she looked at the money. She said, "Oh, you work. That's why you're late?" She had the broom in her hand and was ready to whack them with it. Sammy wasn't afraid of her, but he would act it out. She said, "You're a gooda boy. You bringa money to Mamma."

Joey said, "Mamma, you want me to work the same job, I might come home a little late, ya know." And that was Joey's first fight at thirteen.

So moving forward, in spite of Georgia's sexual descriptions earlier on, Joey was still a virgin. He had seen pictures, but he had no idea how to make love or even seduce a girl. Like most of his peers, he was so afraid of being refused that he dared not try. But his brother Sammy wasn't afraid. He was older and was always telling Joey about his conquests. Joey wanted Sammy to fix him up with a girl but again was afraid to even ask out of fear Sammy would laugh.

Joey probably would have remained a virgin for at least another year if it wasn't for a girl named Ruth. He didn't even know Ruth, but he knew her boyfriend, Max, somewhat from the gay and lesbian bar. One day, they hailed him when he was walking, and Max offered him a ride with them. Max let him drive the car when they got out of the city, and Joey didn't know which excited him the most: driving the car or feeling the warmth of Ruth's thigh up against his. Max guided him to an isolated tavern in the country and got out, saying that he had some business to take care of and to wait for him. When Max went into the bar to get a drink, Ruth moved closer to Joey, exposing even more of her thigh. Joey was wondering what he could say when Ruth slid her hands between Joey's legs and began unzipping his pants.

"Wha … What are you doing?" he said.

"Don't worry, Joey," Ruth replied. "I just like you, and this looked so good swelling in your pants, I just had to see it." She took it in her hands and sighed, sexually.

"But … but what about Max?" Joey stuttered, wanting her to stop but continue at the same time.

"Oh don't worry about Max, honey. He doesn't mind. Besides, he likes you too," she purred.

Joey was confused and said, "I didn't know Max was gay. He's Italian; he can't be gay."

Ruth said, "Forget Max. He's harmless."

Joey wanted her so much more than he had ever wanted anything else but didn't know how to do it. So he confessed—flushing with shame even though he was only fifteen—that he'd never done it before. Ruth wasn't even listening. She guided him, and due to her skill, Joey became less a boy and more a man right there in the front seat of the car. It was over fast, and Ruth chuckled as she asked how he liked it.

"Incredible!" Joey groaned, reaching for her again.

However, before he could begin again, he heard a sound in the trees off to the side of the road. He pulled away, but Ruth said that it was all right, that it was just Max who liked to watch people making love. The idea turned Joey off. He couldn't get rid of the feeling of Max's eyes staring at him. So when Max came out of the trees, Joey moved away quickly. When they returned to Ruth's apartment, she guided him into lovemaking again, despite Max being in the same room, ostensibly reading a magazine. Even though Joey knew he was there, he melted and knew nothing more than desire as she undressed before him. It was the first time he had ever seen a nude woman. They made love for an eternity, and when they were tired, Joey fell asleep on her breasts. He awoke to Max licking his leg and realized that Max was trying to get it on with him. Joey jerked away and jumped up. He got into a boxing pose and stared at Max in amazement as he kissed Ruth's feet while explaining his bisexuality.

Joey yelled out, "You better not touch me, or I'll kill ya!"

And then Ruth bounded out of bed and got in between them. She put her arms around Joey to soothe him as she said to Max, "Get out! Get out, Max!"

After Max left, Joey slowly stopped trembling and became aware of Ruth's breasts pressed up against his chest. He spent the night with her, his first night away from home. In the morning, Ruth began to explain that she was the one with the money and car and that she had been keeping Max instead of the other way around. He was getting ready to go to school at Hutchinson High. It was his junior year. She bought him breakfast and drove him to school. When his friends saw her and the car, their mouths watered. As he leaned over the car door and kissed her good-bye, he could feel their eyes on his back and the feeling of awe washed over him. He stood straight and walked cockily into the classroom, saying nothing in response to the many questions from his peers.

Ruth was there to meet him after school and drove him home. When Rosina saw the convertible in front of her building, she ran downstairs. In a voice heard for blocks, she asked Joey where he had been all night and who the slut old enough to be his mother was. His mother didn't even listen to his stammered reply but screamed at Ruth to leave her son alone and to go back to the streets where she belonged. As Ruth drove away laughing, Rosina cuffed Joey by his arm and dragged him into the house by his ear. His brother asked him a thousand questions that night while his mother was asleep, and Joey answered all of them. The next day, when Joey left the gym, Sammy was waiting outside. They talked until Ruth drove up, and they both got in the car. Joey drove, enjoying the power he experienced behind the wheel. Suddenly, he saw Sammy's hand between Ruth's legs and saw that Ruth only had eyes for Sammy.

Joey turned back around and drove back to the outskirts of Buffalo. They didn't seem to notice. Joey pulled up and got out. He told them he felt like walking. He stood on the walk, looking at them. Sammy stared back and then crawled over Ruth, started the engine, and drove away. Joey kept staring until the car disappeared, not hating Sammy and not hating Ruth. Joey simply felt … alone.

Chapter Two

Life Shining Shoes
(Ages 16–18) 1947–49

On July 30, 1947, Joey turned sixteen. Though he was underage, he had been fighting amateur fights in Canada, Rochester, and Buffalo for the Elks, Italian-American, and other clubs. Usually, amateur fighters had fifty-plus fights before turning pro (professional). Joey had had fifteen fights. He was keeping in shape on his own, and after a few fights, he began thinking he should get a trainer or a manager. The more he asked around, the more good things he heard about an Irishman named Mike Scanlan. Finally in 1948 Joey went to see this Mike Scanlan at Singer's Gym. He walked up the four flights of stairs, paid a quarter for admission, and watched some fighters working out while he waited. Mike Scanlan was a slender, middle-aged man who had a reputation for being a good discoverer. But when Joey told him he was a Golden Gloves champion, he laughed and said Joey looked more like a girl. Still, he looked again. "There is cockiness about you though," he said after the second look. "Go put on some trunks and gloves, kid," he said and then turned away and began talking to somebody else.

When Joey returned, Scanlan put him in with Billy Cox, a professional lightweight who was bigger and heavier. Cox made Joey look bad in the first round and was doing even better in the second when Joey hit him with a lucky right that decked him. Cox jumped up so embarrassed he was ready to kill, but Mike Scanlan was already leading Joey out of the ring and over to a big mirror. He watched Joey do footwork for a minute. "What's your name, kid?" Mike asked.

"Joey, Joey Giambra," Joey replied.

"Joey, huh? Yeah, Joey sounds like a fighter's name," Mike said. His eyes wandered over Joey's body, looking for flaws, searching to see if the body could be developed properly. "Yeah, kid, you might have some potential," he grunted. "Come back tomorrow 'bout this time," he said turning and walking away. "And come prepared to work out," he added to the wide-eyed Joey.

Mike showed Joey every trick when he saw Joey's natural ability after only two months; he set up Joey's first fight. Joey immediately gave up his job, thinking he was on his way to becoming a champion. But after winning his third straight amateur bout, Joey realized he needed to start earning some spending money. Joey got a part-time job driving a truck, which enabled him to train after he quit his previous work.

The boss had a pretty seventeen-year-old daughter, who decided she wanted the handsome Joey. She flirted with him in the office to no avail, as Joey was only thinking about becoming a champion. One afternoon, she called him and asked him to come by the house to pick up something for her father. When Joey arrived, she greeted him wearing only a very thin negligee. Joey hadn't been with a girl since Ruth, and very quickly, all thoughts in his mind of becoming a champion were replaced.

That evening, when he finished his workout at the gym, he was completely exhausted. Mike looked at him funny but didn't say anything until Joey walked up to him. Joey asked, "Mike, how long before a fight should a fighter lay off having sex?"

Mike looked disgusted. He knew Joey looked sluggish training that night, and now he knew why. "Listen, Joey! Sex is out! Ya unnastand? *Out!* From now on, if you do anything to break training, I'm not handling you! You break training, and you get hurt every time. And don' you forget it!" Mike growled.

"I'm sorry, Mike. It won't happen again," Joey said while avoiding Mike's eyes. In spite of Joey's promise, however, the daughter kept trying. She hadn't promised anyone! Finally, after Joey kept telling her no, she threatened to tell her father "something" if Joey didn't make love to her. Joey figured he would be fired anyway because of her hot pants, so he quit.

A few weeks later, after a particularly impressive workout, Mike took Joey aside and said, "You're beginning to look pretty good, kid. If you listen to me, I got a feeling you could go all the way. Here's what I want you to do: I want you to move in with my wife and I, so I can watch your training and your diet and see to it you don't make any more bad mistakes, like shacking up with some broad." Mike was treating Joey like the son he never had, becoming more to Joey than just a trainer.

Rosina was against it at first, but between Mike and Joey, they finally convinced her that it was best. "I will come and see you every day; I won't be that far away," Joey swore.

With tears in her eyes, in her slight Italian accent, she said, "If this is what you want, okay, just don't get hurt."

So Joey moved in with the Scanlans, but all did not go well at first. Mike was somewhat of a slob at home, leaving everything where it fell. Joey began picking up the habit, something he never got away with at home. After a week, Mrs. Scanlan was fed up. She hadn't minded taking care of her husband, but she was damned if she was to become Joey's slave, and she told them both off. Joey took it personally, and being too sensitive, he became terribly hurt, but Mike was able to smooth things over. Joey felt like he had become a burden to her and from then on began making his bed, doing his own clothes and dishes, and in general helping her in any way he could. Soon, Mary Scanlan began to smile again. Joey was training for the 1948 Golden Gloves and his weight of one hundred and thirty pounds put him in the lightweight class. Mike was pleased with his boy's progress but sensed he was becoming lonely and got him a companion. He bought Joey a boxer dog, and they instantly named him Champ. Champ was a beautiful animal. Wherever Joey went, Champ went. They were soon inseparable; they even jogged together, and when Joey lay down, Champ was there beside him. Joey fought his way to the Golden Gloves finals in New York City. He didn't have any time to go sightseeing that first visit to the big city, and though he was awed by its magnitude, he wasn't awed in the ring. He won the Golden Gloves title and took it home to Buffalo. Mike had Joey fight three more amateur bouts, one in Rochester, one in Syracuse, and then one back at the Elks Club in Buffalo. After that, Mike told him, "You're ready to fight pro now, kid."

"But I'm not eighteen yet, Mike," Joey said hesitantly, hating to remind him, fearful that Mike would not let him fight.

"Shit! I'll get you a fight up in Canada. No one will check us up there," he said.

Joey kept working out faithfully while Mike left to set up the fight. When Mike returned, he told Joey he had been approached by Tommy Lippes, an attorney who also promoted boxing shows to buy a piece of Joey. Also, two other men wanted to buy in. Mike told Joey that he decided to wait to see how Joey's first professional fight turned out before deciding what to do about the offers. Six weeks short of his eighteenth birthday, Joey made his professional debut across the Peace Bridge in Fort Erie, Ontario, Canada. It was the middle of June, and as Mike got him ready, he could see that Joey was very depressed.

"What's a matta, kid? You worried 'bout the fight?" Mike asked lightheartedly, because he wasn't worried.

"No, I'm not worried about the fight. My class graduated today, and if I would have stayed in school, I'd be with them tonight; that's all," Joey said.

"Ah, don't worry about graduating. When you become champion, you can get an education and just about anything else you want. Right now, just concentrate on winning the fight," Mike said.

He had matched Joey with Oliver Lee Phillips, an upcoming young pro with fifteen straight wins. Joey and Phillips used to spar every day, so Mike figured Joey could take him. If not, well … it would be a good yardstick. Joey was glad his bout was first, and that he wouldn't have to wait around. He entered the arena quickly and bounced up into the ring. Then, as he was helped out of his robe, he saw damn near all of his graduating class. They still had their white robes on and were standing up, yelling things like, "Good luck, champ!" and "We know you can do it, Joey!" He couldn't believe how many of them had made the trip, how many had come to cheer him on. They would never know how much they cheered him up. In the second round, Joey knocked Phillips out and didn't have mark on him when his classmates piled into his dressing room. They had a party afterward, and when Joey went back to his hotel that night, he was very proud and very happy, and so was Mike.

"Now we're in business, kid. Did you have a good time?" he said joyfully as he greeted Joey.

Joey rambled on for fifteen minutes before Mike could get in another word. Though when he did, he was serious. He said, "Joey, there's something we're going to have to do. We're going to have to come up with some money to work with. Tommy Lippes and Barney Lefcowitz want to buy in on your contract. What do you think?"

"Mike, you're my manager … manage. Whatever you say goes," Joey said with complete trust.

Mike sold 25 percent of Joey's contract to each man for a period of two years. Mike came away with three grand and bought Joey some new clothes and then bought himself a new car.

Mike Scanlon and Joey went to eat his pre-fight dinner at 3:00 PM. His fight was to be a preliminary bout lasting six rounds against Henry Powell in November 1949. This would be the fifth pro bout of Joey's boxing career. Joey sat in a booth eating his steak, baked potato, and Italian salad. His manager left him alone while he talked to the boys (Mob guys).

Suddenly, a well-dressed man sat across from Joey and introduced himself as Vito Genovese. He reached across the table to shake Joey's hand and said, "What kind of Italiano are you?"

"Sicilian!" Joey replied.

"Well, you're one of us," Genevese said. Joey smiled and wondered what Mr. Genevese meant by his remark. Before he left, he said, "You're gonna be champion. I seen you fight … But remember this, paisano, *'Prima la Familia,'*" which meant, "First your family." And he smiled and walked away.

Joey's manager walked back over to his table and said, "Do you know who that man was?" Joey shook his head puzzled. "That's the Mafia underboss, Vito Genevese."

Joey said he was a fan of his and wished him to be champion. Mike Scanlon and Joey moved to New York City to build up his name and get more fights. At the time, Madison Square Garden was the place to be on *Friday Night Fights*. They were staying at a hotel directly across from the Garden. Also directly across from the Garden was the Garden Cafeteria, where the fight crowd gathered. Joey was invited to eat with friends of Mike Scanlon, including Tex Sullivan, owner of the biggest store selling show tickets for all of Broadway. Next to Tex was Oney Madden, boss of the Irish Mob. Through Mr. Madden, Joey and Mike got their first fight in the Garden, an eight-round semifinal. Al Weill, Rocky Marciano's manager and the Garden's matchmaker, took kickbacks ($300.00) through Oney Madden from fighters' managers so they could appear in the Garden. Mike didn't have to pay. But Joey's opponent was one of the toughest guys he had ever fought. Sal Dimartino was undefeated until he met Joey. Joey won unanimously on national television. Joey was so impressive to the crowd that he got a standing ovation. He left the ring, and on his way to the dressing room, he passed center row ringside where all the stars sat: Sinatra, Jackie Gleason, Toots Shore, Don Rickles, and more. In a loud voice, Frank Sinatra yelled, "Nice going, Dago!"

In his dressing room, which was filled with reporters, photographers, and well-wishers, Joey was in awe. He felt he was on the threshold of becoming "the Champ"!

The best sparring partners always worked out at night, so the majority of Joey's training was done at night. He soon found time hanging heavy during the day and decided he needed a job to keep himself busy. Barney Lefcowitz put him to work hauling hay for the cows at his meat-packing company. Shortly thereafter, Joey was sitting atop a corral fence singing, when a cow looked up at him with her big, soulful brown eyes. As Joey kept singing, the cow nuzzled up to him and began licking his hand. He found it tough enough to work around these animals knowing they were going to get slaughtered, but this incident got him running back to the office. "Mr. Lefcowitz, there's a cow out there that I'd like to buy."

"You want to buy a cow?"

"Yeah, how much do you want for her?"

"Joey, what are you going to do with a cow?" Barney asked through a smile.

"I don't know," Joey said, suddenly confused. "I just can't stand to see her get killed."

"And where would you keep her?" Barney added.

"I'll keep her here," Joey said with some hope.

"Look, Joey, you have to understand this is a business," Barney said, trying to be kind. "That cow won't do you any good. She doesn't even give milk. You'd better forget about it."

Joey walked dejectedly back to the corral, petted the cow, apologized to her, and tried to let her know he had nothing to do with the business. But as he watched her get herded away toward the slaughter area, he pictured her being hung up by her hind legs and having her throat cut, and he got so sick to his stomach that a little while later, he went back to the office and told Barney he had to quit.

"You're supposed to be a fighter, a tough guy," Barney said somewhat amused.

"That's different; those cows didn't have a chance," Joey said solemnly.

"Look, I want you to have a job." And he thought for a minute. "How about you work in the office operating the switchboard?"

Joey slowly nodded and said, "Well, at least I won't see the cows getting killed."

Joey learned how to operate the switchboard and ran various errands for a while, but one day, he inadvertently disconnected Barney from an important Chicago call. Joey fully expected to get hollered at, but he got hollered at a lot, and he ran out of the office with his feelings terribly hurt.

"Why don't you forget about the job and keep your mind on boxing?" Mike asked when Joey told him about what had happened.

The next day, Joey informed Barney of his decision to devote himself to fighting full-time, and Barney was very understanding. He even invited Joey to his home for dinner to show there were no hard feelings. After seeing the wealth and beauty of the Lefcowitz home, Joey thought, *There's only one way I'll ever have anything like this; I've got to become the champion of the world.* Joey was eighteen when he had his second professional fight, his first in his hometown. He was matched against Jessy Bradshaw, a warhorse type of fighter. Mike made it clear that he had to beat Bradshaw in order to get better fights. It turned out to be a very rough fight, and though honestly, he thought he should have been given the decision, the fight was called a draw. A rematch was natural, and another rough fight ensued, but this time, Joey did get the decision. Things began to really look better after that. Joey's picture was in the papers, kids in his neighborhood wanted his autograph, and he started getting the adulation of the young ladies. Joey knew this was the way he wanted it to be. And he proceeded to win twelve straight professional fights, during which time, the weight of his lithe muscular body settled in the high one-fifties, making him a natural middleweight. With Joey's reputation growing steadily, Mike was able to get him his first semifinal bout with Johnny Cesario, a hell of a fighter in Willie Peps' stable. Cesario had a hundred and twenty-five fights under his belt. And though Mike knew he was taking a big chance sending Joey up against that kind of experience, he was confident Joey would take him.

Joey was driving Mike's car to his morning workout in preparation for the Cesario fight, and as always, Champ was with him. Suddenly, Champ snuggled up extra close to Joey and began shaking. It was quite chilly that morning, but still Joey wondered. "You'll be okay as soon as we start running, Champ," he told the dog and rubbed him briskly. They arrived at Forrest Lawn Cemetery, which was a beautiful park and a great place to run around. As they began to run, Joey kept an eye on Champ. He was beautiful, graceful, and quick, and soon, Joey forgot about the incident in the car. They were on their second lap when Champ spotted some pheasants in a bush. He made a run at them and then followed as the birds ran across the road. A car going way too fast for a park area killed Champ instantly. Joey ran to him and held Champ in his lap, sobbing almost hysterically, wondering if Champ knew and that was why he had snuggled and shivered. The driver had screeched to a halt and finally arrived back at the scene. He could see at once the dog had expired.

"Why were you going so fast? Are you crazy?" Joey cried.

"Well, he's dead, kid. You'd better call the ASPCA," the man said blandly. As he turned and walked away, Joey wanted to go after him and really let him have it, but instead, he carried Champ to the car, wrapped him in a blanket, and cried all the way home.

"What's wrong?" Mike asked when he saw Joey's face.

"It's Champ … He's dead. A car ran over him."

"What?" Mike said his voice crackling on the single word.

Mike started to blame Joey for not watching him closer, but when his own initial pain subsided, he drove Joey and Champ to a vacant lot, and there, they both buried him. For several days, Joey was inconsolable, and Mike finally said, "Look, kid, if you want, I'll get you another dog, but you've gotta forget about Champ. You've got a fight in the semifinal coming up, and it's very important."

But Joey didn't want another dog, and there was no way he'd ever forget about Champ.

May 22, 1951, the day of the fight finally came, and at the weigh-in, Cesario asked Joey about his mother, if he went to church, and about his life in general. He even said he felt bad about Joey's dog getting killed. Mike was busy with some reporters or he would have told Joey he was being psyched out and that just by finding out Joey was a nice guy, Cesario would try to use it to his advantage. The night was there; the fight was on. Cesario was clever and quick, but Joey was still upset about Champ and had trouble concentrating on the fight. For the first two rounds, Joey couldn't put anything on Cesario, who was making him look bad. Joey caught him with a combination early in the third, and near the end of the round, Cesario butted Joey on the forehead. In the fourth round, Joey started getting to Cesario again, and again, he got butted, this time on the left side of his face.

"What the hell's the matter with you? This guy is really jerkin' you around!" Mike yelled when Joey returned to his corner.

"Mike, look, I know he's buttin' me, but he always apologizes."

"Aww, Joey!" Mike groaned, shaking his head at the streak of innocence. "He's giving you a snow job. Now get out there and knock him out!"

It was the seventh round before Cesario really slowed down, and Joey began hurting him. Two solid punches rocked and staggered Cesario just before the bell rang. Joey was thinking, *One round to go*, as he went crisply back to his corner.

"Joey, those early rounds killed you. He's got you two, four, and one even. If you don't knock him out, you're going to lose the fight! That's the only way you can win! You've got to knock him out!"

The bell rang, the fighters touched gloves, and then Joey hit Cesario with a left-hook, right-hand combination that dropped him. He got up, and Joey pursued him, but the highly experienced veteran had just enough left in him to keep Joey from putting him away. Cesario took a split decision back to his dressing room, and Joey took a split lip, a lump on his forehead, and a closed left eye back to his. And he was alone—no one was there. *Nobody likes a loser*, he thought as he sat down and looked at himself in the mirror. He had never been hurt like this before, cut up, battered, and he thought, *God, this isn't what I want. What if I really get hurt? What then?*

Mike came in and saw the tears in the unhappy young man's eyes. "What's wrong with you, kid? What are you crying about?"

"I don't want to fight anymore; I don't want to get killed," Joey said quietly.

"Relax and learn from your mistakes. The only thing that beat you tonight was experience," Mike said just as softly.

"Look at me," Joey said as he turned away from the mirror unable to look at himself any longer. "No. This isn't my bag; that's all there is to it."

Mike looked deeper than the battered face and left the room. Joey was still sitting there looking at the floor when Johnny Cesario came in a few minutes later. He didn't look any better than Joey, but Cesario had looked like that before, and again, his experience was the difference.

"What do you want?" Joey asked not so politely, thinking maybe Cesario had come to gloat.

"Normally, I wouldn't bother talking to a guy I just beat, but you're one of my people, Italian, and I feel kind of bad," he said in a big-brother tone. "You know you didn't lose that fight tonight. It was your mind that lost that fight. You can punch, box, and you can think in the ring. You really had me going there. The only thing that beat you was my experience, but if we had gone one more round, you'd have taken me anyway. I wouldn't have lasted ten for sure."

"You really think I've got it?" Joey asked sincerely.

"Sure you have. You've got guts, strength, and endurance, everything that counts to be a champion," Cesario said while smiling softly. "That's why I don't want you to give up just because you got beat tonight. But you've got to remember, not everyone will be a gentleman in the ring. Most guys, when they know they're getting beat, will throw away the book."

"I wouldn't ever want to fight dirty," Joey said wincing.

"You don't have to, but if you would have butted me back, after I gave it to you that first time, I wouldn't have butted you that second time."

Joey smiled and nodded his understanding. "Thanks a lot, Johnny. I really appreciate this."

Cesario nodded back and then left, and a moment later, Mike walked back in. "Well?"

Joey realized what Mike had done and thought, *Boy, does he know how to play me.* He looked back in the mirror and said, "I'll try again, Mike."

Joey did a lot of roadwork until he healed, and then Mike worked him hard, mind as well as body. Next, Mike took him to Detroit, where he was victorious over Al Adams and Herbie Phillips. Then after four more quick wins at home, 1951 ended and Mike said, "Joey, it's about time we headed to the big city."

"New York?" Joey asked, knowing the answer and excited.

"They've got about nine boxing clubs; we'll build a good reputation there. We'll get a few main events, and if it goes the way I think, the next stop will be the Garden," Mike continued.

Madison Square Garden was "it" for any fighter at that time, and the chance of appearing on national television whet Joey's appetite.

Joey went home, packed a bag, and then said good-bye to his mother and family.

"Just take care of yourself. Don't get hurt," she said as she held back her tears.

"I won't let them hurt me, Ma, and when I get back, I will buy you a house," Joey promised and kissed her.

"Don't forget to go to church," was all she could say.

Chapter Three

First Time in the Big Apple
(Age 20) 1951

The Capital Hotel, located diagonally across from Madison Square Garden, became home for Joey and Mike. A lot of fighters who fought at the Garden stayed there because it was convenient and the price was right. They got connecting rooms, and the next day, Mike set up a routine for Joey to follow—religiously. He woke up at four thirty in the morning, took the subway to Central Park where he ran two miles around a reservoir, and then took the subway back. He would clean up and rest for a couple of hours and then have breakfast before going to Stillman's Gym for a workout. Later, he would play cards, watch television, and hit the sack early. On Sunday, his day off, he would go to church, then see one or two double features, and then return to the hotel. This went on for nine months, and Joey was fighting every week to ten days and winning. He didn't get a chance to see much of the city, and Mike made sure he stayed away from girls, but the reputation they had started to build was there. Giambra was attracting so much attention, and nobody took him lightly. Finally, Mike told Joey to take a few days off and go out and have himself some fun. To Joey, that meant one thing: to have himself a girl. It was still early, so he walked over to Times Square and then up one side of Broadway all the way to Columbus Circle and back down on the other side of Broadway. He looked at the stores, restaurants, and theaters, but most of all, the girls. He kept wishing he didn't have such a baby face, because the girls he was looking for usually hung out in bars, and with his face, they just wouldn't let him in. As he continued walking, Joey passed a bus terminal. Since it was Friday, he thought some girls might be coming into town for the weekend. He had been sitting for a while, glad for the rest, before a girl carrying an overnight bag and dressed like a nurse came walking by.

"Can I carry your bag?" Joey asked politely as he got up.

The girl seemed surprised and amused, and after a moment's judgment, she said, "Thank you," as she handed him her bag.

"Would you like a milkshake?" Joey asked as they exited the terminal.

Again, there was that surprised, amused look on her face, but she said, "Yes."

Joey told her a little about himself and learned she was a nurse from Asbury Park, New Jersey, who often came to New York for the weekend. She was staying at the YMCA. Two hours later, Joey picked her up, and they went to a movie she wanted to see. Joey felt good just being in the company of a girl. After the show, they stopped for a hamburger and then walked around Times Square. Joey felt great just holding a girl's hand. Finally, not knowing what else to do, Joey simply asked if she wanted to go back to his place to watch some television. She smiled at him subtly but said, "Sure."

They talked more than they watched TV, and when she commented on how beautifully developed he was, Joey mentioned the Batman accident and his lower back and lumbar problem. Being a nurse, she understood and offered to massage his back. He quickly got out of his shirt, and she ordered nurse-like, "Lay down on the bed, while I slip out of this dress, I don't want to get it wrinkled."

Joey gladly did what he was told and was very excited. He watched her attractively slender body emerge from her dress. She was wearing a flesh-colored bra and matching panties, complimenting her light brown hair. After a few minutes of massaging, she fell alongside him saying, "There, is that better?"

"Fantastic!" Joey said as he rolled onto his side and looked at her. She smiled and opened her arms, and he went in.

No sooner had he begun the struggle with her brassiere than the door connecting his room to Mike's flew open. Both Joey and the girl jumped halfway out of their skins, not hearing Mike say, "Joey, I got a ... *Oh*, sorry, kids! Joey, when you're through, I want to talk to you about something." Mike closed the door on the two turned-off people.

The girl decided to leave, so Joey walked her downstairs and put her in a cab, promising to call her the next day. *Damn*, he thought as he watched the cab drive away. "Why the hell did you walk in like that? You should have knocked at least!" Joey yelled as he entered Mike's room.

"Sorry about that, kid. Did you make out?" Mike asked easily.

"No! No thanks to you," Joey said.

"Well, forget about it. You're back in training anyway," Mike said.

"What do you mean back in? I haven't had time to get out. What happened to my few days off?" Joey said disgustedly.

"You're fighting Gus Rubicini up in Ridgewood Grove in two weeks. You've seen Gus; he's a tough Italian kid."

"Okay, okay, but next time, knock," Joey said.

First meet of Tex Sullivan and Machine Gun Oney Madden (top Mob boss connected with Madison Square Garden and boxing friend of Vito Genevese).

Joey knew this would be one of his toughest fights because Gus was a good puncher and had a lot of knockouts to his credit. He knew he would have to be on his toes, so he trained extra hard, and except for getting a boil on his butt, he was ready. The September night of the fight found Joey pacing the floor of his dressing room. The boil was almost to a head and hurt like hell. Mike came in saying, "How do you feel, kid?"

"You asked me that when I came here," Joey said irritably. "Ah ... I'm all right. It's just this boil; it's bugging me."

"Lay down. I'll bust it for ya," Mike said.

"No, not till after the fight."

"Look, it will feel better if I pop it now," Mike said firmly.

"No, forget about it for now; it just feels funny rubbing against my trunks when I move around," Joey said, not wanting to face the pain before the fight.

"Well, at least we can tape a gauze pad over it," Mike said patting the rubbing table.

Teddy Bentham, Joey's trainer at the time, could see Joey was nervous, so he told a story about Gus while getting him ready. "Did you hear the gag Tony Janaro played on Gus?"

"No, what?" Joey asked.

Teddy said as he laughed, "Well, Gus hadn't had a girl his first five months in New York, so Casanova Janaro sends ugly Gusto a bar he tells him he could really make out at. But what Janaro does is send him to a queer joint, and can you believe it? Gus actually tries to make it with a lesbian! After getting a few drinks in her and getting her up to his room, he finally got the nerve to ask her to go to bed with him. 'Are you kidding? I don't do things like that with men,' the lesbian says.

"'How come?' Gus asks.

"'Because I am a lesbian.'

"Gus says, like she shouldn't be too ashamed, 'Hell, I am a Sicilian.'"

Joey and Mike both cracked up. "Gus probably thought she was Lebanese." Joey laughed out loud.

"Maybe that's how Gus got the reputation for being dumb," Mike said still shaking his head.

Joey smiled all the way into the ring and couldn't help laughing when he saw Gus.

"All right, calm down and start thinking. This is going to be a tough fight. Get your mind back on business," Mike said seriously.

The bell rang, and the fighters touched gloves. Joey was on his toes, literally, punching and moving so quickly that Gus didn't lay a glove on him for two rounds. By the end of the fourth round, Gus was puffing and plodding just from chasing Joey, who wasn't even breathing hard.

"You're making him look silly, kid. If you can get him, knock him out," Mike said with pride.

"Okay, Mike, I'll see what I can do." Joey nodded.

Joey hit Gus with his best shot in the fifth and sixth round, but he was a tough kid like Mike said, and he withstood the blows and kept coming. Then in the seventh, Gus got Joey in a clinch and yelled at him in Italian, "Stay still and fight like a man!"

Joey started laughing, and Gus got so mad he actually jumped on Joey, trying to hold him still so he could hit him. Joey fell against the ropes, and then as he slid to one side, the center rope caught his boil and broke it. In a split second, Joey screamed and grabbed Gus and then sighed in relief from the pressure of the boil. The crowd started laughing because Joey had a grin on his face, and the two fighters looked like they were waltzing. The round ended. Blood was pouring down Joey's leg as he went back to his corner. The crowd was still laughing, and so was Mike.

"You look like you just got your period," Mike said, while Teddy cleaned Joey as best he could. Joey couldn't knock Gus out but won a unanimous decision.

"What kind of Italian are you anyway?" Gus asked Joey after congratulating him.

"Sicilian," Joey said with a smirk on his face as he watched a funny kind of look cross Gus Rubicini's.

Chapter Four

Getting Lonely
(Age21) 1952

After Joey's showing against Rubicini, Mike was able to get him his first ten-round main event in New York City and his first fight with a contender. It was early in the afternoon, and Joey was sitting in the room watching TV, thinking about his life and feeling lonely, when Mike came busting in exclaiming, "It's Joey G time! Joey Giambra versus Joey Giardello; 1952's your year, kid."

Giardello. "Giardello's ranked number five," Joey suddenly said, amazed at the thought.

"And you'll take him. I know you'll take him," Mike went on.

"They'll have to rank me then, won't they?" Joey stated more than asked, as his own excitement began to hit.

"Maybe not the top five, but surely the top ten," Mike said, grabbing and hugging him. "Now, look, I got to go back to Buffalo for about a week. I don't want you to do any heavy workouts till I get back. Just go to the gym every day and loosen up. Other than that, think of it as a week off. Relax, and enjoy yourself. You got it?"

"I got it," Joey said.

Mike went to his room and started to pack. Joey's thoughts were on Giardello. He was still feeling lonely. A little later, Joey was in the bathroom cleaning up, while the maid was doing the same thing in the room. Since he was a monthly guest, the linens were only changed once a week, and today was the day. The maid was a black woman; they had talked a few times during the year, and Joey liked her.

"Joey, you're a nice boy. Why don't you find yourself a woman!" Joey heard the maid shout.

Joey went to the bathroom door and looked at her. "What are you talking about?" Suddenly, Joey flushed as red as a beet. He saw her standing next to the unmade bed.

"It's no good for a boy not to have a woman, once in a while," she said.

"You know I'm a fighter and in training," Joey said.

She said, "I know it isn't natural to leave pecker tracks all the time, and sex is as natural as eating and drinking. You listen to me; you have yourself a woman."

Joey was still flushed with embarrassment as he turned back into the bathroom. Later that day, Mike and Joey were having a bite to eat before Mike's drive to Buffalo, and Mike couldn't help but notice Joey's somber attitude, especially under the circumstances. "What's wrong with you, kid? You worried about Giardello?"

"Nah … I'm just lonely," Joey mumbled while shaking his head.

"Lonely?" Mike said loudly. "You're not bugged that I'm going away for a week, are you?"

"It's not you I'm talking about!" Joey said loudly, too.

"Okay, okay, let's keep it down," Mike said lowering his voice. "You want to tell me what you are talking about?"

"I want to have a girl. I need a girl," Joey said.

"What are you, some kind of pussy-hound?" Mike said in a tone of disgust.

"That's a laugh. I haven't had a girl for a year now. I'm only human, you know."

Mike shook his head for a moment before saying, "Joey, you've got a very important fight coming up."

"And I've got a week off, and if I don't get a girl, I'm going to crack up."

"Would you just forget about the damn broads?" Mike said too loudly.

"Aww, hell, have a good trip," Joey said getting up and throwing the paper napkin on the table.

Mike watched Joey move quickly out of the restaurant and thought, *I'd better talk to Angelo before I leave.* Angelo Dundee was a young trainer working in the corner for a lot of fighters just to get experience. He wanted to become a trainer, never dreaming he would one day guide the career of a kid named Cassius Clay. His brother, Chris Dundee, was in control of boxing in Florida, and Angelo did dream of one day taking over boxing there. Angelo had worked in Joey's corner a few times and liked him enough to tell him on several different occasions that he could do more for him than Mike could. But each time, Joey expressed his loyalty to Mike.

Joey was walking in Central Park. Mike's lack of understanding had upset him, and walking in the park had always helped him to relax and to think more clearly. He was also hoping to meet a girl who was as lonely as he was, but the only girls he saw weren't alone. As he came out of the park and started back to the hotel, he saw Angelo leaning against a car.

"Well, I was beginning to think you weren't here!" Angelo called out.

"What are you doing here?" Joey asked as he approached Angelo.

"I want to talk to you. Let's take a ride," Angelo said while opening the passenger door.

"Look, Ange, I already told you I cannot fight for you."

"Joey," Angelo said with mock hurt, "did I commit a crime letting you know I'm interested? Things could sour between you and Mike, and I want you to know who you can come see."

It sounded reasonable, and Joey said, "I'm sorry. I'm just uptight."

"Come on," Angelo said as he nodded at the car for Joey to get in.

"How did you know I'd be here?" Joey asked after he pulled into traffic.

"Mike told me. He was worried when he left. He also told me you were horny as hell," Angelo said simply.

"Ah, it's more than that, Ange … I'm lonely. Is that so hard to understand?"

"Nah, of course not. Frankly, I think Mike's a little too harsh on you. What the hell? You're only human."

"That's what I told him!" Joey almost shouted hearing his own words.

"Sure," Angelo humored him. "Tell you what; I have got a girl I want to fix you up with."

"How come you never fixed me up before?" Joey asked suspiciously.

"Look, I know a girl who saw your fight last night with Gus. She was right there at ringside, and she told me she wants to meet you."

"Well, why didn't you tell me before?"

"I didn't want to break your training and get Mike sore at me."

"And he would've been," Joey agreed.

"When can I meet her?"

"What about tomorrow or tonight?"

"Ah, I'm afraid if she isn't busy by now, she doesn't want to be," Angelo said shaking his head and smiling.

"Oh, what kind of girl is she?" Joey said dejectedly.

"Matter of fact, she's a call girl, but high class," Angelo said.

"What do you mean? She works for a phone company?"

Angelo couldn't help laughing even though he knew Joey was a naive kid. "No, Joey, a call girl is like a prostitute, only more expensive. You call her up, and she meets you."

"Well, how expensive is she?"

"This one is two hundred a shot."

Joey said, somewhat shocked, "Two hundred? You're crazy!"

"Since she wants to meet you, I bet you can get a rate, maybe half price?" Angelo said thinking.

Joey sighed heavily. "I don't know, paying a girl to make love is … I don't know."

"Hey, do it and get it out of your system. It's worth it," Angelo said.

The next morning, Joey was reading the paper. He saw that the Mickey Jelke trial was still getting headlines in New York. He was an heir to an oleomargarine fortune, who had over one hundred call girls working for him. Naturally, there was a big crackdown on vice taking place and that didn't make Joey feel better about a call girl. That afternoon, Joey was exercising at Stillman's Gym when Angelo came by.

"I just got through talking to Ruby, the girl I was telling you about, and what'd 'ya think—"

"She changed her mind," Joey said with mixed emotions.

"Just the opposite, she wants to romance you tonight at her place, and she only wants fifty bucks from you."

"Her place?" Joey questioned him.

"Yeah, and let me tell ya something; that stuff just don't happen. She must have really got turned on watching you fight. Incidentally, here's the fifty. I'll put it on the expense account," Angelo mentioned.

"Thanks, Ange. You know, you're a pretty nice guy," Joey said, taking the single bill.

"Well, here's the address. She has the penthouse; she wants you there at seven."

"A penthouse?" Joey said, impressed.

"She's got a couple of wealthy guys floating the bills. Be happy about it. Now here's what you do. Do it once, give her the fifty, and leave," Angelo said.

And Joey agreed.

Joey was anxious for seven o'clock to get there, so he left early and walked all the way there just to pass the time. He had worked up a sweat in the only suit of clothes he owned before he reached a freshly remodeled brownstone building with Ruby's address on a canopy that went all the way out to the curb. He entered the building and then the elevator and wondered where the operator was. He had been waiting a few minutes when a man stepped in and pushed a button. The door closed, and they were on their way up. When the man got out, the door closed. Joey pushed the penthouse button, feeling like a fool, because he had never been in a self-service elevator before. And he started thinking—thinking about Ruby being a prostitute and that the vice squad could be watching her. The elevator door opened against a steel door to the penthouse apartment. Joey saw a blonde with a bad complexion look through a small window.

"Are you Joey?" she asked.

"Yeah, are you Ruby?"

"No, Ruby's in the bedroom. She'll be right with you."

She smiled as she let him in. "Do you live here too?" Joey asked.

"No, just visiting. I'm on my way. Good-bye, Joey," she said stepping into the elevator, and she was gone.

"Make yourself comfortable. I'll be out in a minute," Ruby called out from the bedroom.

"Okay," Joey called back as he sat on the couch and looked around the luxurious apartment.

"Make yourself a drink."

"No, thanks, I don't drink."

"I should have known. Well, just relax then!"

The *New York Times* was on the edge of the coffee table, so Joey picked up the sports section and glanced through it. He would look up at the bedroom from time to time, and the last time, Ruby appeared in a sheer, ivory-colored negligee. She moved slowly toward him, and he could see her short red hair, her blue-green eyes, and her beautiful face. Then his eyes filled with her *Esquire*-like body on a petite five-foot-two-inch frame, the protruding nipples, the triangular shadow between her legs. Ruby sat beside the blushing Joey and then took a cigarette from the coffee table and lit it.

She asked, "Would you like one?"

"No, thanks. I don't smoke either," he was barely able to say.

"Right … What's the matter?" she asked softly as she sat erect at the edge of the couch letting him see the perfection of her breasts.

"I wouldn't want you to think that I wasn't a gentleman. I mean, I usually get up when a girl comes in the room."

Ruby let her hand slowly move toward his crotch and gently settle. "But you are a gentleman," she whispered just before she kissed him. She sensed his restraint as they kissed, and as their mouths parted, she said, "You're uncomfortable, aren't you?"

"Well, you see, I never paid a woman to make love before. I don't know … What do I do?" Joey stammered.

"Just do what comes natural," she said, finding his innocence attractive.

"Don't you have to do it a certain way when you pay someone?"

"Come into the bedroom," she said as she put out her cigarette. She then took him by the hand and led him to the bedroom. As they entered, Joey heard soft music playing and saw his first king-sized bed. The room was bathed in amber light and perfume scents, and Joey felt as if he were in a palace. Ruby helped him out of his jacket and placed it over the back of the chair. Then she turned back to see him frozen there, looking at her.

"Would you like me to undress you?" she asked coyly.

"Uh, no, that's okay … Isn't it kind of light in here?" Joey said, feeling bashful.

Ruby moved sensually toward a dimmer switch by the bed, and the lighting became a soft glow. Then she slipped the negligee from her shoulders and let it drop to the floor. "Now it's your turn," she said as she slipped onto the bed.

Joey quickly got down to his shorts and then moved quickly and sat down with his back to her.

"You're very shy, aren't you?" she said more than asked as she ran her long nails down his back.

"Promise you won't laugh if I tell you something."

"I promise," she said.

"I haven't had sex for a year," he blurted out.

"You're kidding?" she said, astonished. "I can't believe that."

Joey turned to face her, and his body became a magnet for her eyes. "Mike, my manager, says sex is bad for athletes. He watches me and will not let me break training."

"Take off your shorts," she whispered.

Joey slipped them under him onto the floor and then lay down beside her. "Besides, most girls think I'm still a little boy."

"Well, you are kind of cute, ya know." She smiled as she put her hands on him, saying, "But you sure aren't little, boy." Ruby leaned over and kissed him, and he felt her nipples press against his chest. He grabbed her and held her to him as they started. When the wave of pleasure had passed, the pain of humiliation was there, and Joey jumped into his shorts and started for his clothes.

"What's the matter? Where are you going?" Ruby asked.

"Well, it's over, isn't it? Angelo said to do it once, give you the money, then go."

"But you haven't done anything yet," she said with a touch of a laugh.

"Sure I did. Didn't you feel it?" Joey said with contempt for himself.

"Oh, well, that doesn't count; that was a misfire. Come on, let's try it again."

"But I haven't got any more money."

"Joey, if it was money I wanted, you wouldn't be here. It's you I want," Ruby said sternly.

Joey returned to the bed somewhat confused. He slipped out of his shorts with less shyness, lay down on the bed beside her, and held her firmly in his arms. "I feel like such a baby," he finally said.

"You're a baby in the bed, just like I'd be in the ring," she said kindly.

"You like the fights, huh?"

"Not really," she said, easing out of his grasp. "But I like a beautiful body." Ruby sat up beside him, looked at him, and touched him. "Usually, when guys are young and good-looking like you and have a good body like yours, they don't have to pay a girl like me."

They didn't talk much for the next two hours; they just made love over and over. Joey was lying on his stomach feeling more physically satisfied than ever before, and Ruby was sitting up having a cigarette. "Now don't misunderstand, I like you, Joey, but you're a little too fast for me."

"What do you mean?"

"You're just too fast; you've got to get more control."

"Oh, maybe it's because I haven't had it in so long," Joey said.

"No, I'm going to teach you how to really make love. How old are you, Joey?" she asked as she was inhaling.

"I just turned twenty-one a couple of months ago."

"And I'm not even twenty yet. Boy have we had different sex lives," she said shaking her head.

"Yeah … What are you going to teach me?"

"Anything you want and a lot you probably never heard of."

There was a silent time before Joey asked, "Ruby, when you finish your cigarette, would you massage my lower back?"

"Sure," she said before he had a chance to tell her why. She took her final drag, put out the cigarette, and then spun around and straddled his legs.

"Oh, that's marvelous," Joey groaned as she massaged him, and he had almost fallen asleep when he felt her kissing his thigh and then his backside. "What are you doing?" he asked as he looked over his shoulder at her.

"I am going to give you a trip around the world," she said as she continued kissing him. "I'm going to make love to your whole body."

"What's that? Wait a minute," Joey said as he turned on his side. "Mike told me that it is not normal, and guys who let girls kiss them down there get soft brains."

Ruby just looked at him with disbelief. "I don't know why your manager is feeding you such crap, but, Joey, how can you believe it?"

Joey thought for a moment. "People always tell me I'm gullible. I don't know what to believe."

"Roll over on your back," she said nudging him.

"Are you sure it won't hurt?"

"If it doesn't feel good, tell me to stop," she said lowering her head between his thighs. Joey tried to relax as he watched her, and he had to admit it felt good. He also had to admit he was getting passionate again, but he just couldn't relax. He took her face in his hands and gently brought it to his. "Now, I know it didn't hurt," she teased.

"No, it's not that. I just don't feel right about it," Joey said as he kissed her lightly.

"You're sweet, Joey. We'll just go nice and easy and let things happen naturally," she said as she fitted herself onto him. This was another first for Joey. He didn't know the girl could be on top. He watched her, all of her dancing on him. Joey went right out of his mind. It was almost midnight when Ruby said, "I hope you've worked up an appetite."

"I sure have. I'm starving," he said.

"Good, me too. Let's go have something to eat." And with that, Ruby jumped out of bed and ran into the bathroom. Twenty minutes later, Joey helped Ruby put on a mink coat over a black evening dress. She looked rich as well as beautiful. Ruby phoned down to the garage and ordered her car brought around.

"Do you have a driver's license?" she asked as they boarded the elevator.

"Sure, I love to drive," Joey said.

"Good, it's not one of my favorite 'have-to's.' There are too many creeps out there, and I swear they're breeding."

Ruby's all-white convertible was waiting for them, and Joey loved it. *One of these days, boy,* he thought as he quickly pulled into traffic.

"Where would you like to eat?" she asked.

Joey answered, "You know these places around here better than I do," not knowing where the hell he could take her. It suddenly dawned on him that outside the fifty-dollar bill he hadn't given her yet, he only had a few bucks on him.

Ruby directed him to an Irish restaurant called The Shamrock. One look at the place put a knot in Joey's stomach, and after he saw the menu and had a moment of panic, he then said simply, "Ruby, after I give you the fifty, I won't have enough to pay the bill."

"Good, use the fifty to buy dinner."

"Okay, then I'll owe you," Joey said relieved.

"Joey, I don't want to take money from you," she said as she put down her menu.

She paused, giving Joey a chance to say, "What do you mean? Why not?"

"I want to be more than a call girl to you, and I want you to be more than a john to me."

The waiter came and went with their order before Joey said, "Can you afford to waste time with a guy who can't help you out?"

"Being with you tonight wasn't wasting my time. This is the first time I've been turned on in a month. Let me tell you something, Joey; I don't have to be a call girl anymore. The two men paying for the penthouse and anything else I want within reason are nice, but just don't do it for me. They don't even come over but once a week each. There is no threesome going on. And when they do come over, they call ahead of time. I've gradually all but cut out the rest of my action. You are the first new man in my life in a long time."

"Why are you telling me this?" Joey had to ask.

"I want you to be my boyfriend, my lover." There it was, the girlfriend he had been wishing for.

"What about the two guys keeping you?"

"I've been toying with the idea of easing them out of my life, and with you, I'd do it quicker. We could be good for each other, Joey," she said, pleased with the thought.

Joey looked at her hand, which had come to rest on his. "How did you get into this business?"

"I'd have to tell you the whole story of my life." She laughed.

"I'd like to hear it," Joey said sincerely.

"You really would?" It was a statement and made her smile appreciatively. All through dinner, Ruby outlined her life for him. She told him of her upper-middle-class family in Memphis, Tennessee, and how she had run away from them when she was fifteen because she was boy crazy. So by the time she had gotten to New York, all she had to do was lose her accent. She had taken singing and dancing lessons when she was a kid and dreamed of being a Radio City Music Hall Rockette, and it broke her heart when she found out she was too short. Then she began pounding the pavement looking for work but found a madam at a friend's party instead, and being almost broke and not wanting the folks back home to know where she was, she was prepared to give it a try. The next two years were spent entertaining well-known doctors, lawyers, businessmen, and politicians. After that, she went on her own, and by the time she was nineteen, thanks mainly to a stockbroker client who invested money for her, she owned two apartment buildings in Memphis, Tennessee, that her folks took care of; over one hundred thousand dollars in stocks; and over fifty thousand dollars in cash sitting in several safety deposit boxes. Joey's mouth was still open when he pulled up in front of the hotel. He could hardly believe how rich she had become in only a few years, but he knew she had no reason to lie.

They talked a little while, both feeling the blissful exhaustion of the evening, and then Ruby asked, "How about tomorrow, can we get together?"

Joey eagerly said, "Sure."

"Maybe we can spend the day together?" she suggested.

"That'll be great; I haven't seen Central Park, Stillman's Gym, and Times Square," Joey said.

"Good, I'll pick you up at noon, and we can start off with brunch," she smiled and said with anticipation.

"Beautiful," Joey said as he kissed her.

The next day, they had brunch and then took a boat trip out to the Statue of Liberty. They talked a lot and laughed a lot, and when Joey read the inscription on the statue, he had to hold back the tears, because his family was among those it was dedicated to. The next stop was the top of the Empire State Building. While they were enjoying the awesome sight, Ruby asked, "What do you want to do when you quit fighting, Joey?"

"Since I was a kid, I've always wanted to be a singer or an actor … Surprised?"

"Yes, a little. I mean, if you want to be an actor, why do you take the risk of getting your face all scarred up?" she asked.

"I figure if and when I become champion, people will know me and it will open a lot of doors for me."

"Well, that's true," Ruby had to admit. "But I could open a door for you right now. Lee Strasberg is a friend of mine. He runs a famous actors' workshop called Actors Studio, and I know I could get you in."

"That sounds great, but once I start training for the Giardello fight, I won't have time for anything," Joey said.

"You're such a good-looking kid; I hate to think of you getting hurt," Ruby said while touching his face. They ended the day outside with a patio dinner and then began the night inside with passion. They were young, healthy, and insatiable, and Joey was finding a freedom he had never known. Ruby had Cantonese food brought in around midnight, and that was the only time they left the bedroom. "Joey, I really like you, and I want to make you a proposition. Come live with me. Help me straighten out my life, and I'll take care of everything while you become an actor."

"Gee, that sounds great," Joey said quite bewildered by the offer.

"And don't think about the money. You know I've got plenty, and when you start making money, you can pay it back if you want, but it really doesn't matter."

Joey wiped his mouth and hands as he thought about it for a minute. He seemed to feel he was at a crossroad, a turning point, and thought he had better wait until Mike got back. "Ruby, can I think about it for a few days?"

"Of course, I know it's a big decision, and I want you to be sure," Ruby said without hesitation.

Joey leaned over and kissed her lightly. "You know, I've never slept with a woman before."

"You won't be able to say that tomorrow," Ruby said as she kissed him, but not lightly. The following day, they went on a cruise around Manhattan Island and then had a marvelous time at the Bronx Zoo. After dinner, Ruby settled with a cigarette, looking at the smile on Joey's face and said, "Let's go back to your place. I want to stay with you tonight."

"Okay, but it's just a small hotel room," Joey said almost apologetically.

"I know, but I want you to see me there, so that when you're alone … you'll be able to see me there."

Joey gave Ruby his key, sent her up first, and then followed a few minutes later. "I've never did anything like this before," Joey said as he entered the room. "I felt like a spy or something."

Ruby laughed as she hung her dress beside her coat in the small, almost empty closet. "Is this all the clothes you have?"

Joey was looking at the diminutive redhead in a black bra and panties and thinking how absolutely beautiful she was. "Yeah, but except for these three days, one suit was all I ever needed."

"Tomorrow, I'm going to buy you a present," she said moving onto the bed.

"You don't have to do that," Joey told her as he began to undress.

46

"But I want to. It's making me feel good just thinking about it." They made love, talked, watched television for a while, made love some more, and then fell asleep in each other's arms.

When Joey awoke in the morning, Ruby was gone. Alongside the telephone was an envelope with his name on it, and it was signed, "Love, Ruby." Joey opened the envelope and pulled out three brand-new one-hundred-dollar bills. He looked at them for a minute and then got Ruby on the phone.

"Ruby, what did you leave me this money for?"

"For you, Joey, I want you to have some spending money till your manager gets back."

"I don't want your money," Joey said feeling ashamed.

"Joey, I can't tell you how much you're doing for me, so much more than I'm doing for you. I mean that. So, please, don't let pride or anything spoil things. Okay?"

"Okay," Joey said feeling a little better about it, but not much.

"How about I pick you up in an hour. We can have brunch and then go shopping?"

"It's a deal; I'll meet you downstairs in an hour," Joey said.

As Joey walked through the lobby, he could see Ruby already parked out front. He could also see Angelo Dundee standing beside the car talking to her. Then as he walked out of the hotel, he heard Ruby saying angrily, "Who the hell died and left you boss?"

"Listen, you little slut …" Angelo got out before Joey interrupted him.

"Hey, Ange, don't talk to her like that."

Ruby smiled as Angelo turned to the approaching Joey. "What the hell are you doing with her, going steady?" Angelo spat.

"Look, Ange, I like her, and she likes me. I still have a couple of days off, and I'm going to see her," Joey said a bit irritated.

"She's no good for you, Joey; I want you to stay away from her," Angelo said as he tried to calm down.

"I think you're forgetting something," Joey said as he opened the passenger door. "You're not my manager." Joey got into the car and shut the door on the frustrated Angelo.

"Bye now." Ruby snickered and started pulling away.

"Broads like you always get theirs!" Angelo yelled.

"Drop dead!" Ruby yelled back as she sped away. Ruby took Joey into the Botany 500 men's store on Park Avenue. She showed him a special credit card that she could even buy a car with and told him he could buy anything he wanted up to a thousand dollars.

"A thousand dollars?" Joey said flabbergasted. "Aww, Ruby, that's too much."

"The guy will never question it. Believe me."

"But what if he should." Joey worried. "I'll tell him my brother came to visit, and if he doesn't like it, I'll tell him what he can do with his credit card." She laughed.

Joey felt like a kid let loose in a candy store with a pocket full of pennies. Everything he saw he wanted. He let Ruby guide his selection of two suits, an Alan Ladd raincoat, two pairs of shoes, shirts, ties, belts, underwear, and socks. The spree cost a little over nine hundred dollars.

"Do you want me to drive now?" Joey asked as they walked back to the car carrying everything but the suits.

"No, I'm going to have to be dropping you off; I won't be able to see you for the next two days," she said with a sudden drop in her spirit.

"Oh?" Joey said, a little deflated himself, and he helped her into the car.

"I figured the next two days would go slow, but now I know they'll go slow."

"Are you going to miss me?" he asked.

"Yeah, well, it'll give you a chance to get all of your strength back, and don't worry; we'll make up for lost time." Ruby smiled as Joey got in.

"That almost sounded like a threat," Joey said, and they were both smiling.

Joey spent most of his time at Stillman's Gym the next two days and couldn't stop thinking about Ruby's offer and the Giardello fight. Angelo was there. He half apologized and half continued the harangue regarding call girls, prostitutes, etc. Finally, Joey was able to pick his suits. He was trying them on and was more than pleased with what he saw in the mirror when Ruby called. She set the time and told him which suit she would like him to wear and then picked him up that night. They went to the Latin Quarter. They had dinner, saw the show, and then went back to her place and made up for the lost two days. Joey stayed the night, and they talked about everything but what was primarily on their minds. Neither of them seemed to want to face that reality. But the following day, as they escaped the city on the Staten Island Ferry, Ruby gave in to curiosity, "You know, one of the things I like about you, Joey?"

"Yeah." He grinned.

"Oh, you! I'm serious … It's that you're so understanding. When I hit you with the news about not seeing you for two days, you hardly flinched. I was afraid you'd be upset."

"I don't have any right to be upset with you, for any reason," Joey said logically.

"Joey, have you been thinking about what I said?"

"You mean, coming to live with you, quitting fighting, and going to the Actors Studio? I haven't been able to think about anything else," Joey admitted. "It's like, I want two things, but I know I can only have one."

"You're waiting for Mike to get back, aren't you?"

"I owe him that. We've been together from the beginning."

"You know what he's going to say, don't you?" she said knowingly.

"Maybe not. The reason I trust him so much is because I know he is not just for himself. He really cares about me," Joey said.

"When does he get back?"

"Tomorrow, or the day after."

A long moment passed before Ruby said, "Let's stay at your place again tonight."

"Why?" Joey asked.

"I want my memory there fresh when you guys talk," she said.

That night, Joey and Ruby were in bed watching a late movie on TV between bouts of love, when they heard a door slam.

"Sounds like Mike came home early," Joey said without moving.

"I was hoping he wouldn't, but I had a feeling he might," Ruby said covering herself with the sheet.

The door connecting the rooms opened, and Mike just stood there with a look of disgust.

"You'll never learn to knock, will you, Mike?" Joey said with disgust of his own.

"Get that bitch outta here; I want to have a long talk with you," Mike said caustically. Then he slammed the door shut, and Joey had to take a deep breath to calm himself.

"I'm sorry about that," he finally said.

"Don't be silly. It's okay," Ruby said slipping out of bed.

"I don't know why he called you that," Joey said puzzled.

"I bet you'll find Angelo already got to him," Ruby said as she got dressed.

"I'm going home. You two might as well get your talk over with."

Joey got into his robe while Ruby finished dressing, and there didn't seem to be anything to say. And they held each other for a moment. Ruby said, "Call me tomorrow." And then she was gone.

Joey knocked on the room's connecting door. "Yeah, come in," Mike called out.

"How come you're back early?" Joey asked tensely as he walked into Mike's room.

"Angelo called me yesterday when he saw what's-her-name pick you up last night. He told me the whole story."

"He doesn't know the whole story," Joey said getting angry.

"Look, Joey, can we talk about this like men, or do we have to start shouting like kids?" Mike said using his fatherly voice.

"Now you're Jekyll. You were Hyde a minute ago," Joey said with his anger rising.

"I've been afraid of losin' you; I don't want to lose you, Joey," Mike said softly, and Joey melted.

"Her name's Ruby, Mike. I like her a lot. She's taken me places, bought me things. She's a lot of fun. I'm only human, Mike," Joey said sitting by the suitcase Mike was unpacking.

"I know, kid, but you've worked so hard, and you've gotten this close. If you beat Giardello, you're a contender."

"I know, Mike," Joey said thinking about being champion.

"Give it another year," Mike urged.

"All right, you're my manager," Joey said thinking of Ruby.

"You're going to have to start doing heavy training now, and you can't do it in a bed."

"I know. I'll handle it," Joey said.

"It's this town. After the Giardello fight, I'm going to take you back to Buffalo."

"Okay, just don't embarrass Ruby anymore, and make sure Angelo doesn't either," Joey said feeling rotten.

"Don't worry about it; I'll take care of it," Mike said reassuringly.

The next day, Joey called Ruby. He told her of his conversation with Mike and that he knew he would never feel right living off of her. She told him to call her anytime and that she would be there for him.

1950 Giambra's face was on many fight cards and tickets. He was Known as The Buffalo Adonis.

1951

Chapter Five

First Giardello, Womber, Graham Fights
(Ages 21–22) 1952–53

On October 13, 1952, Joey fought the number-five middleweight, Joey Giardello, in Eastern Parkway Arena, Brooklyn, Giardello's hometown. Joey had now become a number-five contender for the middleweight title! Incidentally, Joey's first ten-round fight in Brooklyn, New York, was the fight against Giardello. They were the first fighters to use the eight-ounce gloves with new padding made for air force crash helmets, because there were a lot of ring deaths from using the six-ounce gloves that were padded with horse hair, which were vulnerable and would break and separate during the match, making the glove leather and knuckles impact on the fighters, causing death to several boxers the previous year.

The Cornell University laboratories had been experimenting on an eight-ounce boxing glove, utilizing the same shock padding used in pilot helmets. Boxing needed the power of a six-ounce, but at the same time wanted less damage done to the wearer's hand and the receiver's face. The boxing commission of New York decided to test the new glove in the Giardello-Giambra fight being held October 13, 1952, at the Eastern Parkway Arena in Brooklyn. The night before the fight arrived, and Joey was in perfect condition. The odds were three to one that Joey would knock him out, but Joey thought they were way out of line. He had no doubt that he would win the fight. As he tried to fall asleep, he thought about Ruby and about how different the past three months would've been if he had stayed with her. He felt bad that he hadn't even called her. If she'd have said, "Come over," he wouldn't have been able to say, "No."

At the weigh-in the following morning, Joey had a very somber look on his face. After he made the weight and passed the physical, Mike asked what was bothering him. "Ah, nothing, Mike," Joey said with a wave of a hand.

"You're not letting the odds makers scare you, are you?"

"No, no." Joey's head shook.

"Because you know those guys are going strictly from 'He's ranked' and 'You're not.'"

"I know, Mike. I know."

"Well then, what's wrong?" Mike pressed, knowing something was eating him.

"I think I broke training last night."

Mike was becoming exasperated. Then, he suddenly thought and said, "You didn't see that whore again?"

"No, I didn't see anybody, and she's not a whore!" Joey answered irritably.

"Well, then, what the hell are you talking about?"

"I had two wet dreams last night."

Mike started to laugh and said, "Boy, you must be loaded, kid."

"I don't know what's so funny," Joey said worriedly. "Do you think it will slow me down much?"

"Let me tell you something, Joey; those things are natural, and it don't wear you out, like having a broad under you. Now it isn't going to hurt you, so get it out of your mind."

"Okay, Mike," Joey said somewhat relieved.

"That mind of yours, that is your own worst enemy," Mike said shaking his head and walking away.

Joey and Mike were alone in the dressing room just before the fight. Joey was ready to go, and Mike was giving him some last-minute reminders when they heard, "Okay, Joey, you're on."

Joey jogged down the aisle to ringside and then quickly climbed into the ring. Teddy helped him out of his robe. He began moving, punching air, loosening up, letting some of his nervous energy escape, and he wondered if Ruby was there. Giardello climbed confidently into the ring, and the roar of the crowd let him know he was their favorite. He was big city, a future champion with the look of an altar boy. Giambra? A hick from Buffalo, a kid stepping out of his class. The two young men looked at each other with slight smiles as the referee gave them instructions, and then they turned to their respected corners. The bell rang for round one. Both boxers boxed beautifully, and as it rang for the end of round four, the crowd knew they were seeing two excellent boxers in a seemingly even match. Neither of them was able to tag the other with anything solid, and only those with money on Giardello winning the fight by a knockout were unhappy. But in the fifth round, Giardello landed a tremendous right that stopped Joey in his tracks. Giardello was so cocky he started for a neutral corner, not wondering if Joey would go down, but whether he'd get back up. As he turned back, he saw that Joey hadn't gone down, and a more-than-surprised look registered on his face. Joey swarmed all over him for the rest of the round. And when Giardello got back to his corner, he seemed to be in a state of shock.

"You all right?" Mike asked Joey as he and Teddy attended to him.

"Yeah," Joey almost angrily replied.

"He really nailed you."

"He's the one that's worried."

"Go get him, kid," Mike said, knowing his boy was okay.

The fight went the full ten rounds. When it was over, Joey was barely breathing hard, but Giardello was puffing and staggering.

"We beat him! We beat him!" Mike screamed as he grabbed and hugged Joey.

Twenty minutes later, Joey stood in the shower, letting the water cool him. He could still hear the jeers when Giardello got a split decision and the cries from the crowd, "You was robbed!" as he made his way back to the dressing room. Mike immediately demanded a check of the scorecards. Two of the scorecards had been erased here and there, and the scores didn't tally properly. The entire fiasco was brought in front of the boxing commission, and the following day, there was a full hearing about the fight. There was no question the scorecards had been tampered with, and Mike wanted the decision to be reversed. The commission said they couldn't do that, but they did grant Joey a rematch in thirty days. Mike insisted the fight be held in Buffalo, where Joey could get a fair shake.

The Mob had a stranglehold on the boxing business and controlled judge's referees, and others. Even though Joey had won the fight, he lost in a ten-round decision. But the boxing commission at that time was untouchable, fair. When they reviewed the scorecards, they found discrepancies and gave Joey a rematch to be held in Joey's hometown of Buffalo, New York, on November 11, 1952.

The Giardello faction agreed on the condition they could bring two New York officials. Joey told them they could bring anybody they wanted, that it wouldn't matter, that he was going to knock Giardello out. Everything was set. And Joey and Mike packed up and went back to Buffalo. It had been almost a year since Joey had been home, so the first two days he stayed with his mother. Rosina stuffed him with Italian food morning, noon, and night and even made him drink a couple glasses of wine, insisting it was good for his blood. Over the two-day period, Joey got to see all of his family, and he was really able to relax and enjoy himself. On the second night, Mike and his wife were there for dinner, and Joey's brother Angelo tried to give him a few tips on fighting. Being a street fighter supreme, Angelo had tried street fighting in the ring but soon learned he was too short for his weight. For some reason, Angelo had no confidence in Joey and figured Giardello was going to kill him this time if he didn't learn a few things.

"Get away from this kid," Mike finally had to tell Angelo. "He knows what he has to do. Leave him alone."

Later, Joey thought, *I'll show him I'm a good fighter. I'll show the whole family. I'm going to be champion of the world.*

The fight was to be held on November 11, 1952, in the Memorial Auditorium, and since it was to be televised on the *Monday Night Fights*, it was being highly publicized. Everything went well during the training period, and finally, the night of the fight came.

Before the fight, in Joey's dressing room, Vito Domiano came in and told Joey, "Giardello is three to one against you. How do you feel?"

Joey then said, "Vito, bet all you got on me. I won't let you down!" Joey won the fight by decision, but his lip was split down the middle, and he was rushed to the emergency room for twelve stitches.

The Buffalo area was blacked out on television. Ten thousand people packed the auditorium, and Joey knew that between the television money and the live gate, he was going to get the biggest purse of his young career. The crowd cheered wildly for the hometown boy as he bounced slowly down the aisle and into the ring. The cheers dropped off and some booing was heard as Giardello entered the ring, and Joey felt inspiration flooding him. This time, when they were receiving their instructions from the referee, Joey had the same slight smile on his face, but Giardello's countenance was serious and almost grim. Very much like in their first meeting, both Joey G's boxed beautifully for the first four rounds, but just before the end of round four, Giardello caught Joey with an uppercut and split his lower lip right down the middle. Blood gushed out, and when the round ended, the doctor came to Joey's corner. Fearing that they might stop the fight, Joey screamed that he was all right. Mike filled the wound with an iodized solution to coagulate bleeding in that era of boxing. solution that stopped the bleeding immediately.

In the fifth round, Joey started to get Giardello. He worked him over with body shots and then cut his eye. From then on, it was all Giambra, and the crowd were yelling themselves hoarse. In the ninth round, Joey looked like he was going to keep his oath and knock Giardello out, but to Giardello's credit, he was able to hang on. The tenth round was a carbon copy of the ninth, with Joey swarming all over the badly beaten fighter, as Giardello just managed to weather the storm.

Harry Kesler, the referee, was a millionaire businessman who donated his remuneration as a referee to charity. He scored the fight, eight rounds for Giambra, and two rounds for Giardello. Arte Aidella, a judge from New York City, scored it seven rounds for Giambra, two rounds for Giardello, one round even. The local official had been more than impartial, scoring the fight five rounds for Giambra, four rounds for Giardello, one round even, giving Joey a unanimous decision. Joey bounced back up the aisle hearing the cheers and cries of congratulations. He seemed as fresh as when he came down that aisle, only his badly cut lip marked the difference. A stocky, dapperly dressed man approached Mike and Joey. The nice-looking, green-eyed, graying man introduced himself to Joey as Buck Jones and congratulated him. When they shook hands, Joey felt the man put something in his hand and then saw him wink at Mike and walk away. Once inside the dressing room, Joey opened his hand and found five one-hundred-dollar bills.

"Mike, look at this," Joey said astonished.

Mike took the money smiling and saying like a proud father, "I'll hold on to that for you."

"Who is he?" Joey asked as he went to the mirror to check his lip.

"This place will be mobbed in a minute. I'll tell you later."

"Well, what did he give me the money for?"

"I'll tell you that later, too," Mike said with a gleam in his eye.

One knock at the door filled the dressing room with Joey's family and friends. Angelo smiled and told him he was lucky. Sammy told him he was going to be champion, and Carmen, Joey's favorite brother, put his arm around him and hugged him. Then Rosina came in and instantly began to cry when she saw his badly swollen lip. Finally, Mike ordered everyone out, and Joey agreed to meet them at Bafo's La Cantina on Main Street. After his shower and rubdown, Joey dressed in one of the suits that Ruby had bought him and put on his Alan Ladd raincoat, and then he and Mike drove to the party. Tony Bafo had a big table set up for Joey and his family and friends. He liked Joey; he had made a bundle on the fight and gave them a good discount on the bill. Joey felt proud of having shown everyone what a hell of a fighter he was, and he felt proud of the way he was dressed, but most of all, he felt proud because he was only twenty-one, and everyone was proud of him. After the party, Mike took Joey home and started nursing his lip.

"Now will you tell me who the guy was that slipped me the five hundred?"

"Sure, they call him Buck Jones."

"Buck Jones?" Joey said trying to remember where he had heard that name before.

"Doesn't that ring any bells?" Mike prodded.

"The Mafia guy?" Joey asked uncertainly.

"One of the nicest guys you'll ever meet," Mike answered.

"Mafia?" Joey repeated softly to himself.

"Don't worry about it. Believe me, he's a nice guy."

"How come he gave me the money?" Joey asked.

"Just before the fight, he told me how proud he was to have a kid from Buffalo making it in the ring, and he wanted to know what I thought of your chances tonight. I told him you were in great shape and that I thought that you would win. If anyone should ever bother us, he said to just to let him know and he would straighten it out."

"Gee, that's great," Joey said.

Mike agreed. "Giardello was an eleven-to-five favorite, and for Buck to lay five bills on you, he must have had to bet a few grand."

"Wow," was all Joey could say, stunned by the thought that someone would bet thousands on him to win a fight.

"Any way you look at it, we've made an influential friend tonight."

Mike made Joey take the rest of the year off, giving his lip more than enough time to heal and giving Joey time to spend the holidays with his family. Running and light workouts kept Joey in shape, and meanwhile, Mike was able to set up a match for January 26, 1953, in Brooklyn, with Danny "Bang Bang" Womber. Womber was a stable mate and protégé of Sugar Ray Robinson. He was a tough kid from Chicago, who got his nickname by being a rapid-fire puncher. Womber was a natural welterweight, ranked eighth in the world, but often fought in the middleweight division. In the past year, he had fought to a draw with both Ralph "Tiger" Jones and the French champion, Pierre Langlois, and had beaten Kid Gavilan, the welterweight champion in a nontitle bout. All this added up to this being one of the best opponents for Joey to date. Joey had a slight a six-pound advantage over Womber, and after an exciting ten-round battle, it was Joey's superior condition and strength that earned him a unanimous decision.

In the following months, Joey took Bernie Docusen in a third-round knockout by decision. And then soon after, he took Otis Graham by decision. By the time an April rematch with Bang Bang Womber came around, Joey had been ranked the number-five middleweight in the world.

The second bout with Womber was held at the Memorial Auditorium in Buffalo. Because of Joey's surge in popularity and the promise of another great scrap, ABC Television decided to show the bout coast to coast on the *Saturday Night Fights*. Again, the fight went the full ten rounds, but this time, Joey gave Bang Bang a boxing lesson. Joey continually pounded lefts and rights to Womber's head and body, and though Womber kept battling back, he eventually lost a rather lopsided decision. Two weeks after his great showing against Womber, Joey began asking Mike when his next fight would be. Mike told him to relax and stay in shape and that he was working on it. Two weeks later, as Mike was driving Joey home from the gym, Joey said, "It's almost been a month, Mike. What's going on? Why aren't you setting me up with any fights?"

Mike grunted and shook his head. He said, "I'm trying kid. Let me tell you what's happening. I've been talking to a lot of people, and I've been trying to get you Chico Vejar, Vince Martinez, Chuck Davey, and Ernie Durando, and all I get is the same thing, they are all asking a fortune to fight you and all the promoters have to pass."

"I don't understand, Mike. They know what the promoters can and can't afford," Joey said.

"Sure they do," Mike agreed as they pulled into the driveway and parked. "They are all afraid of you. They figure if they fight you, they are going to get beat, so they ask for the moon, and there is no fight."

"Is there any way we can force them to fight?" Joey asked.

"How do you force a guy to fight?" Mike said rhetorically. "You have thirty-one wins, and the two you lost to Cesario and Giardello were both tainted. These guys know that. They know you're a smart, aggressive fighter, with dynamite in both hands. They don't want any part of you."

"Well, what are we going to do?" Joey asked Mike as he started getting out of the car.

"You're going to stay ready, and I'm going to keep plugging. Actually, we're pretty close to getting a match with Kid Portuguese. We'll know in a few days."

"Hey, that would be great." Joey brightened, and he and Mike started for the house.

"Great, I am not too sure about," Mike said with concern. "I'll tell you one thing about the Kid, we'll find out how good a punch you can take. That chunky little Costa Rican champ hits as hard as anyone in the division."

The fight with Tuzo "Kid" Portuguese was set for June 20, 1953, at the Memorial Auditorium in Buffalo, the site of Joey's big wins over Giardello and Womber. Joey was very edgy about the fight, because he figured if he beat the Kid, the others wouldn't be able to keep ducking him. Then when he learned that Lou Scozza was to referee the fight, he really got nervous. Maybe it was just chemistry, but he knew Scozza didn't like him, and that for some reason or another, he had something against Joey. The night of the fight rolled around, and Joey was ready. Again, the fight was being televised but blacked out in the area, and again, a packed house let Joey know that he was their choice. The bell rang, and the fight was on. Joey moved and boxed beautifully, and Kid Portuguese couldn't touch him. In the second round, Joey hit him with his best punch, a left hook to the jaw, and the Kid just laughed at him, showing Joey a shining gold front tooth. Joey tried not to show any surprise, remembering the look on Giardello's face when he took his best punch, but Joey was thinking he would have to stay on his bicycle throughout the fight. Still, in the second round, Joey caught the Kid with another good left but felt pain in his left hand and knew that he had hurt himself more than he probably hurt the Kid. For the next three rounds, Joey tried covering up that he was only punching with his right, but when he returned to his corner at the end of the fifth, Mike yelled, "What the hell's the matter with you?"

"My left hand is gone," Joey admitted, but he was moving and boxing so well that Kid Portuguese wasn't getting to him and the fight was all Joey's. In the eighth round, Joey felt his energy starting to go. They were indoors with no air-conditioning, and the body heat of ten thousand people, the hot television lights above the ring, and his own perpetual movement all began to take their toll and sap his strength.

Both fighters fell into a clinch, feeling grateful for the momentary respite, but then Referee Scozza stepped in and told them to break, and as Joey moved back, Scozza stepped on his foot, and he stumbled and fell backward. With Joey's guard down as he was trying to regain his balance, Kid Portuguese hit him with a sucker punch that caught him squarely in his right eye and knocked him flat on his back. Suffering the first knockdown of his professional career, Joey was all but out cold and only instinct made him crawl to the ropes and start climbing. He was on his feet at the count of four, hanging on to the ropes and trying to shake the cobwebs out of his head. But by the time the mandatory eight count ended, Joey's eye was puffed up and closed tight. Scozza didn't even ask Joey if he was all right; he just stepped aside and let the Kid at him. Again, Joey's instinct was there, and he knew the Kid would go for the kill. His one good eye saw the Kid's wild right coming. He ducked, and Kid Portuguese flew through the ropes and was hanging out of the ring. Joey grabbed him to keep him from falling out of the ring and onto the concrete below, and the Kid came back with an elbow that caught Joey right on top of the head, showing him a blinding flash of light. The bell rang, and as Joey staggered back to his corner, he heard the ovation of the crowd, and he knew it was for him. He also knew that Kid had fought dirty, and a wave of anger went through him.

"Wow, what a punch that was!" Joey said as he fell to the stool.

"Yeah, I thought your head was coming off," Mike said as he and Teddy went to work. "I don't know how the hell you ever got up."

Joey's head felt like a balloon, and he could only see through one eye, but his head cleared again, and he thought, *Left hand, I know you're hurt, and I'm sorry, but I'm going to have to use you anyway.*

"You've got a real bad eye, kid; we can either stop the fight or cut it open with a razor," Mike said grimly.

"No, Mike, don't stop the fight, and don't cut my eye open … This guy won't hit me anymore," Joey said firmly.

Just then, the doctor came over. "What do you think?" the doctor asked Mike.

"He's going to be all right; don't worry about it," Mike answered quickly.

The bell rang for round nine. Joey knew that Kid Portuguese was tired too and the heat was wearing him down too, so he went to work on him with body punches. After a minute, the Kid started hanging on, and after another minute, he dropped his guard to ward off the body blows. Joey put everything he had into a right cross. The Kid did a pirouette and flew across the ring. Joey was on him like a panther, again delivering body shots that hurt. As Joey walked back to his corner after the bell, he received a standing ovation, this time for his comeback from the previous round. The final round began with the usual touching of gloves, but Joey only put one glove out, a sign to those in the know that he felt the Kid had fought dirty. Then Joey proceeded to give him an unmerciful beating. He cut his left eye and his lip and had his nose bleeding. He kept pounding him with lefts and rights. Kid Portuguese was a bloody mess by the time the final bell rang, but Joey kept right on punching until the referee stepped in and broke it up. Joey went to his corner hearing the yelling, screaming fans who knew they had just seen a great fight. The two judges gave the decision to Joey, much to the crowd's agreement, but Lou Scozza made it a split decision by making his card for Kid Portuguese and was soundly booed for his effort.

Rosina hadn't come to the fight, but the rest of Joey's family was there and waiting for him outside of his dressing room. They became quite upset when they saw what he looked like, so Mike rushed him inside and locked the door. In a matter of seconds, Mike and Teddy had an ice pack on his eye, and they were wrapping off his badly swollen left hand. Joey was in a lot of pain, and his thoughts went once again to what a rough business he was in. His morale was way down, and he told Mike he wanted to leave by the back door. Mike went out and told them Joey was all right but didn't want them to see him looking the way he did. When they got home, Mike packed Joey's eye with borough's solution, which helped reduce the swelling. The next morning, Mike took him to the hospital for some X-rays. The eye proved to have a broken blood vessel and would heal itself, but the second finger on his left hand was dislocated, had a bone chip near the large knuckle, and required a full hand cast. Then just to make sure Joey hadn't received any brain damage, he was given an electroencephalograph.

"Well, kid, with that eye and that busted knuckle, it looks like you won't be fighting for at least a month," Mike said as they drove away from the hospital.

"Maybe longer. I want to take a vacation. I feel like I need a rest," Joey added.

"Why not? What do you say we go up to Canada?" Mike agreed.

"Hey, bass season starts in a few weeks."

So Joey and Mike went to their training camp in Godfrey, Ontario, Canada. Joey stayed in shape doing roadwork and shadowboxing, but mainly he relaxed by going fishing. Then one night, he went to a square dance and met a young lady. He brought her back to the two-bedroom cabin he shared with Mike.

Mike's only comment was, "Why didn't you bring a girl home for me?"

They shared two beautiful nights and days before the beautiful girl had to go back home to Perth. Since it was only thirty-five miles away, Joey drove her back, and she promised to return for another weekend before his vacation ended. Almost six weeks of fishing and swimming and running freed Joey's body from all stress and injury and painted it a deep tan. That same period of time did as much, if not more, for his mind. Joey and Mike came home in mid-July, and no sign of Joey's injuries remained. They were greeted with the news that all arrangements had been completed for a rematch with Tuzo Kid Portuguese in September. So once more, Joey began a schedule of heavy workouts in preparation for the fight, but this time, he wasn't worried about the Kid.

Joey knew the Kid's style. He knew that he could beat him easily and that if he didn't get stepped on by the referee, the Kid wouldn't be able to get to him. Joey's prediction was borne out. He won a lopsided unanimous decision and went back to his dressing room without a mark on him. "This was like a warm-up, Mike; we ought to line up something right away," Joey said, feeling his oats.

"Well, they want you for a Christmas show in Cleveland."

"Christmas, that's a long way off!" Joey barked.

Mike thought for a moment before remembering, "Hey, Otis Graham's looking for a match. He's on his way out and looking for something to make a few bucks. You want to take him on next month?"

"Sure, I beat him easy when we fought at Eastern Parkway. It'll just be like another warm-up," Joey said.

"Right! Meanwhile, I'll have time to see what I can do about getting you a big one."

"Are we going to fight him at home?"

"Nah, I think we could draw better up in Canada with Otis, and besides, you have got a lot of fans up there. Let me make a few calls tomorrow."

Mike had no problem setting up the fight for early October in the Maple Leaf Garden in Toronto. It was a big arena, and they figured Joey would draw quite a crowd. But as the fight drew near, even though Graham was a tough fighter and a hard hitter, rumors started flying all over town that he was going to take a dive. This both embarrassed and upset Joey, but there was nothing he could do. Joey was sitting on the rubdown table in his dressing room and ready to go, when Mike was called outside. A minute later, he returned.

"What was that all about?" Joey asked.

"Ah, nothing, the boxing commission just told Graham if he tried anything funny, he wouldn't get the three grand he was guaranteed." Mike shrugged.

"That's a shitty thing to pull on a guy just before a fight," Joey said disgustedly.

"Yeah, but the rumors are still hot and heavy that he just wants the money and doesn't want to get hurt doing it."

"Gees, what if I really knock this guy out? Everyone is going to think he took a dive anyway," Joey hissed.

"Well, he told them that he's not only going to fight, he's going to win, so don't you start playing Kid Galahad out there. He could still get lucky and knock you on your ass."

"Yeah, I know. I won't take any chances, Mike."

Ten minutes later, the fight was on. The first two rounds featured good boxing but very little action, and the restlessness of the crowd permeated the arena. Then, in the third round, Joey hit Graham with a beautiful left hook that staggered him. Joey tried to press his advantage, but Graham clinched and covered up until the round ended. The crowd was no longer restless but had come alive.

"I thought you had him, the poor bastard's probably afraid to go down," Mike said as Joey returned to his corner.

"He must need the three grand real bad," Joey said as he got worked on.

The next three rounds found Graham calling on what skills he had left just to make a fight of it and at the same time keep away from Joey's relentless pursuit. But in the seventh round, the inevitable happened. Joey hit him flush in the jaw with his best right-hand punch. Joey knew he had hurt him badly and only the ropes were holding Graham on his feet. Suddenly, another instinct came into play for Joey, and he eased off his punches. Maybe it was all the pre-fight dive talk, or maybe it was knowing that Graham was about to hang 'em up (quit fighting), but Joey carried him the rest of the way (pulled the punches, didn't hit him hard). The following day, Joey made sure Graham got his money and then told the boxing commission what he thought of them for threatening to withhold Graham's purse. Mike kept trying to shut him up, but something told Joey they were out for blood and had maybe even started the rumors themselves so that Graham would take as much of a beating as he could stand, and then some.

As they headed back to Buffalo, Joey's anger subsided, and when he told Mike, "I don't ever want to fight in Canada again," it was with deadly calm.

Joey and Mike knew that another win over Otis Graham wasn't going to further his career, but an unexpected plus did come out of the fight. A ringside photographer got the action shot of his life. He had a close-up lens trained on Graham when Joey hit him with that right in the seventh. The picture of Graham's face, distorted beyond recognition, with Joey's right-hand glove mashed against it and perspiration flying through the air in all directions, made several national magazines and most of the sports sections across the States. With that kind of publicity, Joey Giambra became a recognizable name all over the country.

1952 Giambra on another cover

1952 Madison Square Garden

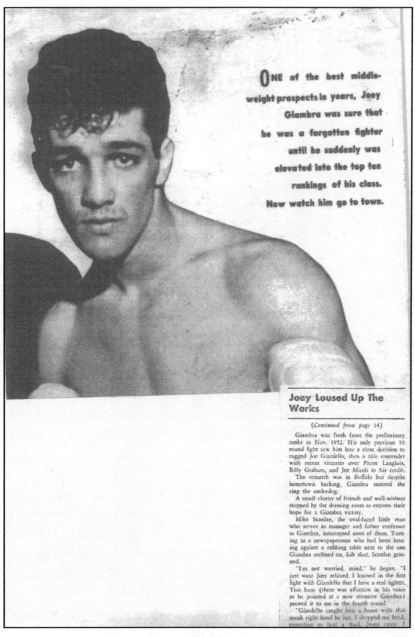

ONE of the best middle-weight prospects in years, Joey Giambra was sure that he was a forgotten fighter until he suddenly was elevated into the top ten rankings of his class. Now watch him go to town.

Joey Loused Up The Works

(*Continued from page* 14)

Giambra was fresh from the preliminary ranks in Nov. 1952. His only previous 10 round fight saw him lose a close decision to rugged Joe Giardello, then a title contender with recent victories over Pierre Langlois, Billy Graham, and Joe Miceli to his credit.

The rematch was in Buffalo but despite hometown backing, Giambra entered the ring the underdog.

A small cluster of friends and well-wishers stopped by the dressing room to express their hope for a Giambra victory.

Mike Scanlan, the oval-faced little man who serves as manager and father confessor to Giambra, intercepted most of them. Turning to a newspaperman who had been leaning against a rubbing table next to the one Giambra reclined on, lids shut, Scanlan grinned.

"I'm not worried, mind," he began. "I just want Joey relaxed. I learned in the first fight with Giardello that I have a real fighter. This bum (there was affection in his voice as he pointed at a now attentive Giambra) proved it to me in the fourth round.

"Giardello caught him a beaut with that sneak right hand he has. I dropped me head, expecting to hear a thud. None came. I

1952

70

Chapter Six

Night at the Rathskeller
(Age 22) 1953

Mike decided to strike while the iron was hot. He had a syndicate connection that he hadn't wanted to use, but he knew that without help, he and Joey could only go so far. He got in touch with Oney "Machine Gun" Madden and asked if he could get Joey a fight in Madison Square Garden. "The kid's good enough. Why not?" was Madden's reply.

Al Weil, Rocky Marciano's manager, grudgingly told him that plans were made for Giambra to fight Sal DiMartino in an eight-round semifinal the last week of October.

"The Garden?" Joey asked with disbelief.

"Madison Square Garden, but you're in with a real tough guy. Sal's a good fighter and puncher," Mike said.

"Yeah, I know, and he's won about twenty straight," Joey said.

"I think Weil wants to see you get creamed because I used 'juice' to get you in," Mike said uncomfortably.

"Don't worry about it, Mike. I'll lay him out." Joey was thrilled just being in the Madison Square Garden dressing room and couldn't wait to get into the ring. And then, Mike had to hold on to him to keep him from running down the aisle. Once in the ring, Joey began jumping up and down, shadowboxing, and filling his eyes with his surroundings. When he heard his name announced and moved forward to take his bow, Joey was almost overwhelmed with the dream come true.

"Take it easy this round; feel him out. You hear me?" Mike cautioned.

"I know I'm wired, Mike, but don't sweat it; I'm okay," Joey said quickly.

He boxed brilliantly, scoring well and making DiMartino constantly miss. At the end of the sixth round, Joey had a bad cut in the corner of his left eye, where DiMartino had caught him with an elbow, but Mike had stopped the bleeding and Joey had been able to protect the eye.

"What's that?" Joey asked as the television lights went on.

"They are going to show the last two rounds on TV before the main event," Mike told him.

"This is going all over the country, isn't it?"

"National television, kid. Now don't let it throw you; just keep fighting your fight."

And that's exactly what Joey did. Joey easily won a unanimous decision. The following day, the switchboard handled dozens of phone calls from people wanting to know about Joey Giambra, and during the week, a bagful of mail came in, all with the same request.

"You're fighting Tony Amato in two weeks," Mike said while Joey worked on a heavy bag at Stillman's Gym.

"At the Garden?" Joey asked.

"Of course, another eight-round semifinal, and they told me if you win this one, they'll give you a main event." Mike grinned.

Joey knew the fight with Tony Amato, a good-looking kid from Brooklyn, was a big chance. He felt the pressure immediately and was more nervous in the following two weeks than he had ever been before. Again, he felt the thrill of just being in the Garden, the thrill of being announced there and of hearing the bell for round one. Both fighters felt each other out during the first round, and Joey fought cautiously during the second and third, holding back a bit. In the fourth round, he started to open up. In the seventh round, Joey hit Amato with a devastating left hook, and he fell like a tree. Amato didn't move while the referee counted him out, and Joey received a standing ovation from the Garden's knowledgeable boxing fans.

Joey was still in the dressing room, savoring his knockout win over Amato, when Mike came in rubbing his hands together. "Okay, kid, now you've made it. Your next fight here is the main event. They'll let us know in a few days."

"I'm glad, Mike. We finally made it, huh?" Joey said understating his true feelings of stardom.

"Yeah, kid, we finally made it."

In Joey's bout with Jimmy Herring, the blond-haired, blue-eyed, German-American "Golden Boy" of New York, Joey was called the Buffalo Adonis, with his brown hair, brown eyes, and Italian-American heritage. The fight was booked as the Battle of the Beauties. This was Joey's debut as a main eventer. The Garden was sold out, even with TV access live!

Joey's first main event at Madison Square Garden was set for December 6, 1953. And Joey's opponent, you ask? Jimmy Herring, the Golden Boy of New York. Herring was a good-looking blond-haired, blue-eyed German. He really looked like a golden boy, and he was also undefeated. After his win over Amato, the sportswriters started calling Joey the Buffalo Adonis and were billing the upcoming fight with the Golden Boy as "the Battle of the Beauties." They also started to call Joey the best fighter they had seen in fifteen years, and with this, Joey began to believe in himself, to the point of thinking he was one of the greatest fighters in the world.

Mike and Teddy were in the dressing room waiting for the semifinal to end. Mike was cleaning his fingernails with a penknife, just to give his hands something to do, and Teddy kept rubbing Joey's neck and back muscles, constructively releasing his nervous tension. As for Joey, he couldn't wait to get into that ring.

"Mike, we are on television in Hollywood, aren't we?" Joey asked.

"Sure, coast to coast, why do you ask?" Mike said.

"Maybe they'll discover me?" Joey said exuberantly.

"What? Are you kidding me?" Mike said, unable to believe what Joey was thinking about at a time like that.

"No," Joey said with a smile.

"You got to be pulling my leg talking like that before the fight of your life."

"I'm not worried about the fight, Mike."

"What do you mean? This guy hasn't lost a fight. He's a tough kid," Mike said with his nerves fraying.

"I've seen him fight a couple of times. I know a few things he does wrong, and when he does, I'll catch him," Joey said confidently.

"Just like that, you are starting to believe all that publicity, and you're starting to get cocky," Mike said.

"Aww, no, Mike," Joey said.

"This guy might hand you your head, and all you can think about is getting discovered by Hollywood."

The semifinal ended, and Joey was on his way. Once in the ring, he began jumping up and down in the classic manner while some celebrity fighters were being introduced and taking bows. Joey was looking over the ringside around his corner, when he spotted Ruby. She waved and smiled. And Mike saw him wave and smile back.

"Who are you smiling at?" Mike asked looking around.

"That girl over there," Joey answered nodding in Ruby's direction.

"Where do you know her from?"

Joey didn't want Mike to know it was Ruby, and since it had been over a year since Mike had seen her last, Joey knew he wouldn't recognize her. "I don't know. I just met her somewhere," Joey said.

"With over fifteen thousand people here, you spot a dame," Mike said shaking his head.

"Look, kid, you get your mind on the fight and forget about Hollywood, broads, and everything else. You understand?"

"Mike, there's one thing I want if I win this fight. If I win, will you give it to me?"

"Joey, if you win this fight, I will buy you a brand-new Cadillac. Just go in there and fight like you know how … What do you want?"

"I want to get laid; that's what I want."

"I don't believe it, blonde or brunette?" Mike said looking over at Jimmy Herring.

"You've got something against redheads?" Joey kidded.

The fighters were introduced, and the reaction of the crowd was like the odds, six to five pick 'em. For the first three rounds, the fight was dead even. Both boys boxed beautifully and seemed equal as far as ability was concerned. Joey returned to his corner and said, "Mike, how's my hair?"

"What the hell are you worried about your hair for?"

"I'm on camera. Hollywood's looking at me." Joey beamed.

"You're in an awfully good mood for a guy who is just holding his own."

Joey winked and said, "Mike, I'm going to knock him out in this round."

"Kid, don't take any chances. This is a damn good fighter, and he's got a hell of a punch!" Mike cautioned.

"I've got him in my back pocket, and I don't have a mark on me either … Hollywood's going to discover me, and I'm going to be an actor."

"Yeah sure, kid," Mike said to Joey, humoring him as the bell rang. "Go on."

The fighters circled each other, and then Joey threw a left jab and let his left hand drop on purpose. Joey knew this action would draw a right lead from Jimmy Herring, and when it came, Joey slipped it with his head and put everything he had into a right into the Golden Boy's jaw. Herring stopped dead in his tracks, gave Joey a surprised look just before his eyes rolled to the back of his head, and with a delayed reaction fell over. Joey went quickly to a neutral corner and resumed his boxing stance in case Herring got up. The black curl that fell to Joey's forehead bounced with each count from the referee. The Golden Boy managed to struggle to his knees at the count of five. He tried to balance himself and then fell back at the count of seven, completely out. Joey rushed over to the fallen fighter to help his manager take him back to his corner, but the previously undefeated Golden Boy's manager angrily pushed him away. Mike was so excited he jumped into the ring as if Joey had just become the champion of the world. Joey hadn't even worked up a sweat and had a smile on his face that let everyone know how happy he was. And knowing that Hollywood was watching, Joey started to ham it up, taking bows and throwing kisses to the crowd and the camera.

Johnny Addy's voice suddenly rang out over the loudspeakers. "The winner by a knockout, Joey Giambra!"

Ruby was standing by as Joey climbed down out of the ring and tried to press a note into his glove. Teddy Bentham saw the note fall, and Joey watched him pick it up as Mike began to quickly usher him toward the dressing room. Halfway up the aisle, a wave of hysterical young women and teenage girls pushed Mike and Teddy aside as they attacked the Buffalo Adonis. By the time the security police got to him, Joey was stripped of his robe and trunks by the screaming females, and the police had to escort him to his dressing room wearing only shoes, socks, and his jockstrap. When Joey came out of the shower hooking a towel around his waist, he found his dressing room full of photographers and reporters and could hear screaming young ladies being kept outside. Joey reveled in it all, and twenty minutes later, he was finally able to sit down and begin to descend from the clouds. Jim Norris, the owner of Madison Square Garden, the Detroit Red Wings, and oil interests, told everyone to leave the dressing room, and a few people of the Mob, including Frankie Carbo, walked everyone out.

Mike and Joey were left alone with Mr. Norris, and he said, "You're going to be the next middleweight champion, and we're giving you a party at the Rathskeller restaurant and dining room across the street from the Garden. I own it, and we'll have a meeting with my partners who decide who gets the title!"

Joey then said, "Who gets the title is the last man standing in the ring."

Carbo just smiled and said, "Now you get yourself cleaned up, and we'll see you in an hour!"

Carbo left, and Mike Scanlan said to Joey, "We're in with the boys!"

Joey later said to Teddy, "Teddy, where's the note Ruby gave me?"

"Ruby is that that whore?" Mike began out of habit.

"Mike, don't talk that way about her. She's not a whore."

"Okay, kid, anything you want, it's yours. You are my champ," Mike said benevolently.

Teddy handed Joey the note which told him she was staying at the very plush Sherry Netherlands Hotel and that she would be waiting for his call.

"I've got what I wanted, Mike." Joey laughed as he started for his clothes.

"Good, now all I have to do is get you the car, but leave your clothes off a while; dry out and cool off completely," Mike said laughing with him.

"All right," Joey said as he sprawled out on the rubbing table.

"We're in the big time now, kid; the big man finally opened his eyes to you," Mike said proudly.

"Yeah, what does it mean?" Joey said somewhat bewildered.

"We'll find out when we talk to him. Well, what are you waiting for? Get dressed!" Mike concluded.

Jocy's nice-looking, brown-eyed, full-lipped brother, Carmen, was waiting when he came out of the dressing room. Carmen hugged Joey in his five-foot-ten-inch, one-hundred-and-ninety-five-pound frame, and they both knew nothing had to be said. Carmen had become even more religious than Joey, spending much of his World War II service time in the hospital reading the Bible from cover to cover. He didn't drink or smoke and rarely went out with girls. He was looking for a nice girl to marry and settle down and have children with, but she hadn't yet come along.

"Are you with me tonight?" Joey asked him.

"One hundred percent." Carmen smiled happily.

"Let's go," Mike called back as he and Teddy crossed the street. When they arrived, they were escorted to a big office in the back room. Joey remembered seeing Norris, Frankie Carbo, and a few boys (made men in the Mafia). He never got their names. They closed the door after they entered.

Two men stood by the door, and Mr. Carbo said, "Vito Genevese met Joey and likes him and told us to buy Joey's contract."

They offered Mike $50,000 (a lot of money in that day!).

Mike said, "I am like the father the kid never had. I'll leave it up to Joey."

Joey then replied, "If Mike works as my trainer, I accept."

Norris and Carbo said, "We have our own trainers for our boxers."

"Mike brought me this far, so I'm staying with Mike."

Carbo yelled out, "You don't tell us! We tell you!"

"Mr. Norris, you seem like a gentleman. Does that mean if I don't sign with you, I won't be able to fight in the Garden anymore?" Joey said.

Norris smiled and said, "Kid, you're the hottest fighter in the country after you KO'd our golden boy Herring! You can still fight in the Garden, but you'll be fighting the toughest Ni***r we can find! If you sign with us, I'll give you a contract for the title."

Joey smiled and told him, "I won't sign, so bring on whoever you want."

As Joey and Mike were leaving, Carbo smiled at Joey and said, "You could've had it all. You have a lot of balls, and I respect you for that."

Joey said, "Mr. Carbo, please give my regards to Mr. Genevese!"

Later that evening, Joey was treated royally when he and his entourage entered the Rathskeller. Norris had a buffet of gourmet food set up, and the bar was open. There were photographers, reporters, guys, and dolls by the score, and Joey Giambra was the guest of honor. He thrived and basked in it and then remembered Ruby. He had to call her. He told her the situation and asked her to come over, and she agreed on the condition she could bring her girlfriend. Joey and Carmen sipped on their soft drinks while Ruby and her girlfriend sat at the bar. Joey didn't want to get a playboy tag, though he joined Carmen and the girls, and after a short while, he suggested the girls go back to the hotel. He told them that he and Carmen would join them in a little while.

Ruby smiled and said, "Just make sure it's a 'little' while."

"Sooner than that," Joey promised.

Five minutes later, Joey walked over to Mike and told him he was leaving.

"You going to see that girl?"

Joey smiled and said, "Yeah."

"Okay, have a good time, and be careful." Mike smiled back as he handed Joey a couple hundred dollars.

"You didn't need any money," Carmen said to Joey as they left the Rathskeller.

"What do you mean?" Joey asked.

"Where'd you get it?"

"I bet on the fight, and I won five thousand bucks." Carmen grinned.

"Five thousand? Gees, you took an awful chance, Carmen. What if I had lost?" Joey said dumbfounded.

"Hey, I got a lot of confidence in you," Carmen said as he shadowboxed in the street. When Joey and Carmen got to the Sherry Netherlands Hotel, they found the girls waiting for them in the lobby.

"We decided we wanted to take a walk. How does that sound to you?" Ruby asked.

"Great," Joey said as they all began a tour of the Times Square area. Joey and Ruby walked arm in arm, and her friend and Carmen walked the same way, close behind.

"I've missed you," Ruby said softly. "I can't tell you how many times I thought of you. It's been over a year."

Joey nodded. "I know."

She nodded back. "I called you a while back, and your phone was disconnected. And I wondered what happened. I also wrote you a couple of letters. Didn't you get them?" Ruby said somewhat surprised.

"No," Joey said picturing Mike seeing whom the letters were from and tearing them up.

"Could your manager have gotten a hold of them?" Ruby asked.

Joey smiled and said, "You're reading my mind. So what have you been doing?"

"Capsule version now, details later," Ruby began and then had to interrupt herself. "By the way, we've got adjoining rooms, and I know Carmen would be welcome."

"He likes her too," Joey said.

"Good, now we don't have to worry about them … Well, when you went back to training, I decided to quit the business and go back to Memphis. I moved into one of my own penthouses, made up with the folks, and went straight arrow. My stocks tripled, and I also invested in several business ventures. I'm really a very rich lady."

They all stopped at a fruit stand and had papaya juice and then walked back to the hotel. Inside of half an hour, Joey and Ruby were alone, and a little while later, they spoke of how beautiful it was to be together.

The next morning, Carmen came in with all the newspapers, and Joey read the glowing reports of his victory over the Golden Boy. He also saw pictures of himself as the girls tore his clothes off. He was holding his crotch with both hands and had a funny grin on his face.

"Let's go have breakfast," Joey said feeling the whole world was on his side. He had money in the bank; he was getting a new car, he had a great future, and right then, he had a beautiful girl.

"You've always done so much for me; let me buy something for you," Joey said to Ruby after they ate.

Ruby glowed softly. "Buy me a bunch of flowers."

"Aww, come on, I mean something real nice."

"Joey, money couldn't buy me anything nicer."

Joey went over to one of the flower hustlers that dotted Broadway and bought her a bunch of daisies.

"Thank you." She smiled, as she kissed his cheek. Later, between passion's fall and passion's rise, Ruby said, "We'll be going back to Memphis tomorrow."

"So soon? I was hoping to have a few more days together," Joey said disappointed.

"I want you to come to Memphis when you get some time off. We can have a lot of fun," Ruby said.

"I'd like that."

"And let's keep in touch this time," Ruby offered.

"I'll make sure of it," Joey said, again picturing Mike.

1953 After the Giambra vs. Portuguez fight standing with manager and trainer Mike Scanlan

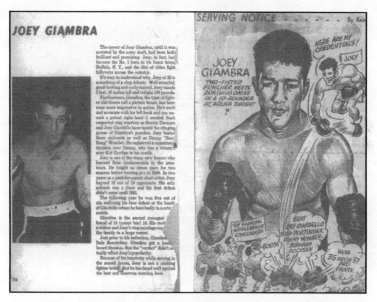

1953 cartoon from the boxing press and the many Giambra fans pleading for Giambra to get a title shot!

*1953 another cover of TV boxing (Giambra
and trainer/manager Mike Scanlan)*

1953 Giambra and his dog Mickey

One of the first Buffalonians to greet Robinson here was Joey Giambra, fifth leading contender for Sugar's old middleweight crown.

"I've seen you fight," Robinson told him, "and you have great possibilities, Joey, if you aren't rushed. Just feel that you're better than any man you fight, and it will help a lot. The only other advice I can give is to keep your hands up and your trunks off the floor."

WRITTEN ADVICE FROM SUGAR—Joey Giambra, left, local middleweight contender, looks over some written advice from Ray Robinson, former world champion. It read: "Keep your hands up and your trunks off the floor."

1953 Giambra and the great Sugar Ray Robinson

SUGAR SHOULD KNOW!

SUGAR RAY ROBINSON, in our midst for the first time a thespian instead of a thumper, classifies Joey Giambra as one the best looking prospects in the game today. "He's definitely championship caliber," said Sugar Ray, whose dance act is curren showing at Shea's Buffalo. Then, turning to Manager Mike Sca ian, he warned: "But be sure to bring him along slowly, as he's s a year or so away from the title." Later, Ray confided to this wri that he likes Joey's chances because he's such a clean-living k always in top condition and without any bad habits. "That's wh you have to have to get up there nowadays," added the former w terweight and middleweight champion of the world.

Asked to name the boxer most likely to occupy his vacat middleweight throne, Ray selected Randy Turpin and Bobo Ols as the two best candidates at the present time. Pressed further as

Sugar Ray, left, offers sound advice to Buffalo's Joey Giambra.

the ultimate winner between the two, Sugar simply smiled and sa "Guess I'll have to sit this one out." He added that Olson is a va y improved fighter and suggested that "he definitely must be doi the right thing." Ray pointed out that Bobo is one of the best-co ditioned athletes he's ever encountered, is a "game, aggressive b and very clever, although he lacks the wallop that Turpin packs."

*   *   *   *   *

AS TO the Berlin rhubarb, which left a bit of sour taste to his European tour in the summer of '51, Ray explained that Gerhard Hecht's handlers charged that their boxer had been hit a kidney punch when he was unable to get up after a blow to the stomach. Some of the fans took up the chant, shouting: "That's what Louis did to Schmeling!" The referee ordered the boxers to continue, and Ray knocked him out again. When Hecht's manager started throwing bottles, the referee became scared and disqualified the champ for using the kidney punch.

1953 Giambra gets some advice from the great Sugar Ray

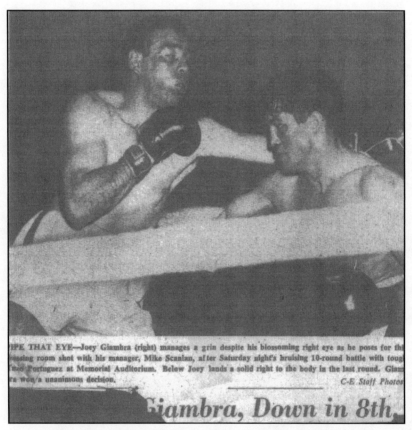

1953 Giambra lands a punishing blow to Tuzos body

1953 Giambra vs.Giardello AGAIN

Giambra's Solid Blows Outpoint Foe In Solid Renewal of Pro Boxing Here

By FRANK WAKEFIELD

BUFFALO'S Joey Giambra, newest member of the big ten in the middleweight class, convinced the majority of the 7273 fans who saw him defeat Joe Giardello, that he is going to be a good fighter.

Whatever lingering doubts there may have been concerning the pink cheeked East Sider's fighting heart and ability were dispelled as Giambra roared from behind to win a unanimous ten-round decision over the fast-hitting and cagey Giardello as boxing returned to the Memorial Auditorium ring Tuesday night after an absence of 12½ months.

The victory not only proved that the 21-year-old Giambra can handle himself against a nationally-ranked boxer, but also helped move Buffalo back toward the prominent position it once enjoyed in the boxing world.

Giambra Squares Accounts

Since the 22-year-old Philadelphian, Giardello, has been ranked ninth among the world's leading middleweights, Giambra practically is certain of gaining a position in the first ten of that division; and he rich awards that go with such ranking.

The bout, ten-round main event of an excellent Hudson Boxing Club show, was a return encounter, Giardello having taken a close and disputed decision over Giambra last month in Brooklyn. Tuesday's victory vindicated the claim of the Buffalonian's management, as well as several metropolitan boxing writers, that Giambra had deserved the verdict in that, his first match.

The story of Tuesday's hard-fought and exciting bout could be told in just two words: Superior condition. Giambra was trained as finely as a race horse by Manager Ike Scanlon and Trainer "Chops" Alberti, and it paid off.

Gains Deserved Decision

It paid off in the early rounds when Giambra had to withstand Giardello's furious attack and heavy hooks to the head and body. And it paid off in the closing rounds when the Buffalonian took the lead from a tiring but ringwise adversary, and finished strongly to gain a popular and deserved triumph, the biggest of his 30-bout professional career.

Although each fighter landed

Joey Giambra, left, scores with a light left as Joey Giardello misses with a wild right in their bout Tuesday night in Memorial Auditorium (Photo by Paul Thomson).

hard and often, there were no knockdowns and the only blood came from a ¾-inch cut inside Giambra's lower lip in the fourth round.

Giambra started very slowly. The Philadelphian repeatedly beat the East Sider to the punch and at the end of five rounds, Giambra trailed 3-1-1 in rounds.

9th Round Victor's Best

The fifth was even, and it was there that it could be noticed that the fast pace was slowing Giardello down to a walk. Giambra stepped it up in the sixth and just about evened the score in the next three rounds, outpunching a back-pedaling and weary Giardello in the seventh, eighth and ninth rounds.

Giambra was glad to do plenty of clinching in those frames, but the powerful Buffalonian shoved him away and renewed the attack. The ninth probably was Giambra's best round when Giardello's low-held right was an open invitation. Giambra accepted and landed a double left hook to the jaw.

He rocked Giardello with the fury of his attack and it looked as if the Philadelphian would go down in Giambra's corner, but somehow he got off the hook and weathered the round.

Giardello, who refused to sit down between rounds, came out with a last-ditch rally in the final round, gained a slight edge, but it wasn't enough to swing the deci...

the other, Willie DiJames, had it 5-4 for the victor with one round even. The referee, Ruby Kessler, and this writer also scored the fight 5-4-1. The two judges are from Buffalo and Kessler is a New York City official.

Referee Gives Winner 6 Rounds

At 154½ pounds, Giardello had a ¾-pound weight advantage over Giambra.

In the six-round semifinal, Billy Mayo, 186, Buffalo, won a unanimous decision over Terry O'Connor, 189, Niagara Falls, Ont.

Jimmy Watkins, 147½, Buffalo, made an auspicious pro debut by stopping Eddie Reynolds, 146½, Syracuse. Referee Fred Stanton of Buffalo halted this scheduled six-rounder in 1:55 of the fifth round.

Dee Antonio, 158, Niagara Falls, scored a TKO over Jimmy Jones, 150½, Utica, in 2:01 of the second round of his first pro start, while another pair of novices, Harry Budniewski, 157½, Dunkirk, and Johnny Barilla, 162½, Syracuse, flailed away to a good draw.

The gate receipts were announced as $14,872.23 by Promoter Tom Lippes.

1953 Giambra vs. Giardello Giambra slips Giardellos left and Giambra counters with a left jab. CLASSIC!

1953 Giambras only knock down in his entire career

ALL OVER — Buffalo's Joey Giambra stands back to survey the damage after knocking out Jim Herring at 2:25 of the fourth round of their middleweight bout last night in Madison Square Garden.

AP Wirephoto

1953 Madison Square Garden Giambra stands over the knocked out Jimmy Herring in front of the sold out crowd

Here is the story-in-a-picture of last night's Otis Graham-Joey Giambra fight in Mutuel St. Arena. That's Giambra' [...] right fist making Graham wince and weave. That sort of thing went on for nine of 10 rounds.

1953 boxing picture of the year. Giambras devastating right against Otis Graham. Sugar Ray Robinson was right!

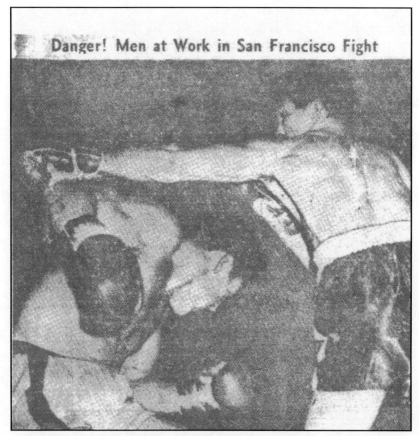

1953 Rocky Castellani ducks under Giambra's long left

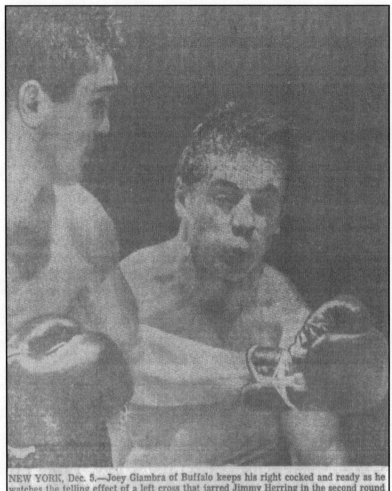

NEW YORK, Dec. 5.—Joey Giambra of Buffalo keeps his right cocked and ready as he watches the telling effect of a left cross that jarred Jimmy Herring in the second round of their Madison Square Garden fight. (A.P. Wirephoto)

1953 Sold out Madison Square Garden
Giambras left cross jarred Jimmy Herring

Tonight's Main-Eventers Square Off at Afternoon Weigh-in

ey Giambra, left, squared off with his opponent, Turzo (Kid) Portuguez, at this after-
on's official weigh-in for their Memorial Auditorium fight tonight. Portuguez tipped
beam at 160 3/4 pounds to 159½ for Giambra. The weigh-in was in the State Office
ding. (Fight story is on Page 13, magazine).

1953 Weigh in before one of the biggest upsets
of the year. Giambra vs. Portuguez

Chapter Seven

Fun with La Motta
(Age 23) 1954

After Ruby left, Joey and Carmen went back to Buffalo. Carmen and Sammy shared one bedroom, and Rosina and Mary (her youngest) shared the other in a walk-up tenement building. The rest of Joey's brothers and sisters were already married. Again, Joey stayed with Mike and his wife, and his routine for staying in shape was reestablished. Every Sunday, Joey would take his mother to church. Afterward, they would go and have an early dinner and then spend a few hours just talking. And then came a Sunday that was to be different. Joey had saved his money all along and treated himself to a luxury. It was an Oldsmobile '98 hardtop. He drove it around the suburbs of Buffalo until he found a track home that wasn't too expensive. He knew his mother would love it. And with a little effort, it could be the best house on the block. After church and an early dinner, Joey took Rosina for a ride and then stopped in the driveway of a colonial house, painted green with white trim.

"Who lives here?" she asked.

"No one, Ma. Do you like the house?"

"It's a nice house," she said, not knowing what to think.

"Come on. Let's go inside," Joey said trying to contain his excitement. He helped her out of the car and up to the front door and then took out some keys.

"Where you get the key, and why you bring me here?" Rosina asked almost frightened.

"I want you to see it," Joey said as simply as he could and led her inside.

"Why? We never going to buy a house."

"Ma, this is your house," Joey said, and his flesh crawled with the magnificence of the moment.

Rosina looked at him with her clouded blue eyes. "Are you foolin'?" she asked.

"No, Ma, it's your house," Joey said, barely able to hold back his tears.

Rosina put her arms around Joey and started to cry, and Joey joined her.

"You something, out of the children I bring into this world, my baby boy buys me a house."

Joey had but an instant to feel proud before Rosina grabbed his hand and started to pull him down. "What's the matter? What are you doing, Mamma?"

"Get on your knees. We are going to thank God."

"But I did it, Mamma," Joey said on his knees beside her.

"Don't talk that way. Without God's help, you couldn't do anything," she said sternly.

Joey nodded as he thought about what she had said. His knees were sore before she finished a ritual of prayers thanking God for the goodness he'd shown in giving them a home. "You a nice boy. God is always going to take care of you."

"I hope you're right, Ma."

When the family was told, they were ecstatic, and the following day, Joey had the entire house filled with new Italian provincial furniture. And then he had a truck come by and bring all their belongings to the new place. Almost simultaneously, a Salvation Army truck came and took all of their old furniture away. Joey drove his mother to the new home, and her first question was, "Who belongs to this furniture?"

"That's your new furniture, Mamma," Joey said proudly.

"No, no, I want my old furniture back."

"But, Ma, that other stuff is over twenty years old, and it's all scarred up and beat from all the moving we've done."

"I want my old *stuff* back; your father bought it when we first came to this country," Rosina said, accentuating the "stuff."

Joey called the Salvation Army and told them to bring everything back to the new address, figuring he could make a den out of the basement. This made Rosina happy, and Joey gave the Salvation Army two hundred dollars for their trouble. Within a few days, he started to have a two-car garage built alongside the house and planned to remodel the house as he went along. Just then, the mailman brought Joey "greetings" from Uncle Sam.

When Mike took over Joey's boxing career, one of the things he had Joey do was enlist in the naval reserve when he was seventeen and a half to keep Joey from getting drafted. Mike had connections enough to keep Joey from going on cruises. To satisfy his obligation, he would go to occasional weekend drills. When Joey told Mike he was getting drafted, Mike tried to get him out of it on hardship grounds, but with Carmen and Sammy both single, he didn't have a chance. Like Carmen, Sammy had been to war. He had been wounded in Korea and came home with a chest full of medals. Joey had him on the payroll for a while, but Sammy went back to being a salesman at the Regal Shoe store. Joey informed his naval commander of what was happening, and the commander assured him he'd be stationed in Buffalo if he joined the navy, because of his five years in the reserve.

"The navy's four years. I've just made a deal to get you assigned to Fort Dix, New Jersey. You'll be the boxing coach, and you'll be able to fight in the Garden on weekend passes, and two years from now, you're out," Mike said when Joey told him about it.

"Are you sure?" Joey asked.

"Believe me, it's all arranged."

Joey felt easier when Mike got him a ninety-day deferment. A month after Joey fought Jimmy Herring on December 4, 1953, he went to Miami, Florida, to box Bobby Dykes, a Mob-owned fighter; he was the number-two contender and very popular in Miami.

When Mike told him he was fighting Bobby Dykes, a contender, on January 7, 1954, in Miami Beach, Florida, Joey was elated.

The holidays came and went, but Joey was training too hard to really enjoy them, and going into the army hung over him like a sword. The year 1954 began. A few days before the fight, Joey and Mike flew down to Miami and checked into separate rooms at the Algiers Hotel. A man named Al Goldman introduced himself that night, while Joey and Mike were having dinner. Al was a fan of Joey's and owned several nightclubs in town, including one on Collin's Avenue, where Belle Barth was the perennial attraction.

"Why stay at a hotel? Wouldn't you feel more relaxed staying with family?" Al said after Mike went to make a phone call.

"What do you mean?" Joey asked.

"I've got a big home on North Bay Road, with a lot of guest rooms. "Why don't you come and be my guest?"

"That sounds good, Al, but right now, I'd better stay with my manager."

"I suppose so. Is this your first trip to Florida?" Al nodded his understanding.

"Yeah, and it's the first time I've been in warm weather in the winter."

"It doesn't take long to get spoiled. Well, look, take care of yourself. I'm bettin' on you," Al said as he got up.

"I'll do the best I can," Joey assured him.

Joey's fight with Bobby Dykes proved to be the third odious decision of his career. He was robbed. Joey won the fight so clearly that when Dykes was awarded the decision, even his own fans booed!

Just like Frankie Carbo (capo for the mafia) and Jim Norris (deal maker for the mafia) had said when Joey left them after their meeting: without the boys behind you, you won't be a winner! The Dykes fight, Joey won but didn't get the decision.

As he sat in his dressing room, half angry and half depressed, Jake LaMotta, the middleweight champion came in to console him. "Gee, kid, you got a bum deal."

"Thanks a lot, Jake; at least you know I won the fight."

"I blew a thousand bucks on ya. A lot of us got robbed tonight."

"Gees, I feel bad about that," Joey said grimacing.

"Don't feel bad. Tomorrow's another day. Meanwhile, get your clothes on, and I'll take you out and we'll have a party tonight."

Two beautiful blondes were waiting in Jake's powder-blue Cadillac when he and Joey left the arena. Jake got behind the wheel and slapped his girl's bare knee. Joey slid into the backseat with the other young lady.

"It's a pleasure to meet you, Mrs. LaMotta."

Jake and the two girls looked at each other and laughed instantly. "This ain't my wife; it's my girl."

"I'm sorry," Joey said terribly embarrassed.

"Aww, don't be silly. Hey, Joey, do you think you can handle Willie Pep?" Jake asked as he put the car in motion.

"Sure, but we'd never fight, because he's a featherweight," Joey said thinking the question was crazy.

"Not in the ring. That's his girl you're with tonight." Jake laughed.

"Hi, Willie Pep's girl," Joey said, joining in the laughter.

"I'm not really Willie Pep's girl. I just see him when he comes into town, and right now, you're in town," she said as she pressed herself up against Joey.

"That a girl, you show Joey a good time. He's tight from losing that fight, and I want to make sure he relaxes," Jake said.

"Jake, you don't have to ask a girl to be nice to me," Joey said defensively.

"Especially this girl," she said as she planted a kiss on Joey's cheek.

"What's your name?" Joey smiled.

"Call me Jest." She smiled back.

Jake took Joey and the girls to the Italian Village, a restaurant where a lot of the boys hung out. One of the owners, Joe DiCarlo, greeted them at the door and immediately told Joey he got a bum deal on the fight. As the night went on, Joey met several boys and found out that DiCarlo himself was wanted in New York, but as long as he stayed away, he was safe. Jake was in a drinking mood and got bombed, so Joey wound up driving the four of them to Jake's hotel, and then he and Jest took a cab back to the Algiers. They had their own party for a while before Joey thought to ask what she did.

"I'm a business girl, didn't you know?" Jest laughed.

"Didn't I know what? What kind of business?"

"You're not kidding, are you? It's just a nicer way of saying I'm a hooker," Jest said after looking at Joey for a moment.

"Oh, I didn't know," Joey said feeling foolish.

"That's okay; Jake took care of everything last night." Joey had breakfast for two sent up to them in the morning, and while Jest was in the bathroom, Mike came by.

"How do you feel, kid?" Mike asked Joey.

"I still feel bad, but I feel good too."

"Did Jake show you a good time last night?"

"He sure did. He wouldn't let me spend a dime, including the girl in the bathroom."

"Oh, well, you get rid of her; I want to have a talk with you," Mike said a bit surprised.

"Okay," Joey said as Jest came out of the bathroom with nothing covering her voluptuous body, not even thinking about trying to hide it from Mike's wide-open eyes.

"I'll meet you down in the coffee shop," Mike said with arched eyebrows and left. Fifteen minutes later, Joey put Jest in a cab and then joined Mike.

"I got a call from New York this morning and got some news that will take the curse off of last night; they want you to fight a main event at the Garden in February," Mike said as Joey sat down.

"Ain't that something. Who?" Joey said shaking his head.

"The Italian middleweight, Italo Scorticini. Now I got to get back to Buffalo, but you can stay here a few days if you want, soak up some sun, have a little fun, and take it easy."

"I'd like to, Mike, but these hotels are awfully expensive."

"Al Goldman's offer still stands, and he's even got a car for you."

"He's quite a guy," Joey said pleased.

"And he thinks a lot of you," Mike said.

Chapter Eight

First Met Shirley
(Age 23) 1954

That afternoon, Mike flew back home, and Al personally drove Joey to his home by the ocean. On the way, Al said, "Joey, I don't want you to take this wrong, I know you're a nice boy and you have a good reputation, but I've got a sixteen-year-old daughter who is nuts about you. I mean, she's got a crush on you, so what I want you to know is that she is still a virgin, and I want to keep her that way."

"Don't worry, Al; I've got too much respect for you to even do anything like that."

Al pulled into the four-car garage of the most beautiful home Joey had ever seen. Mrs. Goldman and Sandy greeted Joey as if they had known him for years and made him feel at home and at ease immediately. Sandy was very cute, but Joey could see that Mrs. Goldman must have been exquisite in her day.

"Sandy, why don't you give Joey a cook's tour of the place and show him to his room," Al said.

"Oh good," Sandy said eagerly, grabbing Joey by the hand and pulling him away.

"Wow, look at that yacht," Joey said as he approached a piece of glass in the front room.

"That's Daddy's," Sandy said, still clinging to Joey's hand.

"No foolin'. Do you go out there much?" Joey asked.

"Sure, we can go tomorrow, if you'd like."

"Oh, I'd like," Joey said, enjoying the anticipation.

Sandy's crush on Joey was at its peak during dinner. Al was understanding. Mrs. Goldman was tolerant. And Joey at twenty-two felt old.

"You want to come to the club with me, Joey?" Al asked after dinner.

"Yeah," Joey said, wanting to enjoy another night out on the town.

Al led Joey into the club just before Belle Barth came on for her first show. They sat at the bar, and Joey sipped on a glass of orange juice while Al translated Belle's mostly Jewish act for him. Joey kept looking at a little dark-haired girl sitting at a table by herself, and when the show was over and Al excused himself for a little while, Joey walked over to her.

"Can I join you? You seem to be alone," he asked and received a rather vacuous look.

"Please," she said, gesturing for him to sit. "No, I'm a friend of Belle's."

Joey ordered a drink for her and saw Al say something to a waitress and start laughing. Joey was still wondering what was going on when Belle Barth came over and sat down. "Hiya, Dago," Belle said coarsely.

"Hello, Miss Barth," Joey said courteously.

"Since you're staying with the boss, you can call me Belle."

"Okay, Belle."

"Do you know my brother, Arte?" Belle asked Joey.

"Do you mean Arte Curly?" Joey said having heard that the manager/trainer in New York was her brother.

"Right, you know him, right," Belle said raucously.

"Yeah, he's a nice guy," Joey said.

"He told me once he wished he had a piece of you." Belle snickered and placed her hand on the dark-haired girl's shoulder. "I hope that ain't what you want from this little gal."

"What do you mean?" Joey asked feeling blood rush into his cheeks.

"What, are you a thick-headed Dago?" Belle said with a smile that wasn't really a smile.

"She's with me."

"Yeah, I know. She told me she was a friend of yours," Joey said.

"No, sweetheart, she's with me," Belle said pedantically.

Al Goldman stepped in at that moment and said, "Excuse us, ladies. Joey, come on back to the bar. There's something I want to talk to you about."

"Sure," Joey said getting up quickly with obvious relief.

As they sat back down at the bar, Al said, "That's Belle's girlfriend; she's keeping her."

"Gee, I didn't mean to upset her. I didn't know Belle was that way."

"It's no secret," Al said.

Joey was still thinking about the dark-haired beauty as a party of seven came in. Belle always drew celebrities and the money crowd, and the way these people were dressed, fur-covered and jeweled, Joey knew they were wealthy. Among them, unattached, was a lovely blond lady wearing a very low-cut dress. Joey's eyes were fixed between her breasts. He was guessing her age to be about thirty-five when she spotted him. He smiled boyishly at her, and she smiled winsomely back. The lovely lady said something to Al, who had greeted and helped seat the party, and Al motioned his hand at Joey to come over.

After the introductions, Estelle, the lovely lady, said, "I don't know what fight the officials were watching last night; you clearly won the fight I saw."

"You were at the fight?" Joey said somewhat surprised, not thinking she was the fight type.

"And I thought you were beautiful," she said with dual meaning.

"Thanks," Joey said simply.

"Will you join us?" Estelle asked.

"Yeah, sure," Joey said and sat beside her.

Joey watched Belle's second show with them, and when it was over, Estelle asked, "Have you any plans tonight?"

"No, I'm just with Mr. Goldman," Joey answered.

"We're going to have a late breakfast now. Would you like to come along?"

Joey just looked at her and then nodded slowly. "I'd better tell Al," he said getting up.

After Joey told him of the invitation, he said, "I know you can take care of yourself, but she's a little out of your league, Joey. That's a very wealthy woman. Her husband died and left her several million."

"Wow," Joey breathed.

"'Wow' is right. She's pretty sharp, so don't make any mistakes."

"Like what?" Joey wanted to know.

"Like taking anything she might say too seriously."

"Al, don't worry. I won't," Joey grunted.

"You've got the number at the house. If you have any problems, just call and I'll have someone come and pick you up."

"Thanks, Al," Joey said.

A chauffeured limo took them to a charming place by the ocean, and when they had finished, dropped the other couples off before depositing Estelle and Joey at the Roney Plaza Hotel.

"Would you like a drink?" the Cuban maid asked as she let them into the penthouse.

"Maybe a cup of tea?" Joey asked.

Estelle nodded, and the maid departed. After putting on some music, Estelle excused herself, and Joey remembered his first visit to Ruby's penthouse. *Which was a toilet compared to this*, Joey thought.

The maid placed a complete, beautifully carved silver tea service on the coffee table. Moments after she departed, Estelle returned wearing a silk negligee. They had tea and conversation, but Joey began to feel quite nervous and out of place.

"Would you like to get comfortable?" Estelle asked sensing his uneasiness.

"Yeah, but I don't have a negligee," Joey joked.

"There's a terry-cloth robe in the bathroom. Why don't you take a quick shower before you get into it?"

Estelle was standing seductively in the bedroom doorway when Joey came out of the bathroom. He stopped short, looked at her, and then moved gracefully to embrace her in their first kiss.

"Let's go to bed," she said.

"You really want me to make love to you?" Joey asked, never having been so uncertain of himself.

"Come on, I'm sure you're not a virgin," Estelle whispered passionately.

During the next two hours, Joey kept hearing her say things like, "You're beautiful," and "Last night, when I saw you crawl into that ring, I thought, oh, he's beautiful, and now I know you're beautiful."

Naturally, he felt manly hearing those things and knowing he'd been pleasing the wealthiest, worldliest woman he had ever known. In the morning, they had breakfast. Then Estelle ordered him a swimsuit and slippers from the hotel's men's shop, and they spent an hour in and around the pool. When they went back up to the penthouse, Joey called Al to let him know that everything was all right.

"Why don't you go home and relax, and then come back for some dinner?" Estelle suggested, while he still had Al on the phone.

"Al, could you send someone to pick me up?"

Al told him to figure about twenty minutes. Joey told Al thanks and hung up.

"I could use one of Al's cars, but I don't know my way around here at all," Joey said to Estelle.

"I'll have my chauffeur pick you up around eight," she said solving the problem.

Joey was waiting in front of the hotel when Sandy pulled up in her convertible. He could see that she was disturbed as he got in and closed the door. "I didn't expect you to pick me up."

"I drive every chance I get. I just got it a couple of months ago. It was my birthday present," Sandy said glumly.

"You're a very lucky lady," Joey said as he settled back into the seat.

"Joey, what do you see in her?" Sandy hissed after about a thirty-second pause.

"You know Estelle?" Joey asked surprised.

"I've met her. Did you sleep with her last night?"

"Hey, you shouldn't talk like that," Joey said in a brotherly way.

"I'm not a baby, and she's too old for you."

"Well, nothing happened. We're friends," Joey white-lied.

"Oh, sure!"

Al saw them drive up. When Sandy ran by him with a quivering chin, he asked Joey what had happened.

"You were right about her having a crush on me. She's mad because I stayed with Estelle last night."

"Ah, kids." Al smiled.

"Maybe I ought to move out, Al. I don't want to upset your household."

"Don't give it another thought. It'll probably help her grow up. I take it you and Estelle hit it off last night."

"Yeah, and we're having a return match tonight."

Joey spent a full week in the Florida sun, and all but two nights of it with Estelle.

"I'm going to miss you," she said as they spent their last night together. "What are you going to do after the fight?"

"Probably just stay home until I have to go into the army," Joey said not trying to hide his feelings.

"I can understand why the army doesn't thrill you. It sure puts a crimp in your plans, I bet," Estelle said.

"It's like cutting two years right out of the heart."

"I know some very influential people; maybe I can do something for you?"

"My manager's got me a pretty good deal, so unless you can get me out of it completely …"

"Ha, Joey, I want you to call me collect anytime, from anywhere," she said as she rolled on top of him.

"You mean it?" Joey had to ask.

"Honey, I think a lot of you, and that's the only way I can let you know I want you to come back without looking foolish."

Al, his wife, and Sandy took Joey to the airport in Miami, and Mike picked him up at the airport in Buffalo. On the way home, Joey told Mike about the vacation but spoke mostly about Estelle.

"Will you forget about those mixed-up broads. All they want is to go to bed with you," Mike said painfully.

"Look, Mike, she's different."

"To you, Joey, they're all different. You're fighting Scorticini on the thirteenth, so get your mind off her and start to concentrate on the fight."

"Okay, Mike. You're the boss," Joey said knowing it was no use talking to him.

When Joey got back from Miami, he got some amazing news. He was being inducted into the army during the Korean War. This was amazing because he had already been an active civilian in the naval reserve for five and a half years and should've had no chance of being inducted into active duty out of the country. In fact, the Korean War was almost over at the time of his induction in Buffalo on March 10, 1954. Still, Joey had to serve two more years. He never tried to refuse to serve his country and avoid the draft, even though they had no right to draft him after his civilian status in the naval reserve.

Again, like the boys said, "Without us, you will lose."

It was as clear as the nose on your face that the Mob had tentacles that reached up into the army. At times, Joey felt tempted to play ball with the Mob, but his mother had raised him a good Catholic, and he always had a conscience and stubborn pride that made him refuse to give in no matter what.

Joey wanted to move into the house he had bought his mother, but Mike insisted that he wait until after the fight. So they trained hard as usual, and then Mike drove to Manhattan for the fight.

Just before the first round ended, Joey started to get to Scorticini. In the second round, Scorticini butted Joey, splitting his left eye wide open. Mike worked furiously to stop the bleeding, and for the next two rounds, Joey almost killed the Italian champion. Round five set the pattern for the rest of the fight. Scorticini kept moving away from Joey, having no more fight left in him, and Joey kept chasing him, cornering him from time to time and working him over. Joey won a unanimous decision. He was taken directly from the ring to the dispensary where Doctor Nardiello was the attending physician. The doctor had to work too close to the optic nerve to give Joey any anesthetic, so he had to be held down as the scar tissue was cut out with surgical scissors. Joey couldn't help but cry, finding the pain of the cutting and the fourteen stitches unbearable.

"Well, you'll have plenty of time to heal; we'll have to wait until you're in the army to find out when you can fight again," Mike said in a vain attempt to comfort him. Joey had less than thirty days until he had to report to induction. He gathered his belongings and moved into the house with his family, planning to spend a lot of time with his mother and just work around the house.

"You're going to the army for two years. Why don't you find a nice Italian girl?" Rosina said to Joey as they ate a spaghetti-and-meatball dinner his first night home. "You go out with Jewish girls, Irish girls, but no Italian girls," Rosina said, berating him.

"What nice Italian girl in her right mind would have anything to do with someone who is leaving for two years?" Joey said defending himself.

"Well, you won't find one if you don't look," Rosina reasoned.

"I know one. In fact, she's so good, and she won't go out with me," Sammy piped in.

"Shut you face," Rosina said, laughing with them.

"Of course, I wouldn't have anything against meeting her. Who is she?" Joey asked.

"Someone I met in the shoe business. She works at a women's shoe store, A. S. Beck's," Sammy joked.

As Joey was trying to get to sleep that night, he found his curiosity growing. Sammy was a very good-looking guy and seldom had a girl turn him down cold. Once again, they were sharing a room, and Joey asked quietly, "Hey, Sammy, what's that Italian girl's name?"

"Shirley Fina. Why don't you drop by Beck's and say hello," Sammy whispered.

"That's just what I was thinking. What does she look like?" Joey asked.

"She's a raving beauty," Sammy said, and Joey knew Sammy wasn't prone to exaggeration. The following afternoon, Joey ambled into Beck's wearing a beautiful suit and his Allan Ladd raincoat. He wore his hair à la Tony Curtis, a black curl hanging down on his forehead. His eye had healed to the point where only a small bandage was needed.

As the manager approached him, his eyes lit up with recognition. "Say, you're Joey Giambra! I've got to have your autograph! I'm a real fan of yours."

After signing an autograph, Joey said, "Mr. Kaufman, I understand you have a girl named Shirley Fina working here. I'd like to meet her."

"She's not for you, Joey," he confided. "Forget it. She's in love with a Jewish boy, Art Sitcoff."

"Oh, well, I'd like to at least meet her anyway," Joey uttered and shrugged.

Just then, Shirley came up from the stockroom and went behind a counter filled with purses and accessories. Joey saw an incredibly beautiful face on a fantastically proportioned body. She wore her strawberry blond hair in the Veronica Lake peek-a-boo style, and Joey felt struck by love at first sight.

"Shirley, I want you to meet Joey Giambra, the famous fighter," Mr. Kauffman said.

"Hello, Mrs. Fina," Joey said at his best.

"Hello, are you Sammy's brother?" Shirley smiled, and Mr. Kauffman moved on.

"Yeah, you know Sammy, huh?"

"I know he's awful fresh," she said and began putting the gloves she had gone for under the counter.

"Sammy's that way, but I don't think it runs in the family. I've got another brother, who is quite shy," Joey said trying to break the ice he felt.

"And how about you?" she asked, trying to hide a smile.

"I kind of fit in the middle," Joey said, also trying to hide a smile.

"Can I help you?" she asked.

"Uh, yeah, I'd like to buy my mother a nice purse," Joey sharply responded.

"What did you have in mind?" Shirley asked.

"Well, what kind of purse would a fifty-year-young woman like?" Joey answered, but that was not how he wanted to respond to her question.

"I bought one like this for my mother recently," she said placing a functional black purse in front of him.

"I understand you are going with someone, but I'd still like to take you out for dinner," Joey said taking out his wallet.

"You'll have to ask my sister," Shirley said looking over Joey's shoulder.

"Your sister?" Joey said as he wondered what kind of game she was playing.

"Her name is Rosella, and she's behind that counter."

Joey looked behind him and thought, *What the hell?* He went over and spoke to Shirley's merely attractive sister, who was thrilled to meet him. "Would you mind if I took your sister out?" he asked.

"Not at all," Rosella said, wishing Joey were asking her.

Joey laughed softly as he returned to Shirley.

She laughed and said, "Okay."

And Joey laughed and said, "So do I … uh, tonight?"

"Tonight," she said.

Later on, Joey arrived at the appointed hour at an apartment Shirley shared with her mother in a project building in the lower terrace area off Trenton Avenue. He knocked and was greeted by Mrs. Fina, a gray-haired woman about his own mother's age.

"Come in. Shirley will be right back. She went to visit her grandmother," she said.

They talked for a while, and Joey knew he was being pumped. Mrs. Fina seemed less interested in his background and his family than his finances. When he told her he had a home and a car that had all been paid for and over twenty thousand in the bank, her eyes popped right out of her head. He also impressed her when he spoke of going into business after he became the middleweight champion. Mrs. Fina then told him she wanted Shirley to marry an Italian boy someday. Wouldn't Joey break up her relationship with the Jewish boy she had been seeing? Shirley finally arrived, took a minute to freshen up, and then was trying to find out what her mother and

Joey were talking about when there came a knock at the door. Shirley answered it, said she would only be a minute, and then stepped into the hall.

Moments later, Joey heard the sound of a slap come from the hall and rushed to the door. As he stepped into the hall, Joey saw a man running down the stairs and Shirley holding her cheek. "Did he hit you?" Joey said, ready to fly down those stairs.

"It's nothing. I'll tell you about it later," she said grabbing Joey's arm.

During dinner, Shirley spoke casually of Tom, the boy she had gone steady with until he went away to college. And then, she had met Art and started going out with him.

"Tom was the guy in the hall tonight," she said.

"Why did he slap you?" Joey asked.

"Oh, he asked me why I went out on him and why I hadn't written to him … You know?" she said.

"Yeah." Joey nodded, wanting her to think he understood. "What about Art? Are you in love with him?"

"No, no, I broke up with him last week. He started getting real serious, wanting to get married and all, and I know my mother would just die if I married a man that wasn't Italian. I'm not going with anybody now."

It was getting late by the time they left the restaurant, so they just drove around and then parked in front of her place. Joey was falling hard and afraid to make a bad move, remembering the remark she had made about Sammy being fresh. Finally, it was time for her to go in. Joey put his arms around her and gave her a gentle kiss good night. Shirley's response was just as gentle. The next night was Friday, and they had dinner, went to a movie, and then parked in front of her place again and talked for two hours. Joey told her just about everything except that he was going to the army soon. After several good-night kisses, Joey said, "I think I'm falling in love with you."

"How do you know?" Shirley asked, wanting to hear more.

"Well, I've never felt like this before. I've never wanted to get engaged before."

"Oh, Joey," she cried into his mouth, and when the kiss ended, she said, "I am game if you are."

Joey wanted to swallow her, to feel her, to do everything with her. But something was different. He knew he was going to marry her, and he didn't even want himself to touch her.

"Why didn't you tell me?" she whispered in his ear.

The next morning, Joey took Shirley to meet a friend who happened to own a jewelry store. "Pick out anything you want, honey," he said, playing the big shot, but knowing in the back of his mind he had a two-thousand-dollar limit. Shirley picked a single-carat solitaire blue-white diamond from a tray and tried it on.

"That's a flawless stone," the jeweler said, approving of her choice.

"You can have something bigger," Joey said, seeing the one-thousand-dollar price tag.

"No, this is good enough for me, and look, it fits," Shirley said demurely.

As they drove away from the jewelry store, Shirley said, "I hope your mother likes me."

"She'll love you; she's been wanting me to bring home a nice Italian girl for a long time now."

"Am I the first?"

"The very first."

Shirley moved closer to him, letting him know how pleased she was about everything. "When are we going to make it official?"

"Tonight, if you like. A bunch of my friends are throwing a big party for me. It's kind of a club I belong to."

"An engagement party, so soon?" Shirley sounded amazed.

"Well, that's what it's going to turn out to be," Joey hedged, knowing she would find out it was his induction party, something the club did for all the members going into the service.

"They say you're fast in the ring, but I'm beginning to think you're just plain fast," she teased and laughed, raising her head up into the wind.

Joey pulled the Olds '98 into the driveway saying, "But we just moved into the place a few months ago, so there's still plenty of fixing up to do."

"Oh, it looks lovely, Joey."

Rosina opened the door, and Joey gave her a quick kiss saying, "Ma, this is Shirley Fina."

"Come in, come in," Rosina said, giving Shirley the once-over, twice. "Fina, Fina, that's a fine Italian name."

After a short inquisition, it was apparent Rosina approved of Shirley, although she was slightly miffed that Joey hadn't consulted her first before getting engaged. That night, Joey picked Shirley up, and they drove to a hall the club had rented in the North Park area of Buffalo. They were both dressed their best and made a strikingly handsome couple. Joey wondered how long it would be before Shirley found out the real reason for the party, especially when there were no direct references made and the innuendos went right over her head. Joey took his good friend Joe Perelstein aside and after swearing him to secrecy asked him to make the announcement of his engagement to Shirley at midnight.

"Oh, you're going to break a few hearts," Joe said slyly. "I know Arlene still has a thing for you."

"Is she here?" Joey asked, looking past Joe.

"Here and headed this way," Joe answered, looking past Joey.

Joey turned and saw the exotic Arlene coming toward him. He instantly recalled having gone out a few times with her, quite a few times, the summer before last. She was a virgin, and not wanting to spoil her, he'd had to stop seeing her.

"Hello, stranger," she said, stopping very close to him. "Who is the girl?"

"Hello, Arlene," he said, unable to resist looking at how full her breasts had become.

"She looks Italian," Arlene said sarcastically.

"She is, so am I."

"I remember us saying it didn't matter one was Catholic and one was Jewish."

"And it didn't." Joey smiled. "Hey, you're looking great."

Arlene softened and smiled. "I'd like to see you before you go away. Maybe we could have a party for two."

"I promise you an answer to that in a little while," Joey said, anxious to get back to Shirley. "Okay?"

"Okay." She smiled mischievously.

It took Joey a while to find Shirley, who had a cordon of men around her. After he broke through to her, she said, "Excuse me, fellas. I want to dance with my man."

Joey liked her saying that, and he liked hearing the men say, "Lucky stiff," and "God, she's beautiful," and knowing how they envied him.

Shirley pressed herself close to Joey, and they began to sway gently to romantic music coming from a record player. "Why didn't you tell me?" she whispered in his ear.

"What?" Joey asked, knowing she had learned the reason for the party, but wanting to play out the hand.

"That you're going in the army soon."

Joey pulled his head back, so that he could read her eyes. "I was afraid I'd lose you."

Shirley pressed her hips more firmly against his and then said, "I'm glad you didn't. I probably wouldn't have seen you again, or let myself fall in love with you."

Joey kissed her tenderly as they continued to sway to the music. "Will you wait for me?"

"Yes, if you will wait ... for me," she answered, and each body shivered against the other.

"I have news for everyone. Quiet, please! I have a very important announcement to make!" Joel Perelstein said. Gradually, the din ceased, and everyone's attention focused on Joe. "Now you all know this party is for our own pal, Joey Giambra, who's going into the army ..." Cheers and wisecracks interrupted Joe and filled the hall. He took advantage of the moment to bring Joey and Shirley up onto the platform that also held the record player. "Hold it! There's more. Our bachelor friend Joey Giambra wants us to know as of this moment, he and Shirley Fina are engaged to be married."

Joey took the ring from his pocket and slipped it on Shirley's finger, and then they kissed fully, in sight of everyone, and all the wisecracks were drowned out. Congratulations were coming hot and heavy, and a few girls and guys let it be known they would still be around if things didn't work out, but then Arlene approached Joey with tears in her eyes. Hatred flowed out on those tears, and without a word, she slapped him and then walked away.

"What was that all about?" Shirley asked, caressing the reddening spot on his cheek.

"Remember when you were out in the hall and Tom slapped you in the face?" Joey smiled. "Well, we're even."

Joey and Shirley hugged each other with laughter. The next morning, Joey took both his mother and Shirley to church and then dropped Rosina off at home. He and Shirley went on a picnic. Rosina spent the afternoon on the telephone, checking up on Shirley Fina through the Italian grapevine. When Joey returned late that afternoon, Rosina was waiting for him.

"Joey, come into the kitchen. I want to talk to you."

"Sure, Ma," Joey said, still on cloud nine from a wonderful day with Shirley. "But I don't have much time. I'm taking Shirley to dinner and a show tonight."

Rosina automatically poured two cups of coffee and brought them to the kitchen table. "Sit down," she told Joey and took her usual place.

"Is something wrong, Ma?" Joey asked, sensing she was troubled.

"Joey, you forget about this girl. She is not for you," Rosina said seriously.

"Ma, what are you talking about?" Joey frowned.

"Today, I call some of my old friends, and I ask about the Finas and Shirley."

"Oh, Ma." Joey sighed, thinking that was a terrible thing to do and hoping it wouldn't get back to Shirley.

"Don't 'Oh Ma' me! This girl. She got nothing. All she wants is your money."

"Ma, you're wrong."

"I'm not wrong. You wrong. You make a big mistake."

"But I love her, and she loves me!" Joey said firmly.

"She no love you. She go out with a lot of men," Rosina said even more firmly.

"That doesn't mean anything today, Ma. A lot of girls go out with guys now before they get married."

"Joey, don't marry this girl. You go in the army and you wait and you see what happens," Rosina ordered.

"That's what I intend to do, Ma, so don't worry, okay?" Joey said kissing her and getting up.

"Okay," Rosina said.

Chapter Nine

Army Days
(Age 23) 1954

On the morning of his induction, Joey kissed his mother good-bye, promising her to at least write once a week and thanking her again for the big family party they had had the night before. His brother Carmen drove him down to the induction center and stood by as Joey and eighteen others from the area were sworn in and then told that their train to Fort Knox, Kentucky, would be leaving in two hours.

"Hey, Sarge, you made a mistake. I'm going to Fort Dix, New Jersey." Joey laughed.

The sergeant looked down at his clipboard and said, "Oh yeah, I'm sorry, kid, but you're goin' to Kentucky."

"But I was supposed to be all taken care of months ago. What could have gone wrong?" Joey said feeling a sense of panic.

"Probably the new directive we got a few weeks back. All New Yorkers are to be shipped down to the Southern states," the sergeant said.

"How come?" Joey wanted to know.

"Who knows? But those are the orders." The sergeant shrugged and walked away.

Carmen told Joey he had a couple of things to do, but he would see him at the station before the train left. Joey sat down wearily, thought for a moment, and then decided he'd better call Mike. "Mike, guess what?"

Before Joey said anything else, Mike said enthusiastically, "You just picked up *Ring Magazine*, and you saw that you're ranked number four in the whole damn world!"

"Isn't that something?" Joey said feeling the irony of it all.

"You don't sound very happy about it."

"Well, that's not why I called. Mike, guess where I'm going?" Joey said.

"Guess where you're going? I know where you're going. I set it up," Mike said impatiently.

"New orders, Fort Knox, Kentucky!"

"You're crazy!" Mike shouted.

"In a couple of hours, I'll be on a train, going a hell of a lot further south than New Jersey."

"Okay, hang on. I'll be right there," Mike said with urgency in his voice. Mike arrived, talked to the sergeant, and then got on the phone with Tex Sullivan, his friend and partner in many ventures. Tex listened, took the phone number at the center, and told Mike he would get right back to him. Minutes later, Tex told Mike that because of the McCarthy-Shine investigations, the heat was on, and there was nothing anyone could do.

"What did he say?" Joey asked hopefully when Mike got out of the phone booth.

"Joey, you gotta go. It's these damn McCarthy hearings. Everybody's scared. It's like somebody pulled the plug on all the 'juice.'"

"What lousy timing. Who do we know in Kentucky?" Joey said feeling sorry for himself.

"I've never, ever been down there. Just make the best of it, kid. We'll keep working on it from this end. I can promise you that," Mike said shaking his head and putting an arm around Joey's shoulders. Mike asked permission to drive Joey to the train station.

"Okay, just make sure you're there. You don't want to get started on the wrong foot." The sergeant obliged.

As the bus drove away, Joey said, "At least this is better than taking the bus ... I'd better call Shirley and tell her what's happened. I probably won't be seeing her as soon as I thought."

"Do you really want to marry her, Joey?" Mike asked as if he still couldn't believe it.

"People don't get engaged, not to get married." Joey managed to chuckle.

"I suppose if I said anything, you'd tell me she was 'different,' and how many times have I heard that?"

"Mike, I don't want you bum-rapping Shirley. She's going to be my wife."

"I wouldn't think of it," Mike said, raising his hands in surrender and then quickly putting them back on the wheel.

Carmen was just helping Shirley out of his car when Joey and Mike arrived at the train station. The two beautiful young people flew into each other's arms, held each other tightly, and kissed.

"That was very thoughtful of you, Carm."

And the two men headed inside. Joey and Shirley came into the train station a few minutes later and joined Mike and Carmen at a snack counter. The bus dropped the other inductees off, and when Joey went to check in with the sergeant, Carmen took the opportunity to get him alone for a moment.

"Joey, I have to say something to you, all right?"

"Well, sure, Carm. What is it?"

"It's nothing you need to answer. It's … you know I like almost everyone. I mean, well, take Shirley, I've been nice to her, right?"

"Sure you have, and bringing her down here was the nicest thing you could have done for me." Joey had to interrupt. "So what are you trying to say?"

"Be careful, Joey. There's something about that girl I don't like."

"What? Has Ma been bending you ear?"

"Naturally, but you know me better than that."

"Ah, don't worry, Carm. I know what I'm doing. We won't be getting married for a couple of years anyway."

Joey kissed everybody good-bye, and then as the train began its laborious effort to get in motion, he jumped aboard. "I'm going to be gone a long time, but I'm going to be true," Joey called to Shirley.

"I love you, Joey, and I'll be true to you!" she called back.

Joey sat quietly for a while before the tears of being lonely and homesick began.

On his first day at Fort Knox, Joey was issued his army wardrobe and gear and then given a series of shots and a promise of more to come. After that, despite his plea, he watched his curly black hair being shaved off with electric shears before he and his bald buddies were put into quarantine for a week. The second week began with their being assigned to a company for the start of eight weeks of basic training. They were marched over to their new barracks where they were greeted by their platoon sergeant, a six-foot-two-inch, beer-dinking, red necked Southerner named Luddy.

"Okay, you bunch of Jews, wops, and micks, inside, and grab your bunks! Fall out!"

Joey was laughing and shaking his head as he passed by Luddy. He had made up his mind that he wouldn't take things personally and he would follow Mike's advice to make the best out of the army.

"What's so funny, boy?" Luddy rasped.

"Oh nothing," Joey said, finding it hard to keep a smile on his face. "It's just the way you called us those names. I'm sure you didn't mean it."

"What makes you think I didn't mean it?" Luddy snarled.

"Because this is the United States Army and we're all Americans," Joey said, and the smile was gone.

"Yeah, that's right; you look like one of those wop Americans. What's your name?"

"Giambra, Joey Giambra," he replied, trying to stay calm.

"See, I was right. It's gettin' so's I can tell wops and Jews as easy as I can tell black folk," he said, although he used a slandering word for the black folk...

Joey bit the inside of his lips before saying, "It's pretty easy to tell what you are, too."

"What do you mean by that?" Luddy said, with his face turning as red as his neck.

"Forget it," Joey said turning toward the barracks.

"Hold it!" Luddy barked, grabbing Joey's arm and spinning him back around.

Joey stiffened, and his face clinched. He just stared at the big man. "Wit a minute … Jam-bra … You that prizefighter I've been hearin' about?"

"Yeah, I'm that fighter, and now I'm that soldier."

"No, you ain't a soldier, yet, but I'm going to make sure you become one … I'm going to give you a break, Jam-bra … You don't do what you're told … I'll break your back."

"Look, Sarge, don't get tough with me. I don't want to be here in the first place, but as long as I am, I'll do the best I can."

"Why do I get the feeling that your best ain't gonna nearly be good enough?" Luddy smiled sadistically.

"One thing right now, don't you ever put your hands on me again," Joey said, knowing the answer to Luddy's question.

"Ooohh … you threatening me, boy?" Luddy said, easily relishing what was happening.

"No, Sarge, I'm not threatening you. Just don't touch me," Joey said just as easily.

"And what are you going to do if I touch you?" Luddy pressed.

"I'll make you part of the pavement," Joey said deadly serious.

"You think you're tough?" Luddy said, relishing his thoughts.

"No, I'm not tough. I just don't want to be bugged; that's all."

"Why, I wouldn't think of buggin' you, boy."

"I'll do my job, Sarge. Just leave me alone."

From that day on, Joey got every rotten detail that came up, and when there wasn't anything special, he pulled KP duty or cleaned out the latrines. He couldn't help feeling a certain amount of bitterness over the injustice of it all, but he knew there wasn't anything he could do about it then. So he consoled himself with the thought that the harassment would soon be over and with the fact that his conditioning kept him from suffering the physical aches and pains his buddies were going through. Then something happened that Joey just couldn't ignore. Marvin Goetz, a little Jewish kid from Buffalo, had lied about his age to get into the army. While waiting for his discharge papers, the seventeen-year-old was required to continue training as scheduled. Sergeant Luddy, who had Jew, Negroes, and Italians at the top of his long "hate" list, just naturally decided to make Marvin's last days as miserable as possible. When Marvin got confused during a manual arms drill session and wound up with his rifle on the wrong shoulder, Luddy grabbed the rifle from him and slammed it into the correct shoulder with enough force to knock Marvin down. Marvin got up holding his shoulder, tears streaming down his face, and started to run toward the barracks.

"Come here, you little Jew bastard!" Luddy yelled as he ran after him and then kicked him in the ass, sending him sprawling flat on his face. Luddy then took off his helmet and whacked him over the head with it. "Now you can go back to the barracks where you belong!"

As Marvin struggled to his feet, Luddy appeared to be deciding whether or not to hit him again with the helmet still in his hand, and that's when Joey ran to Luddy, buried his shoulder in the big man's gut, rammed him into the side of the wooden barracks, and started working him over. Two of Joey's buddies pulled him away to the sound of Luddy's screaming, "Okay, Jam-bra, you're under arrest! Report to the commandin' officer!"

"You chicken bastard, why don't you pick on someone your own size!" Joey screamed back.

"It's your ass now, boy. You guys are still at right shoulder's arms!" Luddy yelled to Joey and then the rest of them, shaking with anger.

Joey told the truth, Luddy lied, and no one else dared to say anything after being sufficiently threatened. And the commanding officer knowing full well what had taken place had given Joey a summary court martial, being the equivalent to a misdemeanor. Joey was fined twenty-five dollars and put on restriction for a week. There wasn't anything else Luddy could throw at Joey, already having given him the dregs, and the next few weeks passed without further incident. The eighth week came, and Joey's platoon was sent on maneuvers to determine if they would get a week's furlough before the start of another eight weeks of training. While they waited for the results to be posted, Saturday night came, and as usual, Luddy took off with two of his pals for Louisville. Joey knew Luddy's routine. He knew Luddy would come back about three in the morning, bombed out of his skull, and climb the flights of stairs to his private room on the second floor of the barracks. So Joey had an idea, and his two closest buddies, who were still ashamed of keeping quiet during Joey's court martial, were more than happy to go along with the idea. At two o'clock in the morning, the three men met at the top of the stairs, and Joey unscrewed the only light bulb that lit the stairway. They sat down and waited until they heard the quiet, drunken singing of Sergeant Luddy. When he managed to reach the top of the stairs, Joey's buddies secured a blanket over his head, and Joey gave him about five good shots in the face and then pushed as his buddies pulled the blanket away. Luddy bounced ungracefully down the entire flight of stairs. The platoon was called out to formation at seven in the morning. The commanding officer and Sergeant Luddy looked over the men, and the men looked at Luddy's swollen black eye and lip and hopefully broken arm in a sling.

"Okay, which one of you guys did this?" Luddy called out, and his eyes were fixed on Joey's face.

The silence was more pronounced than usual, and the commander felt compelled to say, "If anyone knows who did this, fall out!"

While the silence continued, Luddy turned red and his black eye and lip hurt. "I know it was that wop bastard, Jam-bra!" Luddy cried.

"As you were, Sergeant," the commander ordered intensely.

Joey's straight face kaleidoscope into a smirk when he heard that.

"Yes, sir," Luddy said and moved closer to Joey. He said under his breath, "I'm going to get you, Jam-bra. Somehow, some way, I'm going to get you."

"We'll see about that," Joey said as he continued to smirk.

And the platoon was given their one-week furlough home. Joey's train pulled into the station in Buffalo, and he took a cab home. He hadn't been given the exact time or day of his arrival, so he couldn't give anyone else the info, but he was looking forward to surprising his mother. Joey paid the cab driver, and then suddenly became aware of the spring day as he sauntered up the walkway to the house. Rosina had greeted him warmly, but even through the screen door, Joey knew he wasn't looking at happiness.

"Ma, you look worried. Has something happened around here I don't know about?" Joey finally said to her.

"Nothing happen. You brothers at work yet. Everybody's fine," Rosina said with her mind elsewhere.

"Well, something's wrong. If I didn't know any better, I'd think you weren't happy to see me."

"Don't be silly. Come in the kitchen," Rosina said, touching his face.

Joey waited silently as Rosina poured them a cup of coffee. He was able to smile slightly as he watched her and realized that wherever she resided, she lived in the kitchen.

"You home a week. You getting married?" Rosina asked stoically.

"No, Ma, I have no plans of getting married until I get out of the army," Joey added, wondering why she would ask such a question.

"That's not what your brothers tell me."

"Well, I don't know where they're getting their information from, but, Ma, it's not true."

"You two gonna want to live here?" Rosina said not believing Joey.

"No, Ma, this is your house. When Shirley and I get married, we will get our own place," Joey said not wanting to argue about it.

"I want you to stop seeing this girl, Joey. She's no good!"

"Ma, I want you to stop talking like that about Shirley," Joey said flushed with anger.

"She's no good; her family's no good," she said raising her voice.

"What do you mean, 'her family's no good'? We aren't exactly the Rockefellers, you know."

"You got lots of money, and all she wants is you money!"

"Look, Ma, I love her, and I don't want to hear any more about it," Joey said with finality.

"You stupid! You crazy!" Rosina yelled and slapped Joey in the face.

They both sat there for a long moment. Joey's eyes filled with tears as he tried to remember the last time she had slapped him. "Oh, Mamma, with all the children you've had, no one ever bought you anything, no one ever gave you anything, except me … I always brought you money. I bought you a house, furniture, a fur coat. I did everything for you, because I love you. I wanted to get everything for you, and you hit me," Joey said as his heart was breaking.

He got up slowly and left his mother sitting there. Perhaps she thought he was going to his room, but Joey picked up his gear, tossed it into his car, and took off. He just drove for a while, thinking, trying to pull himself together, and then parked in front of A. S. Beck's and waited for Shirley. He greeted her warmly, but as she got into the car, she knew she wasn't looking at happiness. "If I didn't know any better, I'd think you weren't happy to see me." She smiled.

Joey shook his head saying, "I had an argument with my mother."

"Was it about me?" Shirley asked defensively.

"No, it was something about my brothers, and I really don't want to talk about it." Joey said too loudly, not wanting her to blame herself.

"Okay," Shirley agreed. "Take me home so I can clean up and change, and maybe we can go out if you want to."

"That sounds great, although maybe I should check into a hotel while you get ready," Joey said starting the car and driving off.

"You don't want to go home tonight?"

"The way I feel right now, I don't want to go home, period," Joey said bitterly.

"Well then, why don't you stay at my place?" Shirley offered.

"But you don't have any room," Joey said, liking the idea.

"I'll sleep in the room with my mother, and you can take the sofa bed in the front room."

"Hey, I'm all for it," Joey said beginning to feel good again.

"Are you sure your mother won't mind?"

"Positive. You know Mother and I are very close," Shirley assured him.

"That's nice," Joey said with a trace of sadness.

He spent the entire week with Shirley and her mother and didn't go near his mother or family. He knew he was being overly sensitive, but that was how he was. He had been hurt terribly, and it filled him with resentment. Joey spent several afternoons with Mike, and one night, he and Shirley were invited to Mike's house for dinner. Too soon, the week drew to a close, and the night before he had to leave was there. As was her habit, Mrs. Fina retired to the bedroom about eleven o' clock. Shirley and Joey would then neck and talk until around two o' clock in the morning, when she would have to go to sleep. But this, his final night, was to be more. Between kisses, Joey and Shirley made plans for their wedding, which would take place as soon as he got home to stay, and they spoke about their future.

"I love you, Shirley," Joey said as the new day began, and he had to touch her.

"And I love you," she responded, filling his hand with the breast he touched.

"I want to make love so bad, but only to you. I don't want anybody else. I love you so much." Joey groaned.

"I'll be right back," she said and went quickly into the bathroom.

Joey stood up quickly as she returned. She was wearing only a flimsy robe, and he felt her as they embraced.

"My turn," he said and disappeared into the bathroom. Minutes later, Joey returned to Shirley carrying his clothes and wearing an army-issued safety (protection). She greeted him with open arms, and they made soft sounds as they kissed and explored each other.

As Joey was about to enter her, she cried softly, "Don't!"

"I'm not going to hurt you," he whispered.

"What if I get pregnant?"

"Shh," he comforted, "you know I'm wearing a safety, so you can't get pregnant."

They made love quietly, and it was good. Joey went back into the bathroom and cleaned up. He checked the safety to make sure it hadn't broken and then turned to Shirley. They relaxed in each other's arms for a while, before Joey felt her silent tears against his cheek.

"Why are you crying?" he asked, not wanting to move.

"I'll never be a virgin again; I've given you my greatest possession," she said, and her voice trembled.

Joey kissed her tenderly. He knew she wasn't a virgin before the moment he entered her but loved her enough to overlook it. He thought as long as she was true to him from then on, it didn't matter.

"It's not like losing your virginity, honey. We'll be married, and we'll have it with us always," Joey said as he kissed the wetness from her eyes.

"Oh, Joey." She sighed and opened her robe as she rolled on top of him. Joey became excited again, and again, they made love. When it was over, Joey knew how much more he loved her. In the morning, Joey drove Shirley to work, kissed her good-bye, and then picked up three of his buddies at the prearranged time and place. Before going on furlough, everyone was told that they could bring their cars back if they wished, and Joey immediately decided that was what he was going to do. As the four men began the long drive back to camp and started relating their week's adventures, Joey couldn't help thinking about his family. He felt they had no right to interfere in his life and show such ingratitude. He couldn't understand why they hadn't tried to contact him during the week, and with each passing day, his resentment grew and his hurt deepened. So he didn't call to say good-bye; he hadn't wanted to. Joey and his buddies were assigned to a new brick barracks, which was equipped with all the modern conveniences. It was a palace compared to the old wooden barracks. A message on the bulletin board told them to square away, chow down at the mess hall, and then line up for roll call at thirteen hundred hours. It was signed "Sgt. Smith." Everyone wondered what kind of guy Smith would turn out to be, especially Joey. They were hoping against hope that he wasn't a red necked, Southern bigot like Luddy. Finally, they all lined up and heard the roll call by an apparently more refined and educated man. After all were marked present or accounted for, Sergeant Smith outlined what would be expected out of them during the next eight weeks and what was required from them by him personally. The men were buzzing approvingly about the new sergeant.

As they made their way back into the barracks, Joey passed by and Smith said, "Giambra?"

"Yes, sir," Joey said as he wondered why he was being singled out so quickly.

"I'd like a word with you. Let's take a walk," Smith said politely.

Joey followed as Smith merely ambled out of earshot of the rest of the men. "I saw you fight once. I had the wrong corner. It cost me a buck and a beer."

"I'm glad it wasn't more," Joey said and meant it.

"I thought you were good. It's a shame the army isn't utilizing you the way they should, but then, that's par for the course … So I hear you had trouble with Sergeant Luddy," Smith said.

"That's the truth. Are you going to hold it against me?" Joey said thinking it was an understatement.

"Not at all. That's what I wanted to clear up with you right away. I've known Luddy for a couple of years, and invariably, when he says someone's a troublemaker, it turns out he made the trouble," Smith said.

"That's exactly what happened, Sarge," Joey said with sincerity.

"I figured as much, so what I want you to know is, you toe the mark and do your job, you won't have any problems with me."

"Thanks for being fair about things, Sarge; you won't have any problems with me either," Joey said gratefully.

The first six weeks went quickly and smoothly by, not only for Joey, but for everyone. During the seventh week, Joey received a phone call from Shirley.

"Shirley?" Joey asked recognizing her voice.

"Joey?"

"Hi, honey, how come you're calling?"

"Joey, I think I'm pregnant."

"What? You can't be!" Joey said, suddenly with his heart in his throat.

"But I think I am."

Joey sensed her fear. "Have you been to a doctor?"

"No, I keep hoping to get my period."

"Look, you'd better go to a doctor and have a checkup, because the thing I wore was all right. I know it didn't break."

"Well, if I'm pregnant, something was wrong with it. You're the only man I've ever made love to. It had to be you."

"Shirley, don't push it. Just do what I tell you. Get to a doctor, and get checked!" Joey said still trying to overlook the fact that he knew he wasn't the first.

"Okay, but if I'm pregnant, you're going to have to marry me," she said subdued.

"One thing at a time, Shirley. Let me know what the doctor says the minute you hear."

When their final week of basic training began, rumors started to fly that the entire platoon was to be shipped overseas. Joey didn't waste any time calling Mike and informing him of his latest development.

"Oh, those bastards, the more strings I pull the worse things seem to get," Mike seethed under his breath.

"You mean you're still trying to get me to Fort Dix?" Joey asked surprised.

"Sure I am, but I swear there's a conspiracy against us. Well, I'll try to work something out and get back to you in a few days," Mike said irritably.

"Well, you'd better hurry, Mike; I am getting my orders at the end of the week."

Joey found having his car was more trouble than it was worth, and when they told him he would have to store it when he was reassigned from Camp Chaffee in Arkansas, he decided to sell it. He let the word out and accepted a good cash offer the next day. Whether Mike had anything to do with it or whether it was simply the luck of the draw, Joey's orders were cut for him to remain stateside. He and a few of his basic training buddies were put on a bus back to Memphis, Tennessee. He thought of trying to get a hold of Ruby, but he didn't get the chance. Another bus took them to Camp Chaffee in Fort Smith, where they were told to expect reassignment there within a week. On their first night in Fort Smith, Joey and several of his buddies went into town. They were steered to a small beer bar called the Brass Rail, where most of the GIs hung out. They were early enough to get a corner table in the barn-like place, and Joey was suddenly looking at the nicely shaped bare legs of the approaching waitress.

"What'll it be, gentleman?" the twentyish, dark-rooted blonde drawled.

While the others ordered two pitchers of beer, Joey found himself enjoying the exposed bareness of the girl's low-worn peasant blouse. "I can see what your pleasure is, but what'll you have to drink?" the girl teased leaning over directly in front of Joey.

Joey smiled mildly embarrassed by the laughing of the guys, and the very exposed, full enough, rounded breasts before him. He turned his head as he waved them off. "You got ginger ale?"

"Sure do, and by the way, I'm Beth," she said and then turned and walked away, knowing all eyes would be on her.

They're better from the back, Joey thought looking at her legs and enjoying the sensual shifting of her hips with each step. As the evening wore on, Joey was either talking about boxing and his hope of being sent to another camp where he could start working out and get back into his kind of fighting shape, or he was thinking about Shirley. Two full weeks had gone by since she had called, and he had only received one letter from her, which gave him no information on the pregnancy subject. Joey felt confused. There were too many things running through his mind. If she was pregnant, how could he ever believe it was his, and yet how could he ever know that it wasn't? And was she screwing around with someone, maybe Art, and trying to blame him? Were his mother and everybody else right about Shirley?

The second night in Fort Smith was identical to the first, and the third was threatening to be the same when Beth pulled a chair alongside of Joey's and sat down. For a while, between coming and going, Beth shared her conversation with everyone, but gradually her attention became directed at Joey. "You know, you're the only fella that comes in here that hasn't made a pass at me."

"The only one?" Joey asked with mock suspicion.

"I swear," she said coyly.

"Well, I don't want you to think I don't find you attractive. It's just I am engaged."

"Hell, being married don't stop most of you boys. Why should being engaged? I'm married. My husband's overseas." Beth didn't wait for an answer.

"You don't look old enough to be married," Joey kidded.

"Oh, you … so you do find me attractive?" Beth smiled.

"Yeah, sure," Joey said.

"How long are you going to be in town for?"

"Just a few more days."

"I'm off the next two days, and since I think you're one of the nice guys, how would you like to take me to a show or something tomorrow?"

"I don't know," Joey said honestly.

"Aw, come on. I never know what to do with myself on my days off. Besides, since we're both taken, maybe we can be friends?"

"Why not?" Joey said monogamously.

Early the next evening, Joey met Beth at the hamburger joint across the street from the Brass Rail. They had just enough time to grab a quick bite before the show started. After the double feature, Joey walked Beth home, and they sat on the porch of her rooming house, enjoying the warm summer night.

"That's enough about me. Tell me more about you. Will your husband be home soon?" Joey said after talking most of the way there.

"Not soon enough." Beth sighed.

"Can't wait, huh?"

Beth smiled knowing he misunderstood. "Now, don't you misunderstand. When he gets home, I get a divorce … I sent him a 'Dear John' months ago, but I don't want to hurt him. See he's a very nice boy. What happened really wasn't anyone's fault. We were just a couple of crazy kids."

"It's a mistake a lot people make," Joey said marveling at how many stars were out.

"You know something? You're different from all the fellas I've met in this town."

"Oh, how am I different?"

"You're polite," she said, placing herself in position to be kissed.

"Ah, if I weren't so mixed up, I'd make a pass at you just like everyone else," Joey had to admit to himself as well as her.

"I wouldn't mind at all, now that I know ya a little better," she said placing her lips even closer to his.

Joey kissed her, and Beth kissed him. "Where can we go?" Joey asked when they could no longer stay where they were at.

"Can you make love quiet-like?" Beth asked.

"Am I allowed one long, low groan?" Joey asked softly.

"You're allowed two or three of those," she said, taking his hand and leading him quickly into her first-floor room.

Beth knew Joey didn't have to be back until seven o'clock in the morning, and she had no trouble convincing him to stay all night. In the morning, she drove him back to camp. "I'll pick you up at five o'clock sharp."

"I'll be here," Joey said and kissed her.

That evening, they had a long, leisurely dinner and talked for hours. And then, they drove back to her place, went to bed, and made love. "Where do you think you'll go from here?" Beth asked cradled in Joey's arms.

"I have no idea, and I get the feeling the army doesn't know either."

"I have to work till eleven o'clock, but I hope I can see you again before you go."

"We'll see if we can't work something out," Joey said thinking about Shirley.

At roll call the following morning, Joey and the others were told that in twenty-four hours, they would be sent to Fort Hood, Texas, not to be stationed, but again to be reassigned. Joey was passing the day playing cards when he was informed of a visitor awaiting him at the main gate. He found Beth there and led her to the camp's recreational area.

"Where is Fort Hood?" Beth asked after Joey told her of the new orders.

"I don't know. Somewhere near the Arkansas border, they said."

Beth stopped and leaned against a large tree. She thought a moment before saying, "I'm tired of this town and tired of my job. Maybe I can get a job down there."

"What would you want to do that for?" Joey asked knowing Fort Hood wouldn't be any better than where they were.

"To be near you," she said hoping Joey would like the idea.

"Look, Beth, I'm only going to be there for reassignment. Who knows where they'll send me after that?"

Beth wasn't able to hide the disappointment she felt, and then after a moment, she said, "I never wanted to be a camp follower, but ... but if I could be closer to you ..." She left the sentence unfinished and waited for Joey to speak.

"I think you'd better forget about it," he finally said.

"Will I see you tonight?" she asked, wanting one last chance at him.

"Yeah, sure," Joey said wanting to get rid of her but not wanting to hurt her either. That night, Joey wrote a couple of letters and watched television, not wanting to go into town, and the next day, he was on his way to Fort Hood. *Good-bye, Beth,* Joey thought as the bus rolled along, *whoever you were, whatever you were.*

Chapter Ten

Tough Times in the Army
(Ages 23–24) 1954–1955

On his third day in the Texas camp, Joey got another call from Shirley.

"Joey, we got to get married," she said hysterically.

"Now calm down. What did the doctor say?" Joey said, trying to stay calm himself.

"Nothing. I haven't been to a doctor!" she yelled.

"Why not?" Joey yelled back, feeling his guts twist around.

"Because I'm embarrassed! I'm ashamed!" she said, and her voice was still on the rise.

"Okay, okay, I guess you didn't get your period, huh?" Joey said still trying to calm both of them, trying to think.

"I missed my period, Joey. After three weeks, you can't say you're late anymore."

"Well, girls miss their periods sometimes without being pregnant. Something else could be wrong. That's why I think you ought to see a doctor."

"I've never missed my period before. We make love, and I miss it! I don't need a doctor. I need a husband!"

"All right! Let me think a minute," Joey said wondering what the hell to do.

"I love you, Joey. You won't stop loving me because I'm pregnant, will you, Joey?" Shirley began to cry.

"No, of course not. I'll figure something out and call you, okay?" he said, her tears diluting his anger.

"Okay, Joey, tell me you still love me."

"I still love you, Shirley. I love you."

Joey walked around a while and asked God to help him. He went to the chaplain's office. He listened to Joey's story and then told him it would take a few days to arrange a twelve-day emergency leave. From there, Joey went to the post office, sent Shirley a five-hundred-dollar money order, and told her to make arrangements to hold a wedding reception in the church hall. Two days later, his emergency leave came through. Joey sent Mike a telegram, telling him the flight he would be on and asking to be picked up at the airport.

"What the hell are you doing home?" were Mike's first words.

"I'm getting married to Shirley," Joey said as they started the car.

"Why?" was all Mike could think to say.

"Well, between you and me, Mike, she thinks she's pregnant."

"Oh no, I don't suppose a doctor has confirmed it yet?" Mike grimaced.

"She says she's embarrassed, ashamed to go."

"Yeah, sure, sounds to me like she's giving you a story, Joey. I know she's over a grand in hock. I swear that's all she wants out of you," Mike said shaking his head.

"No, I can't believe that, Mike. Besides, I love her and I'm lonely, and I still got over a year and a half to go. Having Shirley with me should make everything a lot easier."

"Something tells me you're making a mistake. Well, do me a favor, don't knock her up if she isn't already."

They reached the car, got in, and pulled away.

"I think you'd better wait until we get to the house. I don't know how the family is going to feel about things."

"It'll be all right. I've talked to your mother a couple of times, and they are all sorry about what happened … Tell you what, you'll need a car while you're here. We'll go to my place, and you could use this one. And I'll use the old lady's for a few days … If things don't go right at home, you can stay with Mary and me."

Joey and his mother had a tearful, apologetic reunion, and when he told her Shirley and he were getting married, she said she knew and was resigned to it. Joey went and cleaned up. He called Shirley and went to go and pick her up. He took her out to dinner. On the way to the restaurant, they were only able to manage small talk, but once inside and seated, they loosened up.

"The way your mother acted, I guess she doesn't know you're pregnant."

"No, I haven't told anyone but you. I was thinking if we were not in town when the baby comes, no one would know it came a little early."

"Yeah," Joey said thinking it was the best way.

"I've made all the arrangements for the wedding. We're going to have to pay for everything, I'm afraid. My mother just manages to get by on her widow's Social Security check."

"That's okay; did you rent the church hall?"

"Joey, I just couldn't. I wanted something nicer for us, and I hope you don't mind, but I rented the Tourine Hotel ballroom for this Saturday afternoon."

Joey laughed. "Why not?" And he continued to listen to Shirley as she explained how she had everything worked out so that everyone in both families could be notified in plenty of time. They made love twice that night at her place before Joey went home, and their lovemaking was so good Joey forgot the circumstances. The following day was busy and the night filled with love. Friday came, and that day was also full. That night found them taking a drive by Lake Erie. The summer night was balmy. The moon was out, and the stars were shining. Joey parked, and while they kissed, his hands began to explore.

"Don't," she said.

Stopping his hand on her upper thigh, he said, "What do you mean 'don't'?" he wanted to know.

"I'm having my period. It started this morning," she said tearfully.

Joey released his hold on her and slumped down against the backseat. He stared out the window for a long time thinking and wondering.

"I didn't know it was going to happen," she said still tearful.

"Tell me something, Shirley. Did you really think you were pregnant?" Joey said quietly.

"Well, I missed my period. I thought I was … If you don't believe me, you don't have to marry me!"

"I want to marry you, but it's hard to believe you could make a mistake like that!" Joey said vehemently.

"Then take your ring back, and take me home." She took the ring off, put it into his hands, turned her back to him, and began to sob.

"I do love you, Shirley, and I do want you," Joey said and gently turned her to him. He placed the ring back on her finger and held her tightly to him, comforting them both. The next day, August 7, 1954, William Joseph Giambra and Shirley Fina were married. There were quite a few people at the church wedding and a mob at the reception. They spent their wedding night at her place, and although Mrs. Fina went to bed early, Joey and Shirley only kissed and cuddled because of her condition. They relaxed most of the following day, and Joey worked on the bills. The wedding ended up costing about seven thousand dollars, and they received almost ten grand from mostly his family, relatives, and friends. When Joey finished, he figured he had enough to see them through until he got out of the army and started to fight again. On Monday, Joey took Shirley around and paid every bill she owed. He wanted her free and clear of any debts before they boarded the train for Texas. Later that day, they said their good-byes to everyone and then picked up Mike and drove to the train station.

"What the hell made you decide to take a train?" Mike asked thinking it to be ridiculous.

"Neither one of us took a real train ride before," Shirley responded.

"Taking a train from here to Connecticut or Jersey is one thing, but from here to Texas?" Mike questioned.

Two days later, Joey and Shirley checked into the Lone Star Motel in Fort Hood and spent two hours getting train grit out of their pores. Joey had hoped to make love to his wife for the first time, but Shirley was having a sixth day of a normally five-day cycle, so they dressed and went out for dinner. Shirley hated the food.

They were both tired of the train ride and decided to never travel that way again. They watched television a while, talked a bit, and then both went right to sleep. The next day, they searched out a nice apartment where Joey could pay the week, because he still had no idea where he might be sent. He knew all of his basic training buddies were long gone, and he wondered if he would ever meet up with any of them again. Once back at the motel, they decided to stay the night and move into the apartment in the morning. Again, they showered, and again, Joey thought they would finally be able to make love. A brief argument later, they went out to eat and see a movie. Shirley hated the heat. The sixth night of their marriage finally saw it consummated. Joey sensed coldness in Shirley at first, but it faded away from his mind as an almost violently passionate night evolved. Friday morning came around, and they moved over to the furnished one-bedroom apartment. They went shopping, and Joey looked forward to the three days of married life he would have before returning to camp at 7:00 AM on Monday. Shirley hated Fort Hood. They had a basically pleasant three days, and then Joey reported back to camp.

Sergeant Roy Blow didn't say hello. His first words to Joey were, "Listen, Jim-bra, I know from your 201 file here, that you were a troublemaker in basic training … Well, boy, you make any mistakes with me, you're ass is gonna git it." The five-foot-seven-inch red-skinned sergeant smiled.

"I'm fine, sir. How are you?" Joey smiled.

"And a smart ass on top of it … Well, well," the sergeant said, his smile gone.

"Look, Sarge, I don't want any trouble from anybody. Why don't we just shake and be friends."

"You Mafia guys think you can get away with anything, don't'chya?"

"Yeah, I'm Italian," he said, knowing he had another winner. Joey had no assigned duty that day, and as he returned home early, he could only pray he would be assigned before the week was up. Shirley was homesick. Joey was only able to get Shirley's mind off of her mother for a little while, and he fell asleep as she returned to the subject. The next day, Sergeant Blow had Joey put on KP duty. When he got back home, he found Shirley pacing the floor. She didn't even say hello.

Her first words were, "I'm going home!"

"What?" Joey couldn't believe his ears.

"I hate this town! I hate the food! I can't stand the heat! You know I'll break out in a rash!"

"Shirley, you're my wife now, and you have to stay with your husband."

"No, I don't. I'm bored, Joey! There's nothing for me to do here. I'll go crazy staying here!" she said emphatically.

"And I'll go crazy if you leave! I'll have to move back into the camp, and I swear if I have to spend twenty-four hours with this new sergeant, I don't know what will happen!"

"And I miss my mother," she said not hearing a word he'd said.

"Look, give it a chance. Stay around a couple of weeks so we can go have a nice honeymoon," Joey pleaded, feeling that he was losing the fight.

"Is that all you have on your mind?" she accused.

"Shirley, after all, you are my wife."

"Joey, I want to go home tomorrow. I can't stay here any longer," she said with finality and no emotion.

Joey just stood there. The fight was over, but he felt feelings of wanting to hit her, but he had never hit a girl and he wasn't going to start now. He wasn't going to be like his father, so he took a good long walk. Early the next evening, Joey put Shirley on a plane and sent her home. He finished out the week in the apartment, missing Shirley but enjoying the time he had to think. He moved back to the camp on Friday morning. Joey thought on his way to clean up the latrine, *It's sure been a long two weeks; it's sure been a full month.* The next four weeks were the longest of Joey's life. He prayed for a reprieve from the prison he felt himself in but only knew disappointment daily. And his loving wife felt she was fulfilling her marital obligation by writing him a short letter once a week. Sergeant Blow had him on perpetual KP or guard duty and wouldn't give him more than a twenty-four-hour pass on weekends, when everyone else was getting seventy-two-hour passes.

"You'll get one when you deserve it," Blow told him when he complained, and Joey just let the whole thing ride.

Joey's back began to act up, so he went to the hospital to have it looked at. On his induction record, it specified he had back trouble, fallen arches, and a sinus condition, and after checking the curvature of his lower lumbar, the doctor gave him a two-week light-duty slip without hesitation.

"Listen, Jim-bra, if you can fight ten rounds in the ring, you sure as hell can do army work," the sergeant fumed when he handed Joey the slip.

"Sarge, my back is bothering me. I can't do it now."

Sergeant Blow tore up the slip and further antagonized Joey by throwing the ripped pieces in his face. Joey ached. He wanted so much to hit him, but he knew that was exactly what Blow wanted him to do.

"I've got a detail for you right in front of headquarters company; we're building a path for the general, a rock path," Blow said sneering.

Joey silently followed Blow, who pointed out the pile of rocks that were to be sunk in the mud between headquarters and Headquarters Company to form a path for the general. Joey judged the rocks to be between twenty and forty pounds each and knew he wasn't about to lift them.

"Sarge, I am not supposed to lift anything heavy for at least two weeks," Joey stated flatly.

"If you can't pick 'em up, roll them," Blow snarled and walked away.

As usual, Joey swallowed the bitter pill and began rolling the stones to the already muddy area. The day was hot, and Joey was glistening with sweat when he became aware of an officer stopping in front of him. Joey stood up and snapped to attention when he recognized it was General Trapnell.

"What are you doing, son?" the general asked quizzically.

"Bringing some of these rocks over to the mud there, sir."

"Wouldn't it be easier if you carried them over?"

"Yes, sir, but I can't right now. I have a back problem."

"If you have a back problem, you should be on light duty."

"I am, sir, at least I was, but my sergeant said I didn't deserve to be on light duty and tore up the slip."

"You had a light-duty slip?" the general asked warily.

"Yes, sir, I saw the doctor this morning."

"Where is your sergeant?"

"He's back at the company, sir."

"Let's go see him," the general said, and Joey walked but wanted to run.

Sergeant Blow jumped to attention as the general preceded Joey into his quarters. "Are you this man's sergeant?" the general asked crisply.

"Yes, sir, I am," Blow said, and Joey heard the worry in him.

"He tells me he had been issued a light-duty slip this morning."

"Sir, do you know who he is? This here is Joey Jim-bra, the middleweight fighter. If he can fight in the ring, he can do army work," Blow began his defense.

"Are you a doctor, sergeant?" the general asked facetiously.

"No, sir." Blow cowered, knowing he had just been shot down.

"Then how do you know what's wrong with this man's back?"

"Let's call the hospital from Captain Bear's office."

Captain Bear was a tall, dark, and very thin man, almost maniacal in appearance. He greeted the General cordially, the General was on the phone and looked blandly at the sergeant, but the look he gave Joey was that of pure hate, as the general picked up the phone.

"Well, son, you're back on light duty," the general said to Joey, hanging up the phone.

"Thank you, sir," Joey said gratefully, hoping that from then on, the sergeant would have to go easier on him.

"From now on, if this man is in any trouble, someone will answer to me," the general said authoritatively to both the sergeant and the captain, and with that, the general left.

"Dismissed, Giambra. I want a word with you, Sergeant," the captain said menacingly.

Joey was getting ready for a shower when Blow came stomping toward him. "Okay, Jim-bra, you got your two weeks, but when that's up, your ass's going to swing."

Joey was the barracks orderly for the next two weeks. He rested and wrote letters, and his back pain gradually went away. The light duty ended, and the harassment began again. One rotten detail followed another, and Joey felt he had been sentenced to two years of hard labor. One day, he was cleaning the windows in the supply room when the sergeant came in with a pail and a mop.

"When you finish them windows, mop the floor," Blow ordered.

"Okay," Joey said keeping the conversation with Blow to a minimum. It wasn't until he had finished the windows that Joey discovered part of the mop handle had been sawed off, forcing him to bend even more than he would have normally. After swearing under his breath, Joey mopped about half of the floor, section by section, to keep traffic flowing, but then his back began hurting again.

Sergeant Blow came around, saw Joey sitting down, and immediately lit into him. "You should have been done by now. This ain't an all-day detail!"

"My back's acting up again, Sarge," Joey said and thought, *Here we go again.*

"You're a goldbricker, Jim-bra. All you Dagos should be put in jail!"

"Don't you call me a Dago; I've had it with you," Joey said ready to explode.

"What are you gonna do? Hit me? Come on, hit me. You're a fighter!" Blow baited.

"You'll get yours someday," Joey seethed, noticing the sudden silence in the room.

"Are you threatening me, Jim-bra?"

"You'll get yours." Joey turned and moved away from Blow and then went flying forward from a kick in the butt. Joey started back toward Blow looking for blood but was grabbed and held by two guys. "Take off those stripes, Sarge, and let's you and me straighten this out!" Joey challenged out loud.

"Get back to work, Dago!"

"Up yours, you son of a bitch!"

"That's an order!" Blow commanded.

"Screw you, and screw your orders!"

"That's it, Jim-bra! Report to the company commander!" Blow's eyes sparkled.

Joey tried to shake loose, while Blow turned and hurriedly left the supply room. Sergeant Blow was with Captain Bear when Joey arrived.

"What happened between you and this man, Sergeant?" Captain Bear asked to make it official.

"He disobeyed a direct order and refused to work," Blow stated.

"Okay, court-martial him," Captain Bear said.

Joey was given a special court martial and was fined seventy-five dollars and restricted to the post for a month. He didn't mind the restriction because he wasn't going anywhere, and he didn't mind the fine, but that he couldn't get any satisfaction was eating him up. The month restriction ended, and though Sergeant Blow continued his campaign against Joey, for one reason or another, he had to give him a weekend pass. Tony Affrunti, a friend of Joey's from New York, had the misfortune of being assigned to Fort Hood. Joey also knew Tony's mother and father, who owned a leather company in New York, but Joey didn't know Tony's close friend, Frank Sinatra. They had been able to commiserate on several occasions, but this was the first time they were able to get away from camp together. They decided to go to Temple, Texas, which was about thirty-five miles from Fort Hood. It was a Baptist community, and they only served 3.2 beer. Tony drank, and Joey sipped, and after a while, two girls joined them. Tony immediately began to pitch, but Joey couldn't help but think about Shirley.

"What's the matter? Don't you like girls?" one of the girls who had joined them asked.

"That's not it. I'm … married."

"Where's your wife?"

"Back East."

"Why don't you take advantage of that, and why don't you take advantage of me?" she said, and if that wasn't obvious enough.

Joey was getting nervous; he wanted to be with a woman. He was desperately trying to hold himself back, thinking of his church wedding, knowing he would be committing adultery. "No, thanks. Tony, I'll see you when you get back to camp," he said and got up.

Joey walked over to the bus stop thinking about Shirley and missing her. It took him almost two hours to reach his barracks, and he was still thinking about Shirley. He spent most of the night composing a letter to her, telling her how much he needed her and begging her to rejoin him. Joey managed to get in an hour of sleep in before Sergeant Blow rudely awakened him.

"Okay, Jim-bra, you're on KP, so snap to!"

"Hey, Sarge, it's Sunday. I have a weekend pass," Joey managed to mumble.

"Rise and shine! As long as you come back early, you're on detail!" Blow bellowed near Joey's ear.

Monday morning arrived, and while waiting for a full field inspection, Joey got a letter from his brother Sammy. Sammy had mentioned seeing Shirley at the beach with her former boyfriend, and Joey felt his stomach knot up. He didn't know what to think or what to believe. Sergeant Blow came into the barracks to conduct his own inspection before the "brass" arrived. Joey, as always, had everything neat, clean, and ready. Blow looked but couldn't find anything wrong with Joey's preparations, so he moved over to the window beside Joey's bunk and said, "Hey, Jim-bra, your window's dirty."

"There's nothing wrong with that window, Sarge. I just cleaned it," Joey said in no mood for any of Blow's crap after Sammy's letter.

"Well, if you just cleaned it, what's this?" Blow said snidely and pointed.

"What's what?" Joey snapped.

"That!" Blow spit on the window.

Joey reached down and grabbed the bayonet he had laid out for inspection, pulled it from the scabbard, and chased Blow right out of the barracks yelling, "I thought you were a combat soldier, you bigoted bastard!"

The entire barracks was suddenly howling with laughter and congratulating Joey on doing what most of them wanted to do. Their demonstration was still going on a few minutes later when two MPs came in to arrest Joey. They marched him to the company commander's office where Captain Bear and Sergeant Blow were waiting.

"Well, Giambra, we've got you now, and we're throwing the book at you. You Mafia guys belong behind bars anyways." The captain smiled.

"Sir, I am not a Mafia guy, but I am Italian and proud of it. I'm also a human being, and I'll be damned if I'm going to stand for any more harassment from you guys!"

"This is your third court martial, and this one's going to get you to the stockade. You don't know what harassment is, but you're going to learn!"

"You guys don't care. You're not Americans; you're Communists!"

The two MPs grabbed Joey as he started for Captain Bear, who then screamed, "Throw him in the guardhouse! Get that animal out of here!"

The guards had their hands full as they dragged the screaming Joey away, but once outside, one of them said, "Paisan, I'm Italian too! Take it easy! I'm going to testify for you tomorrow. Those mothers are so prejudiced it's sickening, and the way they badgered you, they're the ones who should be behind bars."

The next morning, Joey met with the second lieutenant assigned to defend him, and the young officer's deficiencies were soon made apparent. The lieutenant had not only been unable to reach General Trapnell, he couldn't find the Italian MP.

"What do you mean you can't find him? What did he do, disappear?" Joey asked intensely.

"No, no, I heard he was transferred out of here this morning."

Joey listened to Sergeant Blow's lies corroborated by Captain Bear and several privates and corporals.

"They're all lying. Isn't there something you can do?" Joey said, nudging the doodling second lieutenant.

"Yeah, if you're smart, when they get through, I'll throw you on the mercy of the court."

"Not until I tell them the truth," Joey said and just looked at him with contempt.

"They won't listen to it," the lieutenant forewarned.

"Maybe not, but they'll hear it," Joey said adamantly.

He took the stand, was sworn in, and then was told to answer yes or no by the prosecutor. On the third question, Joey said, "Yes or no won't answer that."

The prosecutor succeeded in frustrating Joey to the point of flustering him. "What am I doing here, and why am I all alone? When do I get a chance to tell you people what really happened?" Joey finally asked, gathering himself.

"Later on. Right now, you must answer the question," the presiding officer said curtly. "What later on? I'm on the stand now."

With that, the presiding officer informed Joey of extenuating mitigation, when he would have the opportunity to tell his story without being under oath.

"Okay," Joey said reluctantly, thinking the army didn't make sense at all. The jury finally retired, and a few minutes later, Joey was escorted into a back room, where a major, a captain, and two lieutenants called him to attention.

"We find you guilty of charge one and charge three, specification B. Before we pass sentence, you may tell your side of the story. Extenuating circumstances could entreat the court's leniency," the major read.

As Joey told his side of things, from the first day of basic training to the present, his eye filled with tears, his voice with emotion. He swore he was telling the truth, pleaded for their understanding, and even cited his spotless civilian record. Joey was sent out of the room, and while they were deciding his fate, he couldn't help thinking of the rumors he didn't want to believe about the stockade.

Again, he was summoned, and sentence was pronounced by the major. "Three months in the stockade."

Joey's righteous indignation grew to hysteria as he said, "You're no good, and you're all rotten! You know what you are? Communists!

That's what you are. You hate Italians, and that's why I'm getting what I'm getting now!"

"That's enough, Giambra, or we'll double your sentence!" the major ordered.

"Listen to me! Be quiet, and I'm sure the general will cut your sentence when he reads the report," Joey's attorney said intensely, getting between him and the quartet.

"Leave me alone," Joey said but the seed of hope had been planted.

The MPs took Joey to his barracks, helped him collect his gear, and then took him to their compound and locked him in a truck with barred windows. After a short drive, Joey got his first look at the stockade, a fort-like edifice of wood and barbed wire; once inside, he was taken to the headquarters of the command and was given a routine indoctrination speech. As he listened, he saw the nameplate, which read "Lieutenant Perelli," on the desk and remembered Perelli had been a fairly well-known college football player.

"Relax, Joey. You're from New York, right?" Perelli said when he finished the automatic little speech.

"Buffalo," Joey said almost inaudibly.

"I'm from New York. I understand how you feel," Perelli said, but Joey stood there in no mood for chitchat. Perelli glanced over Joey's file. "Your civilian record is excellent. How come you're having so much trouble in the army?"

"It's all there in front of you. You can see what they've given me."

"Yeah." Perelli nodded. "I'm Italian too. In this part of the country, they just don't like Italians, Negroes, or Jews, but you have to hang in there."

"I don't belong in here. Officers and sergeants lied to screw me into this place, and I don't belong here," Joey said.

"Joey, I'm going to make out a special report on your court martial and send it to General Trapnell. All I want you to do is stay loose, do what you're told, and I'm sure you'll be out of here in a week."

Joey looked back at Perelli for a moment before stating, "If I'm not out of here in a week, I'm running."

146

"Don't be foolish, Joey. Don't worry; I'm working for you." Perelli sympathized with him.

"Thanks," Joey said and thinking he had been dismissed, started to go.

"Wait, don't you want to make a phone call?" Perelli called.

"Can I?" Joey brightened.

"Sure, as long as you call collect, you're entitled to it. Hell, I'll let you make a few more if you want."

Joey wasted no time getting Mike on the phone and telling him the whole story. He summed everything up saying, "They're really jerking me around, Mike; you have to find a way to get me out of here."

"Okay, kid, you keep your nose clean, and I'll take care of everything. We'll blow the lid off that joint!" Mike said angrily.

Joey was assigned to a barracks and then put on "police the grounds" detail. He picked up cigarette butts, gum wrappers, anything and everything that marred the "beauty" of the dirt. He was then returned to the barracks and given fifteen minutes to clean up for chow. Though the barracks were kept reasonably clean, Joey noticed that the place was infested with cockroaches, and he knew he would go nuts if he had to live in that for three months.

After marching to the mess hall, Joey realized the majority of the prisoners were Negroes and that the majority of the food was leftovers from the main company. The only thing he was able to eat that night was an apple. Later, two of the prisoners in his barracks started a fight. One ripped off a toilet seat and hit the other with it, splitting his head open. That triggered several of the others to start ripping off toilet seats until there weren't any left. The MPs finally got things quieted down and took several men to the hospital. Twice that night, Joey and his fellow prisoners were awakened and forced to march around the stockade for a half hour before being allowed to go back to their bunks. When reveille sounded, one of the Negroes was found dead, having apparently slit his own throat with a razor blade. Joey was able to eat the cereal and milk served at breakfast, but that wasn't enough fuel for the hard labor ahead. And due to the previous night's ruckus, the entire barracks spent the entire night digging trenches. The slop served for lunch was inedible as far as Joey was concerned, and a single orange was all he had. After lunch, Joey and the others began to fill the trenches they had dug that morning. During the rest period, Joey lay flat on his back, already feeling twinges of pain returning to the lower lumbar area and knowing he wouldn't be able to last another day.

One of the MPs came over and began talking to Joey, telling him he was also from New York and that he had seen him fight once. By the time the rest period was over, the MP told Joey there wasn't much he could do but talk to the other guys about not coming down too hard on him. In the mess hall that night, Joey traded his tray for an apple, but two apples for dinner weren't enough to stop the gnawing in his stomach. Two of the Negroes started jawing at each other when they got back to the barracks, and Joey quickly stepped in. He made it very clear that he didn't want to suffer anymore for their goofing off. That he was a professional fighter automatically earned Joey a certain amount of respect, and the rest of the evening passed with relative ease. They were only called out and marched once that night, but a maniacal laugh woke Joey again just before reveille. He had heard that "Crazy," a skinny little Southern kid, flipped out from time to time and spotted him crawling around in his corner catching cockroaches and eating them. Joey was dry-heaving in the john when the bugle sounded. He managed to get the cereal and milk down, and then after breakfast, he had the friendly MP take him over to Lieutenant Perelli's office.

Joey talked to Perelli a while, but to no avail. Finally, he said, "There are a lot of sick people here that should be in a hospital."

"Forget about it, Joey. Guys will try anything to get out of the stockade. There is no way to tell how sick they really are," Perelli said.

Joey stood silently for a moment and finally realized, "I guess I'd better learn to mind my own business."

Perelli agreed. "You can't go wrong. Meanwhile, I made sure my report got to the general yesterday, and I wouldn't be surprised if we heard something this afternoon."

"I sure hope so, and thank you, sir," Joey said.

On the way back to the barracks, Joey told the MP what was happening with his case, and Joey summed up, "One way or another, I will be out of here before the weekend."

"Don't try to run, Joey. Even I'd have to shoot you if you did," the MP said as a friend.

No sooner had Joey gotten back to the barracks, wondering what kind of detail he would be sent on, than a truck screeched to a halt outside, and two MPs came in quickly. One of them called out saying, "Is Private Giambra here?"

"Yeah, I'm Private Giambra," Joey called back.

"Come on!"

"Where are we going?"

"Don't ask questions. Let's go!"

The MPs drove Joey back to Lieutenant Perelli's office.

"Things are going to break for you now, Joey," Perelli said very pleased.

"What happened?" Joey asked, anxious to hear something good for a change.

"I understand the general received a phone call from the Pentagon this morning. It seems that some VIPs are very upset with the treatment you've been getting."

"Not nearly as upset about it as I've been," Joey said, thinking, *Beautiful.*

"Go take a shower and shave, and put your uniform on. You're going to see the general."

"Thanks again, sir. For what it's worth, they're going to know you're one of the few decent people I've met in the army."

"Thank you, and good luck," Perelli said.

Someone is finally going to help me, was all Joey could think as he cleaned up. When he was ready, he went outside and found the general's staff car waiting for him.

"Climb in, man. You must be some kind of cat!" A Negro sergeant grinned.

"What do you mean?" Joey asked.

"I've been driving for the general for a long time, and I've never seen such hell break loose. There's a big shake-up coming down at headquarters," the sergeant said, putting the shining black limousine in motion.

"How come?"

"What I hear is some big people have been callin' Washington about you, and I mean big, Walter Winchell for one, some senator from New York for two—"

"Senator Mahoney?" Joey threw in.

"That's him, and the mayor from your hometown," the sergeant remembered.

"Mayor Sedita?" Joey thought aloud.

"Right."

Joey arrived at Fort Hood headquarters and was met by a general's aide, who immediately took him into a private room and asked him to tell his story. From there, Joey was brought before General Trapnell, who remembered the stone-rolling incident.

"Joey, I imagine you've heard that some important people have asked for an investigation where you're concerned."

"Yes, sir."

"I hope you believe that without those calls, you would still be standing here right now. Once I read Lieutenant Perelli's report, I began this investigation."

"You were fair with me before, so there's no reason for me not to believe that, sir."

"Good. Now there are definite discrepancies in the statements made by almost everyone at your court martial. They've all been summoned, without knowing why. This way, they won't be able to cook up any stories. I will personally interrogate them with you present, but I don't want you to say a word unless I ask you to. Is that understood?"

"Yes, sir," Joey said, jubilantly.

One by one, Captain Bear, Sergeant Blow, and the others who testified against Joey were brought in, questioned, and dismissed. When all had been heard, it was obvious all had lied. Captain Bear, they learned, had court-martialed almost two hundred men in less than a year. He was sent to a hospital for battle shock. Sergeant

Blow was busted to a private, and all the details were entered into his service record. The others were given fines and restrictions.

The general said, when it was all over, "Joey, I've got a major who has been pestering me for almost two years about forming a boxing team. It strikes me that I can get him off my back and at the same time, make up for what the army has put you through. Would that appeal to you?"

"General … Fantastic!" Joey said, trying to hold back a yell of joy.

As Joey left the general's office, he felt elated about everything, but especially pleasing was his remembrance of the looks that crossed the faces of Captain Bear and Sergeant Blow when they entered the general's office and saw him sitting there.

1954 Madison Square Garden SOLD OUT! Giambra won unanimous decision against the Italian Champion Italo Scorticcini

Chapter Eleven

The U.S. Army Recieves World Class Coaching (Age 24) 1955–1956

Major Marsinkouski was in charge of the Fourth Armored Division Tank Battalion. He was a stocky, balding man in his late forties and an avid boxing fan. "Come in, kid. Sit down and relax. Would you like something ... cigar or a drink?" he said to Joey not bothering to move his feet from the desk.

"No, sir, I don't drink or smoke."

"That's right. I read you were always in top condition. That's great!" the major remembered.

"Sir, I want you to know this is the only break I've had in the army, and I want to do a really good job for you."

"And that's great. The general filled me in on what went on back in headquarters. I tried to get you transferred here when you first came to camp for reassignment ... Well, anyway, that's yesterday's battle. Now, here's what we're going to do. First thing, I'm going to put you in Special Service; that way, you won't have to deal with all that army jazz. You'll be like a civilian, and even wear civilian clothes, if you'd like. You'll get your own room, and you'll get the best food. You'll be in complete charge of the boxing team, which you'll put together and coach ... How does that sound to you?"

"I just hit a home run with the bases loaded," Joey said, collapsing in his chair and staring wide-eyed at the ceiling.

"But there's one thing that I want from you, and I want it so bad I can taste it. I want champions!" the major said with a touch of fanaticism.

Joey got his private room in a new brick barracks. He ate special food, and he called Mike Scanlan to tell him all that had taken place and how grateful he was. Mike was elated for him. The call for Joey's boxing team was posted, and for the next few days, Joey looked at all of the men who wanted to try out. He finally selected two for each weight division and scheduled daily workouts for everyone, including himself.

"Major, some of this World War I equipment won't last very long," Joey said to his already frequent visitor.

"You've got a carload of the best already on its way." Major Mars, as he was affectionately known, grinned around his cigar.

Joey's days were suddenly full and looked forward to, but the nights were not. Christmas was only two weeks away, and Joey missed his wife. He called Shirley and told her of his new position and how he had it made. He told her how much he loved her and missed her, and he said he would get a really nice apartment off the post if she would come back. Joey was ecstatic when she agreed to rejoin him after Christmas and thankful he had decided not to mention Sammy having seen her at the beach with Art. Joey bought another Oldsmobile '98 convertible as a welcome-back gift to Shirley. It was all white with a blue interior, and since Shirley didn't know how to drive, Joey planned to teach her.

It was a Saturday afternoon when he and Tony Affrunti drove to the airport to pick her up. When she got off the plane, Joey could hardly recognize her. She looked like a burlesque queen, wearing heavy makeup with tinted dark red hair and a tight dress provocatively cut. But it had been four months since he had seen her, so she still looked beautiful to him.

As Joey came in for a kiss, she said, "Don't, you'll smear my lipstick," turning her head aside.

Joey couldn't believe her acting that way but managed to keep quiet by introducing her to Tony and then telling her about the new car. They dropped Tony off at the camp on the way to the new apartment. Joey couldn't wait for her to see it. When he told Major Mars about his wife coming back and needing an apartment, Mars had sent him to a fight fan and friend, Carl Curly. Curly was a wealthy old Texan, who drove an MG Roadster, refusing to submit to age. He owned the finest apartment house in town and was tickled to have Joey move into an all but luxurious two-bedroom apartment at half the price. Shirley was impressed with the apartment, and after she washed the trip away, she and Joey got reacquainted. Joey took her to see a friend who had a house off the post, where she learned she was the reason for a dinner party. Joey introduced her to Mr. and Mrs. Curly and to a dozen other couples. He hoped that the apartment and having girlfriends would keep Shirley from the loneliness she had felt the last time around.

Two weeks passed by with Joey enjoying his new duties in the army and at home. Shirley had made several new friends, one quite close, and she and Joey had dinner twice a week with Carl and his wife. One of Joey's friends, named Lenny Cohen, who owned a men's clothing store in Killeen, Texas, offered Shirley a job. She and Joey agreed it was a good idea. The time would pass more quickly if she would keep busy. So everything was going fine at this point. Mike called Joey one night and suggested that he come and visit for a while and help him get back into shape to fight again.

"Sure, the bedrooms are at each end of the apartment, and Shirley and I only use one of them. When will you be out here?" Joey said.

"The end of the month, early February for sure," Mike answered.

"I should be able to get permission to fight on a weekend now and then," Joey said.

"You leave the army to me; I'll take care of the army." The glib-tongued Irishman laughed. Mike arrived at the end of January. He brought two cases of the impossible-to-get, very expensive Crown Royal Canadian Whiskey and passed it out to all the army VIPs, right up to the general. By the end of February, Mike felt Joey was ready. Every day, he went to camp with Joey and was invaluable to not only Joey personally, but to the entire boxing team as a whole. When Mike asked Colonel Fogarty, the head of Special Service there, if he could set up a professional fight for Joey in the area, the answer was, "Anytime."

Mike had already talked to some promoters around Dallas, who were all anxious to get Joey and set up his first fight since he joined the army.

"Well, kid, one year down, one more to go, and this army life will be behind you," Mike said after telling Joey the fight was set for the following weekend.

"Yeah." Joey smiled softly. "In the meantime, eight or ten fights around here and you'll be ready for the Garden again."

"It's hard to believe I haven't fought in over a year," Joey said.

"That's okay; things are working out good now."

But all was not working out well there concerning Shirley. Working only seemed to make things worse, and she quit her job after only two weeks. She didn't cook, hated cleaning house, and missed her mother, her friends, and the big city. She complained about Mike living with them and told Joey she didn't like him, but most of all, she hated Texas.

"I don't want to stay here any longer. I want to leave," she told Joey during the week. "Shirley, I'm telling you right now, if you leave this time, it's all over," Joey said deadly earnest.

"We're married, Joey, and there's nothing you can do about it," Shirley said viciously.

"I'm telling you, you go, and we're through!"

"Well, I'm going."

"I've had it with you!" Joey said on his way out of the bedroom slamming the door shut.

Mike was watching television in the front room and was shaking his head. He said when Joey plopped on the couch, "I couldn't help hearing, kid."

"I'm sorry, Mike," Joey said with fury and heartbreak twisting him.

"Joey, get rid of her, send her home, forget about it."

"I should have listened to you, to everybody who tried to tell me about her," Joey said with regret.

"No I-told-you-so's, Joey; you loved her so you couldn't believe what was pretty obvious to everybody else … Is she packing?"

"Yeah."

"Good, I'll take her to the airport and put her on a plane tomorrow. Meanwhile, you just concentrate on the fight and becoming champion … When you get out of the army, we'll go to court and get rid of the bitch, permanently."

Joey had four fights during the next three months, winning them all by knockouts. He hadn't heard from Shirley, nor had he tried to contact her in any way. The boxing team was shaping up well enough to keep Major Mars happy, and though Joey felt lonely at times, he was slowly putting his emotional forces back together again. The month of June began, and the heat became unbearable. Joey closed the gym. He had his boys do their roadwork early in the morning and then spent the afternoons doing laps in the enlisted men's pool. Joey was not only respected; he was loved. Mike had been putting off going to Buffalo to straighten out several interests that needed his personal attention, but the heat convinced him it was time to go.

"You sure there's nothing I can do for you back home?" Mike asked as Joey walked him to boarding at the airport.

"Just call Ma and tell her that I'm all right, but I can't think of anything else," Joey said wishing he were going too.

"Okay, I'll be in touch with you in a couple of weeks and let you know what's going on," Mike said shaking Joey's hand.

Joey had officers' pool privileges and took advantage of them. The officers enjoyed having Joey around, considering him as somewhat of a celebrity, and to the wives and kids, he was a celebrity. He thoroughly enjoyed playing in the pool with the kids, and he also enjoyed the company and conversation of women again. Deep down, Joey still knew he felt bad about Shirley. He couldn't help feeling regret and, occasionally, longing for her.

Joey and Tony Affrunti were driving into town in the Olds '98. Joey was happy he hadn't signed it over to Shirley. They pulled in to a drive-in to grab a quick bite to eat before taking in a movie, and a carhop he'd never seen before took their order.

"Pretty kid," Joey said to Tony who was still watching her retreating figure.

"Sure is, I could go for a piece of that," Tony said lustfully.

"Yeah," Joey concurred.

"Ahh, her ol' man probably just got transferred down here," Tony said realistically.

"Aren't you Joey Giambra?" the girl asked as she attached the tray to the car.

"Yeah, how'd you know?" Joey smiled at her recognizing him.

"I'm from New York. I saw your picture in the papers a few times and thought you looked cute for a fighter."

"I think you're cute too. What's your name?" Joey said handing her a five-dollar bill with the check.

"Dina."

"Dina, this is Tony."

Tony waved back. "Hi, I'm Tony, and I'm from New York. And I also think you're cute."

"Well, thank you. There's enough New Yorkers down here to start a revolution, and in case you're interested, Joey, I get off at twelve," Dina said. She smiled, laughed, and made change.

"I'm interested." Joey nodded, and Dina smiled and walked away.

"You lucky stiff," Tony said with friendly envy as he again watched the girl walking away.

"Pays to be famous, my boy. She sure didn't sound like she was from New York," Joey said doing a bad imitation of W. C. Fields.

"Neither do you anymore." Tony chuckled.

"You mean I sound like that?" Joey couldn't believe it.

"Don't I?" Tony laughed.

"You know, now that you mention it …" Joey nodded, and they were both laughing. Joey dropped Tony off after the movie and got back to the drive-in restaurant at eleven thirty. He had a nice, cold strawberry milkshake while he waited for Dina to finish up.

"I've got to ask, how did you end up in Fort Hood?" Joey said.

"Oh, my ex-boyfriend got sent here two weeks ago for assignment, and well, we pretty much had it anyway. And this time, when they transferred him, I decided to make a few bucks together and head home."

Twelve o clock rolled around and Joey walked out with her. "I've got my own car," Dina said, motioning to a green Kaiser-Frazer car parked nearby.

"Well, what do you want to do?" Joey asked.

"Go back to my motel and take a steaming shower in cool water," Dina said at her sultry best.

"How do you do that?" Joey asked curiously, knowing the question was expected.

"I don't do it; we do it, and you've got to help," Dina said wickedly.

Joey followed her to a nearby motel that advertised weekly and monthly rates, and once inside, Dina punched on the air-conditioning and stripped. Joey was one step behind her, and they frolicked in the shower like kids in front of a fire hydrant. When the frolicking ended … So the affair with Dina lasted one full week. Joey was relieved to find no apparent guilt feelings about committing adultery. He justified his actions with the thought of Shirley leaving him, and no longer fooled himself with the thought that she had been faithful, ever. Joey took Dina to Temple, Texas, on her day off, and while having dinner at Temple's finest, Dina said, "Take me back to your place tonight, Joey."

"I've really wanted to, you know," Joey said apologetically.

"I know," she said knowingly.

"But …" Joey began and then stopped.

"I know. There's only one way to get her out of that bed: by putting someone else in it!" Dina punctuated the sentence.

"I know; you're right," Joey admitted.

"Let me be that someone else," Dina begged.

Joey got rid of a lot of Shirley and a lot of pain that night. He and Dina were lying naked in Joey's room, watching a late movie on television. Dina turned in his arms when a commercial appeared and said, "Do you know what I like best about you?"

"What?"

"You didn't get hung up on me."

"Shouldn't that bother you?"

"It would have a few years ago, but I've learned when a guy gets hung up on me, I've got problems."

"It's easy to understand why most guys could get hung up on you; you're the most sexually free girl I think I've ever known."

"Maybe even freer than you think." She smiled.

"What do you mean?"

"Joey, how would you like to turn me out?"

"You mean pimp for you?" Joey asked with disbelief.

"Why not? I know you don't need much dough, and I could really put together a stake in a couple of months. I can't do it carhopping."

"I don't think I can handle that sort of thing; it's not my bag, but I'll tell you what I'll do … You like Tony, right?" Joey said after a moment.

"Your friend, sure. He's almost as cute as you are," Dina said caressing him.

"He really wants you. Tony is a sharp guy, knows how to handle chicks, and for him to want you so bad means he thinks you're pretty special."

"Do you?" Dina fished.

"Where am I?"

"Here with me."

"That says it all," Joey finished.

The next day, Joey told Tony what Dina wanted, and he was elated.

"Have you ever done anything like that?" Joey asked.

"Nah, I'm like you, I couldn't pimp, but if she'll take care of me for nothing a couple times a week, I'll set her up with as many guys as she can take on."

That night, Dina said to Tony, "It'll be a pleasure paying you off this way."

And she was in business. Tony took her out four nights in a row. He bought her dinner and gifts, but he didn't fix her up with anyone.

"When are you going to help me make some money?" Dina finally asked.

"In ... a couple of days," Tony said passionately, wanting her again.

"This is great, but it won't pay for the freight," she said as she slipped the pillows under her hips.

"I can't get enough of you." Tony sighed painfully, and she knew he was hung up on her.

Damn, she thought. The following day was Friday, and she said she had a girlfriend who wanted to meet Joey, so a double date had been set up. Joey drove Tony over to the motel at the specified time, but all they found was a note taped to the door.

"'Sorry, we'll do it another time. A good friend in a nearby town got sick. I'll be back in a day or two. Love you, Dina,'" Tony read.

"What do you say we go to Temple?" Joey suggested.

"Yeah, let me check the office first," Tony said thinking.

They went into the office, and Tony approached the manager. He asked, "Would you happen to know what town Dina went to, you know, the girl in number nine?"

"Waco ... Some officer came looking for her and then asked me what the best way to get to Waco was," the grizzly old man said through bad false teeth.

"Thank you," Tony said politely.

"He didn't happen to say where in Waco?" Joey thought to ask the man.

"Nope ... Just Waco," the old man said and went back to watching television.

Tony went quickly out, and Joey had to catch up to him.

"Hey, Tony, what, are you sore?"

"Sure I'm sore. Have you ever been to Waco?" Tony snapped.

"No."

"Great town. Let's go. I'll show you the sights."

"Why not? How far is it?" Joey said amicably.

"About a hundred miles," Tony said climbing into the Olds.

"Good, you're Dago temper should be cooled off by then." Joey laughed.

"Oh, I'm all right, Joey."

"Sure you are. You've got no reason to be sore. You knew up front what she wanted." Tony gave Joey the easy directions as they started away from the motel, and they then settled back looking at the star-filled night.

"Do you have any idea where we'll go when we get there?" Joey asked.

"Yeah, there's a nightclub hangout called Bottle Clubs. I'll show you once we hit Waco."

"I take it you didn't set her up with this guy," Joey assumed.

"I never set her up with any guy," Tony said and Joey knew he hated the idea.

"Hey, Tony, you sound like you're in love."

"Ah, I don't know what I am. You gotta be nuts to get serious with a hooker, don't you? And I don't figure I'm nuts yet."

"Boy, you just clicked off a memory for me. Getting involved with a hooker isn't the worst thing that could happen." Joey grinned, thinking of Ruby. They arrived at Bottle Clubs in Waco and immediately saw Dina dancing with a first lieutenant. Only this wasn't any lieutenant, this was Lieutenant Trapnell, the general's son. It took a while, but Dina finally spotted them sitting at the bar. She became perceptively nervous, and a few minutes later, she and the lieutenant left the club. Joey stayed well behind them as they drove back to Fort Hood and then parked across the street from the motel. They watched Lieutenant Trapnell kiss her good night at the door and then leave.

Tony waited two minutes and then got out of the car.

"What are you going to say to her?" Joey asked, knowing he wanted to be alone with her.

"I don't know. Wait for me. I'll let you know right away if I'll be staying or not."

"Don't cause any trouble," Joey said as Tony got out of the car.

"Don't worry."

Joey did worry though; he knew Tony could get mean if he felt put down. A scream-like sound came from the general direction of Dina's part of the motel, and then Tony came running out. A profane exclamation came from Joey before Tony reached the car and jumped in.

"Home, James," Tony said coolly. James was a termanology used for saying chauffer.

"What did you do?" Joey asked as he pulled away.

"I belted her," Tony said as he looked at the back of his right hand.

"Aww, Tony." Joey groaned.

"She's okay. How about putting me up for the night?"

"Sure," Joey said.

"Thanks, I'd hate to waste a weekend pass," Tony replied.

The phone woke Joey up early Saturday morning.

"Do you know what Tony did to me last night?" Dina asked, obviously still very upset.

"Yeah, I hope you don't think I had anything to do with it," Joey said feeling ashamed about it.

"I know, Joey. I just can't understand why Tony acted that way. Is he crazy?"

"Remember telling me how guys keep getting hung up on you?" Joey said.

"So he's hung up on me, big deal! I'm still going to have his ass arrested."

"Aww, Dina, don't do that," Joey said feeling terrible.

"You should see my right eye," she said and began to cry.

"Don't, baby. Look, jump in your car and come on over, and I will cook breakfast for us okay?"

"Okay, but today, I'm calling Lieutenant Trapnell and telling him about Tony and what he did," she whined.

Joey rousted Tony out of bed and told him what Dina had in mind. While Tony was swearing, Joey got through to him that he'd better try to smooth things over, unless he wanted to wind up with a general court martial.

"Better give me a few minutes with her before you come out," Joey suggested.

"Why don't I just wait till you figure it's right," Tony said sensibly.

"Fine," Joey said slapping him on the shoulder. He headed toward the kitchen. The doorbell rang, and Joey hardly recognized Dina hiding behind large sunglasses.

"The body looks great. Let's have a look at the eye," Joey said lightly.

Dina's eye was several shades of red and purple, but not cut or too swollen. As he prepared bacon and eggs, he tried to talk her out of taking action against Tony, but Dina was resolute. As a last resort, Joey got Dina and Tony together over a plate of food, and although Tony was contrite and apologized a few times, Dina refused to accept his apology.

That afternoon, Joey took Tony to the post and accompanied him to Lieutenant Trapnell's office. Tony was wavering between being afraid and angry enough to want to kill Dina. "I can't believe she's making all this trouble over a slap. I wonder what kind of story she told him," Tony said intensely.

"It won't matter if you do what I tell you. Just keep your mouth shut and let me do the talking," Joey said firmly.

The boys were called into the office and stood at attention until the lieutenant said, "At ease ... Do you understand this is a private inquiry into an alleged incident that took place last night?"

"Yes, sir," Tony replied to the question directed at him.

"And I understand you were with Private Affrunti last night," the lieutenant asked looking at Joey.

"Yes, sir, and if you let me, I think I can straighten everything out," Joey said.

"I hope you can," Lieutenant Trapnell said sincerely.

"Well, sir, I know for a fact, officers and gentlemen don't knowingly associate with prostitutes. I myself spent quite a lot of time with Dina, until she asked me to pimp for her. She then made the same proposition to Tony here. I have also been told by two other guys she tried to hustle them. Now obviously, you didn't know this, or else you wouldn't have gone out with her, right?"

"Ah ... right." The officer nodded lightly.

"There's no question Tony was out of line, and he has apologized, but just like I wouldn't want to see Dina get in trouble, I wouldn't want to see Tony get in trouble either," Joey concluded.

The lieutenant slowly smiled and said, "You know, you're pretty sharp."

"Oh, I just figure no woman like Dina is worth any one of us getting in trouble over." Joey smiled back.

"And you're right, gentleman. I suggest we forget about the whole thing," Lieutenant Trapnell said, getting up from behind his desk.

Joey and Tony expressed their gratitude, shook hands with the lieutenant, and left. On the way back to Joey's car, Tony said, "You should have been a lawyer. How can I thank you, Joey?" Tony said.

"By doing what I'm doing, staying away from Dina. I think we've both had it with her. Nice girl but not for us."

The days of June ended, and the days of July were almost gone, and hopefully some relief from the oppressive heat was on the way. The boxing team won their first two camp versus camp tournaments, and Mike decided to stay in Buffalo until the heat broke in Texas. Joey began counting the months, less than eight more and he would be free! Joey watched a ballgame on TV and then decided to go to the officers' pool and pass a few more hours on Sunday.

After playing in the pool with the kids for a while, Joey climbed out and was immediately called over by one of the officers' wives that he knew. He was introduced to a lovely girl named Kara, the wife of a captain from West Point. Her hair was long, straight, and black, and her skin was the glow of dark orange sun. Joey found his eyes continually drawn to different portions of that skin, and during a private conversation, he was invited for dinner at her home that night. Joey was wondering what kind of guy the captain would turn out to be as he arrived at five minutes to seven. Kara opened the door to the quaint little house and gestured Joey in with the sweep of a hand. Joey met the other dinner guests, an officer's wife and child, and was then informed that the captain had been sent to Washington for a week and wouldn't be back for a few days. Dinner went smoothly enough, although Joey felt some anxiety that he couldn't place the reason for. Then the wife and child had to get back home, and Joey knew the reason.

"Maybe I'd better leave too," Joey said as Kara closed the door.

"Not yet," she said with mock hurt.

"But won't it look bad, you and me alone?"

Kara drifted to Joey and settled against him. "I know you want me, just by the look in your eye, and the first time I saw you, I knew I had to have you."

Joey eased Kara to arm's length as she tried to kiss him.

"Are you kidding? You're married. You're an officer's wife! I can't get involved with you!"

"We're smart enough not to let anything happen, aren't we?" Kara said, worming her body against his again.

"No way! One thing about the army, you get involved with an officer's wife, they'll shoot you!" Joey didn't even say, "Thank you," as he dashed out of the house and drove away quickly.

The night passed, and as the sky brightened, Joey returned to his car and put the key in the ignition but was looking at a gift-wrapped package in the passenger seat beside him. He gingerly picked a note from the bow and read, "I want you, Joey."

Inside the package, Joey found a blue cashmere sweater, matching socks, and a romantic Nat King Cole album. Early that afternoon, Joey went to the officers' pool, knowing Kara would be there. He swam a few laps, played with the kids a while, and then clung to the edge of a lounge chair Kara was bathing on.

"You must have been up early." Joey smiled.

"No, I was up late. Did you like the gifts?" Kara smiled back.

"Yeah, but you shouldn't have done it."

"I thought we could listen to the album together sometime."

"Kara, please understand. I'd be too scared to ever relax with you," Joey said uncomfortably.

"Maybe at first, but I'd relax you. I want to see you tonight," Kara whispered leaning and exposing herself.

"Kara, we can't," Joey said without conviction.

"Oh please, Joey. I'll call you tonight. We can meet somewhere, go somewhere … You do want to, don't you?"

"I won't be able to get out of the pool for a few minutes," Joey admitted and then swam away from the hunger he saw on her face. Kara called Joey the moment night fell, and they arranged a clandestine meeting on the outskirts of town. Joey pulled alongside Kara's car, and she wasted no time joining him. A full minute went by before she took her mouth away from his and allowed him to proceed to one of the many motels in and around Belton, Texas. The twenty-five-mile drive passed quickly, but took forever due to Joey's guilt. Joey felt pangs of guilt as they made love, but Kara was warm, affectionate, and marvelous in bed, and Joey soon forgot they were married to other people.

As they drove slowly back to Fort Hood, Joey again expressed his fears, and Kara again attempted to assuage them. "I wish we could have spent the night together," she said as he helped her into the car.

"I wish you weren't married to an officer," Joey said as it was still on his mind.

"Will I see you at the pool tomorrow?" she asked.

"Probably ... Although, there is a big inspection going on at the post in the morning," Joey answered.

"Joey, we can really get something going between us, and you'll never get in trouble. I've got too many connections," Kara said, clutching his hand to her cheek.

"I've heard that before." Joey shook his head.

"Believe me, and don't worry about my husband. I rule the roost."

"I can believe that," Joey said.

"One thing, Joey, I do have my pride, and once I let a man know me, he's got to do the pursuing," Kara said with a different sound in her voice.

After a final kiss good night, Joey watched her drive away, waited for a few minutes, and then drove home. A few hours later, Joey staggered out of bed, put on his full army regalia for the first time in weeks, and went to the post for inspection. An hour later, he came home, started getting undressed, and watched a scorpion fall out of his boot. Moments later, a partially dressed Joey jumped in his car and sped to the base hospital.

"How long did you have your boots on?" the doctor asked as he examined Joey's foot and ankle.

"About two hours," Joey answered quickly.

"Well, if it had stung you, you would have felt it, and your foot would have swelled. Evidently, the scorpion was asleep, and when you put your boot on, you killed it before it stung you."

"Then there's nothing wrong with my foot?" Joey asked relieved.

Again, he drove home. He thought about going to the pool, but then thought better of it. But the following day, he again ventured forth to the officers' pool, hoping he would find Kara surrounded by other wives. Kara was there, and sitting alone with the wife he had had dinner with at her house. Joey jumped in the pool and swam over to them. He said hello, heard it, and then swam over to the kids and began to play. A short time later, Joey climbed to the high board and executed a beautiful swan dive. The kids loved it, and scattered applause from around the pool sent Joey up again. This time, he walked to the edge of the board, fell on his butt, sprung up and out, and dove perfectly into the water. The kids were still laughing when Joey reached the board again and then became quiet as they watched him do a jackknife. As he kicked back, his left heel caught a sharp edge beneath the aluminum board and was badly gashed. Blood spurted out as he hit the water, and he got quickly out of the pool. The lifeguard called a medic while Joey tried to stop the bleeding, and he was soon in the hospital being sewn up. He was bandaged, taped, and told to stay off the foot as much as possible. Joey stayed around the house for several days, reading, watching television, and resting. And then one night, after August arrived without a break in the weather, Joey got a call from Mike.

"Joey, you're fighting Bo Bo Olson!" Mike said very excited.

"You're kidding," Joey said, catching the excitement.

"No, you're fighting him in San Francisco in three weeks."

"Mike, you're crazy; he's the middleweight champion of the world."

"What, are you afraid of him?"

"No, but how can I fight for the title if I'm in the army?"

"Hold it; it's a nontitle fight, a ten-rounder, but if you beat him or even give him a hell of a fight, you can get a title fight out of it!" Mike corrected.

"Wow! Hey, why does he want to fight me?" Joey said feeling somewhat overwhelmed.

"Because you're in the army, his people figured you are rusty, not in shape. At the same time, you are popular, and with all the Italians in San Francisco, you'll draw."

"That doesn't make sense, Mike. What does he want a nontitle fight for?"

"Well, there's rumors that Sugar Ray's going to come out of retirement and try to get the title back. I figure Bo Bo's using you for a tune-up."

"What? He thinks I'm a bum, huh?" Joey uttered, his ego hit.

"Oh, Joey, I know you can beat him. He's ready to be taken. I want you to get in the best shape of your life," Mike implored.

"Mike, I've got some bad news there." Joey was forced to remember his injury.

"What is it?"

"I hurt my left heel."

"How'd you hurt it?"

"I dove off the high board at the officers' pool."

"Why, you stupid bastard Dago? How bad is it?"

"It's pretty bad; I've still got stitches in it."

"Joey, the fight's set for August 26. That's just over three weeks. Let's not blow it."

"Mike, how can I train hard with a bad foot?"

"We'll think of something. You're always in great shape anyways. Just work around it. A couple weeks of hard work is all you should actually need."

"When are you coming out?" Joey asked.

"In a couple of weeks, I'll spend a few days there, and then we'll fly to San Francisco and have a week there before the fight."

"That all sounds great, but what if the army doesn't think that way?"

"I told you before; I'll take care of the army. What do you think I'm spending a few days there for?"

The next morning, Joey paid a visit to the doctor, and while the doctor unwrapped his heel, Joey said, "My manager didn't know about the accident and set me up with another fight … I was wondering if there is any way you could fix it so I could run without doing any damage."

"Sure, I'll tape you up good and give you a box of cotton padding to put in your shoe, because you're healing fine. But I suggest you jog easy for at least three days, and then you should be able to run," the doctor said without hesitation, as he examined the wound.

As he left the hospital, Joey decided to take a few test laps around the track by the athletic field. After changing in the gym, Joey began jogging over to the track. He soon realized he had to favor the heel, but he still managed to get in two miles before returning to the gym for a workout. The next morning, Joey got up at 6:00 AM and thought he'd save himself a trip to camp by jogging in a big empty field near his apartment. He passed what he judged to be a two-mile mark, still favoring the heel, when he stepped on what appeared to be a piece of rope. Only the piece of rope came alive. It hissed and snapped. Joey stopped, watched the copperhead wriggle away, and then ran home. He knew he felt something hit his foot when the snake struck and was terrified thinking he had been bitten, but the moment he took off his shoe, he saw the fangs hadn't penetrated. Joey decided to do his running on the track from then on.

By the time Mike arrived, Joey was running, but still with a limp. The doctor left the stitches in to accommodate the added stress as the deep cut was healing as expected. Joey and Mike talked to Bo Bo Olson that night, and the next morning, Mike went with Joey to the camp. While Joey went to the gym, Mike ferreted out Colonel Fogarty. He told the head of Special Service that Joey had a chance to fight Bo Bo Olson and then proceeded to elaborate on the reams of publicity Camp Hood would get, not to mention what an asset it would be to the Third Corps and the Fourth Armored Division to have one of its men fighting the middleweight champion of the world. Colonel Fogarty gave Joey a ten-day furlough. Two days later,

Colonel Fogarty gave Joey a dinner party at his home and then wished him bon voyage. The following morning, Carl Curly came to Joey's place while Joey and Mike were packing and talking about Bo Bo Olson. Carl had been to all of Joey's fights in Texas, and having won them all by knockouts, Joey began looking on him as a good luck charm. So when Carl said he would like to go along, Joey was grateful for the opportunity to do something for his generous landlord, as well as have his good luck charm around. Joey had the stitches removed just before he, Mike, and Carl drove to Dallas in Carl's Cadillac and took a plane to San Francisco.

Mike had alerted the press ahead of time, so when they arrived, they were met by dozens of reporters and photographers, all covering the story of "GI Joe from Buffalo." The three men checked into a hotel near the Cow Palace, the site for the upcoming bout. After they cleaned up and dressed, they went to a big party the Italian community was giving for Joey at DiMaggio's restaurant on Fisherman's Wharf. The reason for the party was to welcome Joey, to let him know the Italians wanted a champion, and to cheer his official signing of the contract to fight Olson. A big banner reading, "Welcome GI Joe," was the first thing they saw when they arrived at Fisherman's Wharf, and a wave of pride shot through Joey's veins.

"You're the great olive hope!" Mike laughed in response to the all-out thinking that Joey could beat Olson. While he was being naturally gregarious under the circumstances and falling in love every minute, not having seen so many beautiful girls at one time since he left New York, Joey had to admit to himself that he was really nervous. Because of his heel and not having had any real sparring partners, Joey knew he wasn't in the shape he wanted to be in. But most of all, he was nervous because he was about to fight the champion. Bo Bo Olson hadn't come to Joey's party, but his rotund manager, Sid Flaherty, was there for the signing, and he and Mike got together and made arrangements for Joey to join Bo Bo in a public workout at Newman's Gym the following afternoon.

"You'll go three rounds with the California middleweight champion, then three more with the same ex-contender Bo Bo works with," Mike informed Joey, as they and Carl were being driven back to their hotel.

"Beautiful, I hope you can line me up a couple of guys to spar with every day this week," Joey responded.

Newman's Gym was charging a dollar admission to watch the champion and contender work out.

The place was packed with three tiers of people sitting and most of the standing room taken. Bo Bo was the first on to work out. His first sparring partner was an ex-middleweight contender, an older, well-scarred veteran. His second sparring partner was much younger, much quicker, and much more like Joey. Bo Bo was very good; he looked great. Joey got a rousing reception from the boxing fans as he replaced Bo Bo in the ring.

"These guys might want to show off a little, so don't get careless," Mike warned.

"I won't," Joey said looking across the ring to his stocky opponent.

"I hear this guy's a real puncher," Mike went on.

"Hey, put your headgear on. I don't want to cut you up!" Joey yelled across the ring.

"Cut me? You won't even touch me!" his opponent cockily yelled back.

As the first round progressed, it was apparent to everyone that the California champ was trying to butt Joey, elbow him, and work him over unprofessionally, in general. Only Joey showed him exceptional speed and his superb finesse, and the San Francisco fans quickly realized they were seeing a classy fighter at work.

"This guy's trying to do me in," Joey said as he returned to his corner after the first round.

"I know. Pull out all the stops! Teach the punk a lesson!" Mike said angrily.

"Yeah, sure. Easier said than done." Joey chuckled humorously.

"Go in there and finish him off!" Mike ordered as the bell rang.

Joey boxed and moved, making the California champ look bad. Again, Joey evaded the obvious attempt to butt him and then spun the charging bull to the left, hit him with a left hook under the heart, and followed up with a right cross. The bull spun on the way down, landed flat on his face, and didn't move. It took a full minute to revive him and two guys to help him out of the ring.

"You've never knocked any guy out in two rounds and with no boxing behind you at all," Mike said with intense delight as the applause died down and the buzzing increased.

"I kind of surprised myself, but I really caught him flush." Joey grinned.

"Now you saw the guy go three rounds with Bo Bo. He's rough like Bo Bo, but he's no middleweight anymore. He's got you by ten pounds," Mike said as the ex-contender climbed back into the ring.

"So be careful," Joey finished for Mike. He wanted to box and move and go the full three rounds. He knew he needed the work, but before the first round was over, he had been hit low for the second time.

"What the hell are you doing? Keep 'em up!" Joey spit out after purposely clinching.

"Fug you, grease ball!" the fighter growled and then pushed Joey away and against the ropes.

Joey sidestepped as the fighter came at him quickly and then nailed him with a six-inch punch, right on the button. He was out cold as he went through the ropes and clear out of the ring. Mike was thrilled as the crowd watched Joey circle the ring, waving at the people.

"Boy, can you handle yourself," Mike said when he returned to the corner.

"Yeah, but I didn't get much work in," Joey complained slightly.

"You didn't need much the way you took care of those two … Now watch the odds drop!" Mike said.

"You think so?" Joey asked.

"The way some of the reporters dashed out of here, those five-to-one odds are going to drop in half."

Although Joey worked out daily at Newman's Gym, even Mike couldn't find him any decent sparring partners. Joey was taking a breather during his last workout before the fight, when a distinguished-looking man approached him.

"I'd like to talk to you a minute," he said handing Joey his card.

Joey read the card which told him he was a casting director with Metro-Goldwyn-Mayer. "*The* MGM, Mister?" Joey asked.

"There's only one MGM, and just call me Al." The man smiled.

"What do you want to talk to me about, Al?"

"Well, you've probably heard we're going to film the life story of Rocky Graziano, and I'm out scouting for a new face to play the part. You're a middleweight, you're Italian, and though you're much better looking than Rocky, I don't think that will bother anyone."

Joey smiled. "You know, ever since I was a kid, I've always wanted to become an actor."

"I'd like you to come to Hollywood and take a screen test, but of course, if you're marked up after the fight, we'll have to wait," Al said sincerely.

"There's something else we might have to wait for; I've still got six months left in the army."

"Six months, that could present a problem, but if your test is good enough, things could probably be worked out," Al replied thoughtfully.

"Hey, Mike!" Joey called out and then waved for him to come over. "I want you to meet my manager; he does all my business for me."

"Glad to," Al said.

"Yeah, what do you want?" Mike asked, eyeing Al as he approached.

Joey introduced the two men and filled Mike in on what Al had proposed.

"How much do we get for it?" was all Mike was interested in.

"We'll pay all expenses, and if Joey should get the part, we'll negotiate a contract," Al said professionally, though he was somewhat irritated by Mike's callousness.

"Look, my kid's no actor, and he ain't gonna be no actor. He's gonna be champion!" Mike said tearing up Al's card.

Al started away briskly and then turned back. "It was nice meeting you, Joey," he said pointedly and left.

"Damn it, Mike! I'm not going to be a fighter all my life. You know I want to be an actor!" Joey seethed.

"Joey, that's years from now; forget about it. You'll be making so much money and get so famous, when the time comes, they'll be begging for you!" Mike said placatingly.

"Yeah, sure, I hope you're right," Joey said feeling he had blown the chance of a lifetime.

"You get your mind back on the fight," Mike commanded softly.

"That's what's important?" Joey said.

"That's what's important, and that's what you concentrate on."

"Okay, Mike," Joey said, forcing a smile.

"How's the rib?"

"A little sore. That kid gave me a hell of a shot."

"That's the trouble sparring with young studs; they're always trying to impress."

"He impressed me all right," Joey said gingerly feeling a lower rib.

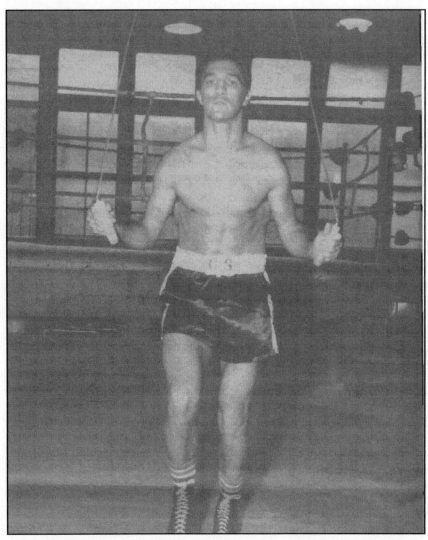

1955 Giambra training to fight Champion Carl Bo Bo Olsen

1955 Giambra fully focused on beating Olsen

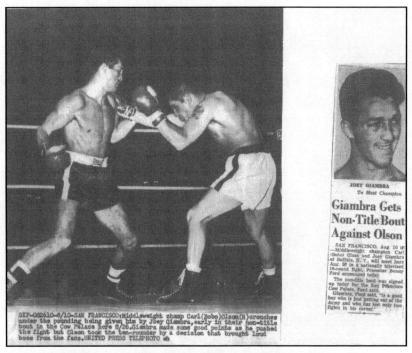

JOEY GIAMBRA
To Meet Champion

Giambra Gets Non-Title Bout Against Olson

SAN FRANCISCO, Aug. 16 —Middleweight champion Carl (Bobo) Olsen and Joey Giambra of Buffalo, N. Y., will meet here Aug. 26 in a nationally televised 10-round fight, Promoter Benny Ford announced today.

The non-title bout was signed up today for the San Francisco Cow Palace, Ford said.

Giambra, Ford said, "is a good boy who is just getting out of the Army and who has lost only two fights in his career."

SFP-082610-8/10-SAN FRANCISCO:Middleweight champ Carl(Bobo)Olson(R)crouches under the pounding being given him by Joey Giambra,early in their non-title bout in the Cow Palace here 8/26.Giambra made some good points as he pushed the fight but Olson took the ten-rounder by a decision that brought loud boos from the fans.UNITED PRESS TELEPHOTO eh

1955 middleweight champion Carl Bo-Bo Olsen afraid to put his title on the line agreed to a non title fight at the Famous Cow Palace in San Francisco.

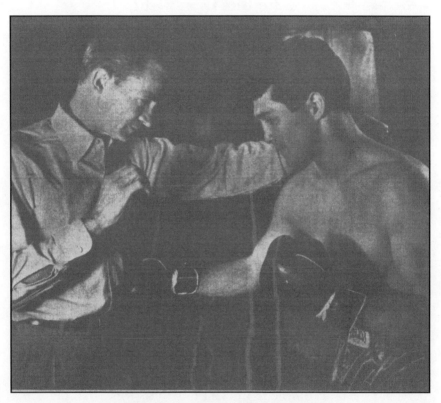

1955 Training with Mike Scanlan

Chapter Twelve

Bo Bo Olson Fight
(Ages 25–26) 1956–57

The weigh-in ceremony was scheduled for 11:00 AM. Because it was a nontitle fight, both managers agreed to have their fighters come in over one hundred and sixty pounds. Bo Bo made it easily, usually having to lose weight for a title go, but Joey weighed his usual one hundred and fifty-eight and was forced to eat bananas and drink beer all day. Joey was surprised at the size of the Cow Palace. It was quite a bit larger than Madison Square Garden, but when he heard there were only five thousand-plus people there, Joey was disappointed.

"Don't be silly. The fight's being televised locally as well as nationally; five thousand's a damn good crowd. How does the foot feel?" Mike said.

"Better than the rib," Joey said stretching.

"Don't worry about a lousy rib; you've got twelve more of them." Mike chuckled.

Joey laughed for the first time that day. He felt nervous. He was nervous. The odds on the fight went exactly as Mike had predicted. They had gone down to two and a half to one after the public workout. Then as the week passed, the articles appeared in sports sections, telling of his having only four fights in a year and a half and with mediocre talent at that, and the odds climbed back to five to one against Joey. Mike answered a knock at the door and then returned saying, "The last preliminary is almost over."

"So early?"

"What early? It's five to seven."

"Oh, that's right; it's five to ten in New York," Joey remembered.

The door was knocked on and simultaneously opened. "Okay, Giambra, you're on!"

Joey boxed his imaginary foe as he jogged down the aisle, looking around the arena. *It looks like more than five thousand people,* he thought.

"Okay, kid, start moving around. Get warmed up," Mike said as Joey jumped into the ring. Joey was glad to be moving, jumping around; he was afraid if he stood still, his knees would shake.

What are you nervous about, Joey? he asked himself. *What have you got to lose? So what if he takes you apart? He's the champion of the whole wide world; you won't be disgraced.*

The introduction took place, and of course, Bo Bo, being a San Francisco boy as well as the champ, received a tumultuous ovation. Joey received a polite applause and enough vocal encouragement from the Italians to keep from being embarrassed. While they were receiving instructions from the referee, Joey was thinking about his foot, all those bananas, and all that beer.

Everything he was feeling must have registered on his face, for when he returned to his corner and awaited the bell, Mike said, "You were ranked number four in the world, and you are better than that!"

In the first round, Joey and Bo Bo both fought their own fights. Bo Bo bobbed and weaved and was very difficult to hit, and Joey boxed, moved, and jabbed. When Bo Bo would try to swarm all over Joey, his basic style, Joey would run like a deer, leaving Bo Bo flailing at air.

"How do you feel?" Mike asked at the end of the round.

"All right. This guy's kind of rough; he likes to butt with that head of his, but I think I can handle him," Joey said.

"Okay," Mike acknowledged, having heard that for a week, and the bell rang for round two.

The boxers circled each other and continued the feeling-out procedure of the first round, and then Bo Bo threw a right hand under the arc of Joey's left. As he did that, Joey bounced off the ropes and came back with a right uppercut that caught Bo Bo right on the chin. Bo Bo was out like a light on his feet, but his instinct made him stagger forward and hang on to Joey for dear life. For the rest of the round, Joey tried to put him away, but each time the referee would separate them, Bo Bo would go into another clinch. The crowd was still on its feet and roaring when the bell ended round two. Joey went back quickly to the corner, but there was no one there. He looked down and saw that they were administering to Carl Curly. Mike jumped back up and threw the stool under Joey.

"What happened?"

"Carl got so excited he passed out." Mike grinned, and Joey knew it wasn't serious.

"I couldn't get to him, Mike," Joey said exasperated.

"Hey, listen, that's no sparring partner out there; that's the champ! Just settle down. You got him going, keep him going," Mike said.

Bo Bo bobbed and weaved throughout the third round. He wanted more time to get himself back together before really starting to fight again. Joey kept trying, but just couldn't get to him. During the fourth and fifth rounds, Bo Bo came on a little stronger, but still seemed reticent to go after Joey. He started his swarming tactic again, so Joey got back on his bicycle. Moments later, Joey caught Bo Bo with a left hook that cut his right eye and then followed up with a right that staggered him. The seventh and eighth rounds patterned themselves after the sixth, but in the ninth, Joey caught Bo Bo with a solid right, followed by a combination left hook and right again. Bo Bo was wobbly the rest of the round, and Joey began to feel the fight was his. The tenth round was even bigger for Joey than the second. He staggered Bo Bo again with a left hook, and Bo Bo was in bad shape. Joey cut his right eye with a sharp right, and he was puffed up and winded. The bell ended the fight with Joey hitting the champion at will. Joey started back to his corner, knowing that the cheers were for him and that the fight was his and that he would finally get a shot at the championship.

"You fought the greatest fight of your life!" Mike screamed, hugging and kissing his "champion."

While they waited for the decision, Mike sponged and wiped Joey's face. Except for a small cut on his right eyelid, Joey didn't have a mark on him. The crowd cheered their approval as the first judge called the fight for Joey. They booed when they heard the second judge score for Olsen, and the crowd rioted when the referee made Olson the winner of a split decision by two points. Bottles were thrown, fights broke out, one man literally dropped dead of a heart attack, and the Cow Palace became a madhouse. Olson left the ring quickly and was rushed out of the arena by his managers and handlers. Joey held on to the ropes on both sides of the post he leaned against. Mike had kicked the stool out of the ring and remained silently by Joey. Suddenly, Mike grabbed Joey's right hand, raised it high, and walked around the ring. The rioting stopped, and a standing ovation replaced it. That night, the Italians threw a victory party for Joey at DiMaggio's Restaurant. Even Joe DiMaggio was there with several other baseball players, and nobody allowed Joey to feel any other way than victorious. Jocy felt victorious again the following morning when he read accounts of the fight. It was unanimous; King Carl Bo Bo Olson had won a hometown decision. Joey Giambra had been robbed! Mike got together with Sid Flaherty for lunch, and they began discussing giving Joey a shot at the title. Sid disclosed Bo Bo's upcoming fight with Sugar Ray Robinson, which was set for early December, and he and Mike signed a contract for Joey to fight Bo Bo late in February 1956.

Mike knew Joey's army stint would be up in March and also knew Joey had done the army proud, so there wouldn't be any problem getting GI Joe to fight again. Late that afternoon, while Mike was showing Joey the contract and telling him of the afternoon with Bo Bo's manager, the telephone rang.

"Go ahead, Mrs. Giambra," Joey heard the operator say and wondered why his mother was calling him.

"I love you, Joey, and I want you. Let me come back to you," Shirley whined.

When Joey heard her voice on the phone, he felt funny inside, knew he had feelings for her, and wondered if he still loved her.

"Who is it?" Mike asked, reading Joey's sudden drop in emotion.

"Joey?" Shirley began crying at his silence.

"Hold on, Shirley," Joey said and then covered the mouthpiece with his hand. "It's Shirley."

"Don't tell that bitch anything," Mike said protectively.

"Why?" Joey asked feeling confused. "Because she's no good for you, and you'll probably divorce her when you get out of the army anyway," Mike said.

"Yeah, you're right," Joey said gloomily and then spoke into the phone again. "Shirley, I'll be going back to camp tomorrow, and you know you can't stand Fort Hood."

"But I love you, Joey, and I miss you so much," she pleaded.

"Look, I'll be home in about six months. Just take care of yourself until I see you," Joey said, thinking she hadn't stuck with him when he needed her.

"Do you still love me?" Shirley asked, still crying.

"Yeah, sure," Joey said, wanting to end the conversation, and he hung up.

"What's the matter? You still care about her?" Mike wanted to know.

"I don't know. I'm not sure," Joey answered thinking that his being in the limelight again was the reason she wanted him back.

"Well, don't waste any time thinking about it now; you'll have plenty of time to think about it when you get out of the army," Mike advised.

Joey, Mike, and Carl flew back to Dallas the next day, and when Joey emerged from the plane, the army band began to play the camp song. While Joey was wondering what was going on, General Walters and his aide shook his hand, and the army photographers kept snapping pictures.

"It was a great fight, Joey. You've brought honor to the Fourth Armored Division," the General said.

"Thank you, sir," Joey said proudly.

"Have you ever been in a helicopter before?" the general asked.

"No, sir," Joey said almost frightened at the thought.

"Well, you're going up in one now. I want you to fly back to camp with me. There is something I want to talk with you about," the general said.

A few minutes later, Carl was driving Mike back to Fort Hood, and Joey was beginning to relax and enjoy a more personal sense of flying than he had ever known in a commercial plane.

"How would you like to get out of the army three months early?" General Walters asked.

"That'd be great, because I am anxious to get back into boxing full-time," Joey said eagerly.

"Boy, the way you fight, I can see why. Tomorrow night, you and your manager come to my house for dinner. You're going to do something, and I'm going to do something for you." The general shook his head.

Joey wanted to ask a dozen questions, but the general had ended that portion of the conversation. Early that following evening, Joey and Mike were enjoying a lovely dinner with General Walters and his family. Mike finally couldn't stand it anymore and had to bring the subject up.

"So Joey tells me you might discharge him early?"

"Yes, what I want to do is promote goodwill, not only for the Fourth Armored Division, but for the army as a whole. The Olson fight has made Joey very valuable. Now, I can order what I want done, but I'd rather pay 'in kind,' 'sweeten the pot,' you know what I mean? So here's the deal; Joey, for the next three months, you make personal appearances and speeches for the army, and I'll see that you're discharged around the first of December."

"My time is your time." Joey grinned.

"You're a hell of a man, General," Mike said with admiration.

While Joey spent the next few months promoting the army and the Fourth Armored Division in the area, Kara began giving Joey more gifts, insisting she wanted to see him and be with him again. Joey was grateful every time he was sent to Austin, San Antonio, Dallas, or Fort Worth, just to get away from the officer's wife. Finally, he told Kara he was going to be discharged from the army even though he still had a month to go, and that did the trick. He never heard from her again. As December approached, Joey finished his personal appearances by answering telephones on a muscular dystrophy telethon in Waco, where he helped raise quite a bit of money. He also got a kick out of meeting Leo Castillo, one of his movie favorites! A week before the Olson versus Robinson fight, Mike called General Walters from Chicago.

"General, I think we can do you a favor … You're discharging Joey, right?"

"His papers are being prepared now," the general answered.

"Good, now look, Joey's going on national television, and he is gonna be introduced before the Olson-Robinson fight. I'm sure you see the possibilities. He appears in his uniform, and they announce he's with the Fourth Armored Division."

"That would be a fine way for him to bow out," the general said appreciatively.

"There's one problem. If Joey walks into that ring without a stripe after almost two years, it's gonna be embarrassing for the army as well as Joey. Even one stripe would take the curse off," Mike said.

"I believe you're right. Those court martials he was involved with are almost impossible to get around, but of course, that's what a general's for; I'll see that he's a private first class in three days," the general said after a moment.

Joey's stripe came through, his discharge came through, and he was on a plane to the Windy City. He took a cab to the hotel where Mike had a room waiting for him, and then they enjoyed dinner as they talked of the future. Joey had a beautiful Texas tan and looked great in his officer-of-the-day uniform. When he was introduced by the ring announcer, Joey climbed into the ring, acknowledged the fine round of applause he received, and then yelled into the microphone, "I'm Joey Giambra, the uncrowned champion!" He walked over to Sugar Ray Robinson and said, "Good luck, Sugar."

"Thank you, Joey." Sugar Ray smiled.

"Maybe if you win the title, I'll get a shot at you?"

"We'll talk about it later." Sugar kept smiling, but his mind was on the fight ahead of him.

Joey crossed the ring to Bo Bo's corner. "I'm pulling for you, Bo Bo. Beat this guy, because I want another shot at you."

"Don't worry, Joey. If I win, you got it.

If I win, Joey thought, *he didn't sound very confident.*

Joey sat ringside under the apron and watched his first fight from the press point of view. Bo Bo looked good in the first round, and Joey began to wonder if Sugar was really through. Robinson had lost a tune-up against Tiger Jones, his first fight on the comeback trail, and he just didn't look like the Sugar Ray of old. In the second round, Sugar Ray caught Bo Bo with a devastating left hook, and Bo Bo didn't move as the referee counted him out. Joey's heart sank. He felt sick. His title shot was gone. Mayhem hit the arena. Robinson had a comeback, and it wasn't expected. Reporters and photographers swarmed the ring, and Joey jumped in there with them. He worked his way toward Robinson, who was already being interviewed on television, and when he got next to him, Joey yelled, "I want to challenge you for the title, Sugar! I think I deserve a shot!"

Joey was seen and the challenge heard on national television.

"What do ya think, Sugar?" the sportscaster asked.

"Right now is too soon to talk about it, but I'll be defending the title in about six months, and Joey's definitely championship caliber," the classy Robinson answered.

Robinson did not want to put his title on the line against Giambra, because at that time, Giambra was unbeatable and Robinson knew it.

Mike had driven to Chicago and was driving Joey back to Buffalo when Joey said, "Mike, you know something? We're never going to get a fight with Sugar Ray. You know the way he is now. He picks out the fighters he wants to fight, and he doesn't want to fight me."

"Well, I'll tell you what we're gonna do; we're gonna put a twenty-five-hundred-dollar bond against Sugar in New York; we'll force him to fight us!" Mike said, feeling Joey's pain.

"I hope you're right, Mike," Joey said knowing that ploy didn't always work.

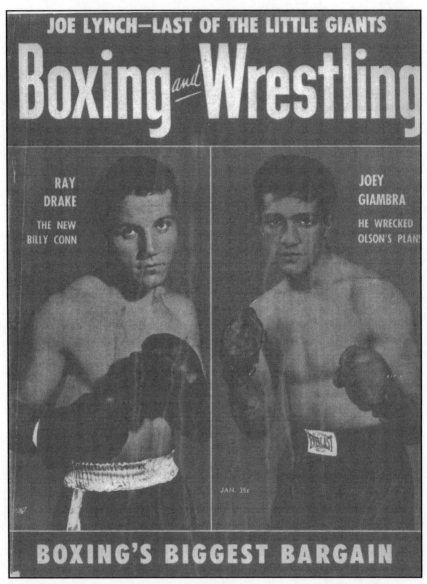

1956 Boxing and Wrestling cover one of many covers for Giambra

Chapter Thirteen

Will Joey Get a Shot at Sugar for the Title?

Joey was thinking about his wife as they approached Buffalo and wondering what he was going to tell her and how he was going to break it off. "I don't know what the hell to do, Mike."

"That came out of left field. What do you mean?"

"Being Catholic, being married in church, how am I going to get a divorce?"

"I took care of the army; I can take care of Shirley. I want you staying with me anyway. You're back in training, starting now, and I'll have you fighting in a month," Mike said with certainty.

Mike's wife, Mary, was very happy to see her "boys" again. They unpacked, cleaned up, had dinner, and then watched television. Joey didn't call anyone, figuring tomorrow would be soon enough to let everyone know he was back. The next afternoon, he called Shirley.

"When did you get into town?" Shirley asked.

"Last night," Joey answered.

"Why didn't you come home to me?"

"I wanted to relax last night; it was a long drive."

As their conversation went on, Joey began wondering if it was the army that had destroyed their relationship, and if things could be different.

"Mike, I think I'm going to see Shirley and have a talk with her."

"Don't get involved with her again, Joey, and for God's sake, don't break training."

189

Joey's heart began to flutter the moment he saw Shirley, and he took her in his arms. He kissed her and knew he still cared for her and still wanted her. Shirley's mother decided to spend the night with her other daughter down the hall, so Joey and Shirley had the bedroom. They made love, and it was still good. Joey thought things might work out between them. He began training the next day and stayed with Shirley and her mother for a week, but he was unhappy there.

"I got to either get an apartment or buy another house," Joey told Mike.

"Why not move in with me and Mary? You can each have a bedroom; this way, I'll know you ain't breaking training."

"I'm all for it, but I'll have to ask Shirley," Joey said.

"Don't ask her; tell her."

That night, after making love, Joey told Shirley how he felt and what Mike proposed, and she agreed to give it a try. Then Joey told her how lonely he had been the last time she left him and that he hadn't intended to stay married. He felt he was doing the right thing by telling her of his affairs with Dina and Kara after she'd left, but his honesty didn't pay off. Shirley was terribly upset.

"I'm going to live at Mike's. Are you coming with me?" Joey asked his petulant wife the next morning.

Mike greeted them at the door with the news that Joey was fighting Alan Andrews on January 6 in Norfolk, Virginia. He then showed Joey and Shirley to their rooms, which were on either side of his. That night, after they had all gone to bed, Joey decided to sneak over to Shirley's room for a while. As he passed in front of Mike's door, a board squeaked and then another. Mike opened his door wearing glasses and carrying a book.

"What are you trying to do, kid, break training?"

"No, no, I was going to get a glass of water," Joey said with a sheepish grin.

"You can get one in the bathroom."

"Oh yeah," Joey said and started back.

"Joey …"

"Yeah?"

"All these boards squeak, and I read late every night."

"Every night?" Joey asked helplessly.

Mike laughed as he closed the door.

Joey's fight with Alan Andrews was televised. It was a damn good fight, and Joey came away a clear victor. His second fight was his return back to Madison Square Garden, and again, he won. Then John L. Sullivan came over from England. He was a strong middleweight, and they wanted to find out just how good he was. Joey beat him, but it was a good enough fight to warrant a return match. Thirty days later, Joey won an even more decisive decision.

"Take a little vacation with your wife; four good fights in a row, you deserve it," Mike said after the second Sullivan fight.

Joey and Shirley drove to New York and stayed for three days. He had picked up a beautiful Jaguar, but they needed the room in the Olds, which had been driven back to Buffalo by one of his Texas buddies. They shopped, saw a couple of Broadway plays, and visited the recently discharged Tony Affrunti in Brooklyn. Tony had all the latest boxing magazines and was the first to inform Joey that he was now ranked the number-one contender for the middleweight title.

Three weeks later, Shirley told Joey she thought she was pregnant, and a week after that, the doctor confirmed it. Joey was so elated he stopped at Buck Hart's cigar store, which was merely a front for his various operations. When the greetings were over, Joey said, "Let me have two boxes of your best cigars."

"What do you want cigars for? You don't smoke," Buck asked.

"No … But my wife is going to have a baby, and I want to give them out."

"Congratulations!" Buck beamed.

"Thanks, I just found out she's a month pregnant." Joey almost blushed.

"That's cute, only one month and already buying cigars."

"Have a cigar," Joey said handing the first one to Buck.

"You know you're a good kid, Joey. Don't forget, anything you ever need at all, you just ask," Buck said as he took a cigar and put his arm around Joey at the same time. Joey's next stop was home at Mike's.

"I already know about it," Mike said unhappily. "Shirley told Mary and Mary told me … You stupid Dago. I told you not to knock her up till you were sure things would work out."

"I think we're okay, Mike. I love her, and she loves me. Things are going to be beautiful now," Joey said.

"I wish I was as sure as you are. Your mother and I seem to be the only ones who can't shake our original feelings about that girl," Mike said lighting a cigar.

"I'd better call Ma. She'll get sore if she thinks I didn't tell her right away," Joey said reaching for the phone.

Rosina's reaction wasn't what Joey had hoped it would be. "Well, I hope she gives you a son. All your sisters have boys, and all your brothers have girls. There's no one to carry on your father's name."

Joey felt somewhat deflated after the conversation with his mother but finally said, "Mike, I think I'm going to buy a house and some new furniture and really set it up nice for Shirley and me and the kid."

"You'll be making another mistake, Joey; I feel it in my bones."

"Nah, with her being pregnant, it's time we have a little privacy." Joey expressed his feelings.

"Am I going to be able to trust you?"

"What do you mean?"

"Well, after all, when you're training for a fight …"

"Ah, you know, I'm a scary type. I know I can't do my best if I'm not in shape, so I'll be able to control myself, especially the last couple weeks before a fight." Joey dismissed his concern.

During June of 1956, Joey and Shirley bought a house they both liked and new furniture they both liked, and almost immediately, Shirley began her campaign to have her mother move in with them.

"Look, Shirley, I don't want your mother or my mother living with us! I don't want anyone living with us!"

"Why not?"

"Because I think we should have our privacy; I bought this house for just you, me, and our kids!"

"We have three big bedrooms, and you know you travel a lot! I'll be left alone!" Shirley persisted.

"We have neighbors and friends you can socialize with, and besides, I'm only gone about five days a month! If you want to see your mother; go see her!"

"You know I can't drive!"

"So take driving lessons! We can afford it."

"No! I'm carrying our baby, and I'd be worried!"

"Then take a cab!"

July rolled around, and Joey went into heavy training for an August 3 bout with Rocky Castellani. Shirley didn't stop nagging Joey; she didn't skip a day.

"I want my mother to come live with us and help me take care of this house and the baby," was her constant cry.

"Shirley, don't you love me?" Joey responded one night.

"Yes, I love you, but I want my mother to come live with us!"

"No, and that's final!" Joey yelled.

Mike drove Joey to New York for the televised fight with Castellani. Joey came out of the fight with a win and without a mark. After they had a quick snack, Mike drove Joey back to Buffalo and dropped him off at his house. Joey heard the television going as he closed the front door.

"Hi, honey, I'm home," he said walking into the living room.

Shirley and her mother, both in nightclothes, were sitting on the couch watching TV.

"Oh, how do you feel?"

"A little tired. Will you draw a hot bath for me?" Joey said hoping he wouldn't have any trouble getting Mrs. Fina out of there in the morning.

"I don't feel good. Draw it yourself," she said, her eyes never leaving the television set.

Joey cocked his head, hearing the same strain of coldness he had heard before. He went into the bedroom, unpacked, and then started filling the tub. After soaking for a while, Joey hooked a towel around his waist and went into the living room.

"Joey, you shouldn't walk around like that with Mother here!" Shirley said startled.

"What are you talking about? I'm more covered up now than when I am in the ring."

"It's not the same thing!"

"Okay, I want to go to bed anyway. I'm really tired," Joey said not wanting to argue.

"You must be after screwing all them girls in New York," Shirley said, just before he was going to say good night.

"What are you talking about?" Joey said a bit startled himself.

"I know what all you fighters do; you all cheat when you're away from your wives," Shirley said abrasively.

"When would I have time to cheat, even if I wanted to, which I don't? We drove back right after the fight!"

"Oh come on, I know better than that. What about before the fight?" Shirley rasped.

"You know, I don't even mess around with you before a fight," Joey said becoming incensed.

"Just because I'm pregnant, you don't love me anymore!"

"Jesus! Shirley, I don't want to argue with you in front of your mother. Just get these foolish ideas out of your head." Joey threw his hands in the air and stared through the ceiling. He went to bed, but he couldn't sleep. The night was hot, the TV was loud, and his adrenaline was pumping. He kept thinking about Mrs. Fina staring at the television but listening to every word they said. He wondered how much of Shirley's attitude had been instigated by the seemingly quiet woman.

"Why are you going to sleep?" Shirley wanted to know, turning on the bright overhead lights.

"Shirley, I'm tired from the fight and the drive," Joey said trying to be patient.

"You're being very rude. My mother is still up; you can at least wait until she goes to bed."

"Look, babe, this is my house! I'm working very hard to give you what you want! Now please, I'm tired, and I want to get some rest!"

Shirley kept nagging, and finally Joey slipped into his robe and went into the living room. Mrs. Fina finally went to bed, but Joey was no longer sleepy.

"Are you coming to bed?" Shirley asked as she got up.

"No, I'm going to watch television for a while; I'm too hot to sleep right now."

"Well, turn down the TV," Shirley said heading for the bedroom.

"What for?"

"Mother's trying to sleep."

Joey cringed but lowered the volume. After a while, he fell asleep on the couch. He awoke to the odor of eggs frying, so he got up and asked Shirley to fix him some bacon and eggs as he washed up.

"Make your own breakfast; I'm not your slave," she started.

Joey was dressing quickly. He knew he was headed for trouble, but he was taking his mother-in-law home. "Come on, Mrs. Fina. I'll drive you home. When I get back, we're going to have a talk," Joey said firmly and then looked at Shirley.

"You're not driving my mother home; she is staying here from now on," Shirley commanded.

"I told you she's not going to stay here, and that's all there is to it!" Joey shouted.

"Joey, if my mother leaves, I leave," Shirley threatened.

"Hey, if you want to leave, leave!" Joey threatened back. He slammed the door to the house, slammed the door to the car, and drove recklessly to Mike's house.

"What's the matter? Have a beef with your wife?" Mike asked the moment he opened the door.

"How'd you know?"

"I ought to know; I practically raised you."

"Her mother's there, and Shirley wants her to live with us," Joey confided, feeling depression taking anger's place.

"I warned you not to get her pregnant; now she's got a hammer over your head with that baby coming."

"I think it'll be okay if I get rid of her mother," was all Joey could think.

Joey spent the afternoon with Mike and Mary and then accepted Mary's invitation to stay for dinner. Shirley's cooking was limited at best, so Joey enjoyed his first good home-cooked meal in quite a while. After dinner, he phoned his house, but there was no answer. When he got home, he found the place dark. He went into the bedroom and found a suitcase and several maternity dresses missing. He called Mrs. Fina and then Shirley's sister, but neither would tell him where she was. All day Sunday, Joey waited for her to call or come home, but the phone didn't ring until Monday morning. Shirley's lawyer informed Joey that she was filing for a separation.

"You've got to be kidding?" Joey said in a state of shock. "Why?"

The lawyer read Shirley's charges, and Joey knew she had fed him all kinds of stories.

"Look, I haven't done anything wrong. My wife is expecting a baby, and she's mentally upset. That's all there is to it. You'd better forget about it."

Joey knew Shirley was staying with her mother, but it was a full week before she allowed him to visit with her. After a minute of polite conversation, Mrs. Fina excused herself, leaving Joey and Shirley alone.

"I can't believe you're doing this, Shirley. I am your husband. I love you. I've been good to you, and now you're going to have our baby. Honey, come home."

"No, thank you, I prefer being with my mother to you," she said sarcastically.

"Shirley, what's the matter? What's wrong?"

"Nothing's wrong. My mother just happens to be more important to me than you are or ever were."

"You mean to tell me you married me but didn't really love me?" Joey said incredulously.

"You think you're so great. No, I never loved you!" Shirley said, her face lined with cruelty.

"What about the vows in the church? Didn't they mean anything to you?"

"At the time, I thought I loved you, but I don't love you anymore. All I want now is money and security!"

"Okay, fine, if that's how you really feel," Joey said, his pride shattered, and he walked away. On the way to Mike's, Joey felt he hadn't done anything wrong to deserve what was happening to him, and he cried. He knew her charges were false and that she had no proof. So when he arrived at Mike's, he said, "I'm going to fight her in court."

"Joey, forget about all that court shit," Mike advised.

"She wants seven hundred a month, the house, and the Olds. She left me; I didn't leave her. She doesn't deserve a damn thing!"

"You're gonna be the champion of the world. What she's asking for is chicken feed," Mike said trying to calm him down and buck him up at the same time.

"Mike, I want a good lawyer. She might wind up getting what she wants, but I am not going to make it easy for her."

Joey wanted to be alone for a while; he had a lot of thinking to do. He just stayed around the house for a couple of days, trying to figure things out and then got a phone call from his brother Carmen.

"Joey, Ma's been getting on me something fierce, since you're alone over there. I was wondering if I can stay with you for a while?"

"Sure, Carm, come on over," Joey said understanding.

He was grateful for his brother's companionship, friendship, and love. Carmen introduced Joey to a place called the Suburban House in Williamsville, New York. It was a private club, and the owner and a few other well-to-do people played poker twice a week. Joey was both good and lucky and came away with over five hundred dollars each of his first few visits. Carmen, on the other hand, seemed to press and usually lost. One morning, Carmen grabbed the paper from the front doorstep, but instead of plopping on the couch with it as he usually did, he handed the whole paper to Joey. "Here, save it for me; I've got to go see a guy about some dough he owes me."

Joey thought it was funny that Carmen hadn't mentioned it before but shrugged and opened the paper. The lead story concerned the third successful bank robbery in the area within a month. Joey pulled out the sports section. When Carmen returned an hour later, Joey knew something was wrong.

"You look like you just lost your best friend."

"Joey, I'm in trouble," Carmen said simply, quietly.

"What's the matter?"

"I got myself in a bind with some gamblers. I owe them three thousand dollars, and I can't come up with it."

"You're broke?"

"I've sold everything I had that is worth anything and even took out a loan on my Cadillac."

"Well, hey, don't worry about it, Carm. I'll lend you the money."

"No, forget it. You've told me often enough not to gamble. No, I'm just going to take off," Carmen said, shaking his head no.

"Where?"

"I'm still in the merchant marines, and my papers are all in order. When I get it together, I'll come back."

"Keep in touch, Carm. Let me know where you're at now and then."

"I will, kid."

Joey began training for an October 16 fight with Gil Turner at Madison Square Garden. He called Shirley from time to time, hoping she would come to her senses, but she kept living up to Mike's favorite description of her: "bitch."

One afternoon, when Joey was planting sod, two hood types suddenly appeared. "You Joey Giambra?" the spokesman of the two asked, while the other just stood there looking mean.

"Yeah, what are you doing back here?"

"Where's your brother, Carmen?"

"What do you want him for?"

"He owes us three grand."

"Yeah, I know about that. Well, he hasn't got it right now, but he's working on it."

"Where is he?"

"He's out of town."

"And we're out of patience. You tell him if we don't get our dough soon, we're gonna start doin' stupid things."

"Show me the marker," Joey said thinking this whole thing had gone far enough.

He took a look, recognized Carmen's signature, and said, "Come here at two o'clock tomorrow afternoon, and you'll have your money."

"We can't go for anything but cash."

"Okay, now let me tell you guys something, and you pass the word. I am a deputy of New York City, and if my brother gambles with you again and I find out about it, I'll have you busted. I'm not a fink, and I'm not afraid, but my brother's not a gambler, so make sure he stays away from your tables," Joey said and took the offensive.

"Okay, you get the money, and we'll forget about it."

The next day, Joey counted out thirty one-hundred-dollar bills and put Carmen's marker in his pocket. A few days later, Joey got a letter from Carmen and was able to write back telling him that the debt was paid and to come home. Carmen arrived the last week in September, having been gone less than a month.

"Maybe you shouldn't have paid them," Carmen questioned after he and Joey greeted each other warmly.

"Carm, you sure as hell know these people don't play games. Just stay the hell away from them."

"Thanks, Joey."

Joey's schedule didn't allow him to see much of Carmen during the following week, but they always managed to at least have breakfast together. Mike decided he and Joey would fly to New York City a week before the fight, and Carmen didn't come home their last three days in Buffalo.

"I was sure he'd be there this morning. He knew we were leaving today," Joey told Mike over the phone.

"Well, don't worry, Joey. He's a big boy. He can take care of himself."

Joey was packed and ready and thought Mike was early when he heard the doorbell ring. "Joey Giambra?"

"Yes," Joey said, seeing two nice-looking, well-dressed men.

"FBI. May we ask you a few questions?" one of them said as they both showed their credentials.

"What do you want with me?" Joey asked feeling intimidated.

"Nothing. We're looking for your brother, Carmello, and we understand he's staying here with you."

"Yeah, but I haven't seen him in a few days. Why? Is he in some sort of trouble?"

"We just want to ask him about some characters he's been hanging around with."

"I'm flying to Manhattan this afternoon, but I'll leave a message for him," Joey said.

"Thank you," the very polite FBI men said.

While he trained at Stillman's Gym, Joey kept waiting to hear from Carmen. He always felt more comfortable with him around at fight time, but as the days passed, he began to doubt that Carmen would show up. The morning of the fight, Joey was on the weigh-in scales when a beautifully dressed Carmen walked in. He wore a very expensive suit, a cashmere coat, and a big grin.

"Carmen! I've been worried sick about you. Where have you been?" Joey said jumping off the scale and putting his arms around him.

"Around, kid. You knew I'd be here for the fight, didn't you?"

"I was beginning to wonder."

"No matter where you're fighting, you know I'll be there. Can we go get something to eat? I'm starving." Carmen kept grinning.

While they were having breakfast, Joey asked Carmen what the FBI men wanted, but Carmen said he hadn't bothered getting in touch with them. After breakfast, they took a walk. Joey tried to find out where Carmen had been, but Carmen kept evading the subject. Joey saw two beautiful leather coats he knew would go great with his sporty Jaguar and said so.

"You like those?" Carmen said, looking in the showcase window.

"Yeah, after the fight, I'm going to buy both of them."

"Why wait? Come on. I've made a score."

"What do you mean?"

"Did you ever see a roll like this?" Carmen said taking out almost nine thousand dollars in ninety one hundred dollar bills.

"Where the hell did you get all of that? You've been gambling again?" Joey asked.

"Yeah, kid," Carmen said with a sheepish grin.

"Well, what are you carrying all that on you for?"

"I like the way it feels. Come on, let's pick up the duds," Carmen said with his grin broadening.

On their way back to Joey's hotel, Carmen said, "Remember you wanted us to get some kind of business together? Well, now that I could hold up my end, why don't we start looking for something?"

"Sounds good. Just don't blow it," Joey agreed.

"No, I've learned my lesson," Carmen said, and Joey assumed he was referring to the three-thousand-dollar gambling debt.

Joey was in his dressing room, waiting for the last preliminary to end, when Carmen came in.

"How do you feel?" he asked.

"A little nervous, but I'll be okay once the bells rings." Joey dismissed him.

"I'll be right out there, and don't you worry about a thing. You're a good kid. God is with you." Carmen encouraged him.

By the time Joey climbed into the ring, he felt great. He spotted Carmen and saw him pointing across an aisle and a few rows back. When Joey's eyes got there, they saw Ruby with the same girlfriend Carmen had liked so much. Joey gave them a nod and a wave of a glove and then turned to face the tough Gil Turner. The fight was rated a toss-up, six to five pick 'em. Ten hard rounds later, Joey came out of the ring having won a unanimous decision.

Carmen yelled, "You were great!" And he fell in behind Joey.

As they passed Ruby and her girlfriend, Ruby made certain that Joey held on to the note this time. When they got into the dressing room, Carmen said, "Joey, you just made us another five grand!"

"Five grand?" Joey's eyes widened.

"I made some bets around ringside, and I got even money."

"I'm glad I didn't know about it. Boy, I hope your luck has really changed," Joey prayed more than said and laughed.

Joey and Carmen met Ruby and her girlfriend that night, and they all partied for three days before the girls returned to Memphis and the boys went back to Buffalo. Again, they settled down to their bachelor life, and once more, Joey made the futile attempt to reconcile with Shirley. San Francisco wanted Joey to fight there again, and the tough Rocky Castellani wanted another shot at Joey, so Mike set up the match for December 10.

Meanwhile, Carmen disappeared again, and as before, on the third day, the FBI showed up. Two days later, Carmen came home, and Joey insisted he go and find out what the Feds wanted. Carmen reluctantly agreed to go, and when he came home, he seemed relieved.

"They've got nothin' on me. What you don't know won't hurt you," was all he would tell Joey.

Mike and Joey flew to San Francisco, and a few days later, Carmen joined them. The fight with Castellani was a replay of their first meeting, with Joey again winning the unanimous decision and Carmen picking up another easy two thousand dollars. Afterward, the Italians threw a party for Joey at Harry Dellis's excellent restaurant, the Villa de Lapaix in Oakland. Mike flew home alone, and Joey and Carmen decided to take a little vacation in the Bay Area. They made the Villa de Lapaix their headquarters, and Harry Dellis liked Carmen so much he wanted him to become a host for the restaurant. They both decided to go back to Buffalo, settle things there, and then return. Joey could fight out of San Francisco, Carmen could take the host job, and they could invest in an apartment building and start a whole new life.

"I think that's a great idea," Mike agreed when Joey returned and told him what he and Carmen planned to do.

"We'll straighten out this thing with your wife, give her what she wants, and be free of her."

"Mike, I told you. I don't want to give her anything," Joey repeated.

"Then you'll be paying lawyers and courts till you're an old man," Mike said with a disgusted wave of a hand.

Chapter Fourteen

Little Joel Anthony Giambra arrives

Joey felt lonely during the holidays. Once more, he had tried to get Shirley to come home, knowing her time of giving birth was approaching, but she refused to even see him. Carmen helped Joey get through the old year and into the new. On January 8, 1957, Carmen and Joey had dinner at the Suburban House and then played poker for several hours. When Joey picked up the paper and turned to the sports section as Carmen began driving them home, he said, "Carmen, look! I'm a father!"

Carmen stopped the car and turned on the overhead light, and they both read the article caption: "Joey Giambra, middleweight contender, proud father of an 8lb 2oz boy!"

The brothers put their arms around each other and began to cry softly. Joey called Mike the minute he got home.

"Big deal! So you're a father!" was Mike's negative response.

Early the next morning, Joey called his mother.

"I'm glad it's a boy. I wonder if I'll ever get to see him," she said without emotion.

Carmen drove Joey to the hospital, and when they arrived, Carmen said, "Let's go to the maternity section and see if we can spot my little nephew through the window."

"Just look for the best-looking kid there." Joey laughed.

They couldn't see any of the names on the baskets, but the baby in the corner had a full head of black hair and was sleeping with his little fists clutched alongside of his face.

"I'll bet that one's yours; he's already got his guard up." Carmen smiled.

"Whose baby is that in the corner?" Joey asked the nurse.

"Oh, that's the fighter's, Joey Giambra."

"Hey, that's me!" Joey grinned.

"Really? Can I have your autograph?" The nurse brightened. She took a small notepad and a pen from her pocket and handed it to Joey.

"Can I hold the baby?" Joey asked as he signed, "To my kid's nurse, Joey Giambra."

"Well, we were given orders that you weren't to touch the baby," the nurse sputtered.

"Who gave you that order?" Joey demanded.

"Mrs. Giambra."

"Look, I want to hold that baby. That's my baby!" Joey's voice rose.

The ward doctor came by to the nurse's relief, and he told her to go get the baby. "I hate vindictive women," he said helping Joey into a white smock.

Joey held his son in his arms and smiled at him before the tears came. He felt an instant love he had never known before, and he prayed that Shirley would feel differently now that the baby had come. Minutes later, Joey and Carmen stood outside of Shirley's private room.

"I'm going to talk to her, Carm. I'm going to try and convince her to come to California with us," Joey said pulling himself together.

"It's okay by me. I'll wait out here."

Joey walked into her room with a broad smile on his face. "Hi, baby, how do you feel?" he said and thought how beautiful she looked.

"Do you really care how I feel?" Shirley said, and Joey knew she hadn't changed.

"I was never called, or I'd have been here."

"I know. I didn't want you here. I wanted my mother here."

"My God, Shirley, what is this thing with you and your mother?"

"Joey, I told you. I love my mother, and she belongs with me."

"Shirley, marriages were not made to include mother-in-laws from either side. If you couldn't stand leaving her, then why did you marry me?"

"I didn't know it then. Did you come here to argue with me?" Shirley said, becoming upset.

"No, no, I came to tell you I love you and to thank you for giving me such a beautiful son."

"He's not yours; he's mine!"

"Well, I helped," Joey said trying to at least get her to smile.

"Never mind, what do you want here?"

"I want you back. We can have a beautiful life together, the three of us."

"On my terms?" she said.

"The three of us, Shirley."

"The four of us, Joey."

"You still want your mother to come and live with us?"

"And I want you to quit fighting and leave Mike Scanlan," Shirley added.

"What? Are you kidding?" Joey couldn't even believe she was serious. "No way."

"Then there's no way for us either!"

"What have you got against, Mike?"

"He's no good, and you know it!"

"He's my manager, and he got me where I am today. I'm a fighter. That's who you married. You can't just tell me to quit. Shirley, I'll take care of your mother, and she can come and stay with you when I'm away, but I won't live with her, period."

"You're no good, Joey. You're no good!"

Joey stood motionless for a moment before saying, "Shirley, we have a baby. Make your requests more reasonable. Let's try to make it together."

"I already told you, on my requests only."

"We'll talk about it later," Joey said as he leaned forward to kiss her, but Shirley turned away.

Carmen was leaning against the wall by the door when Joey came out. He put an arm around Joey's shoulders, and they walked away.

"I didn't even get a chance to tell her about California," Joey said shaking his head.

"I know. I heard most of it; I hate to tell you, kid, but she's not in your corner. Don't get tied up with her again; she'll destroy you."

That night, Joey and Carmen went to the Suburban House again. They ordered a bottle of champagne with dinner and drank it toasting the baby's' birth, health, and happiness. Joey had never tasted champagne before and thought it appropriate to celebrate that way, but even champagne couldn't cut the underlying sadness. They played poker for a while and then picked up a paper and headed home. Joey didn't try to read, preferring to watch the snow, which was coming down heavily. When Carmen stopped for a red light, he flipped the paper open to see the headlines and saw that the third and fourth members of the bank robbery gang had been captured.

"Joey, I'm going to drop you off. I've got to meet a guy at Santora's."

"The pizzeria? What for?"

"He owes me money."

"You need some help collecting it?" Joey offered.

"No, it's friendly."

"You should stay away from that place, Carm. Too many of the racket guys hang out around there," Joey said concerned.

"Ah, they're okay as long as you stay on the right side of them."

Joey lay in a hot tub for a while and then went to bed. It took him a long time to go to sleep, and at five in the morning, the phone woke him up.

"Who is it?" he grumbled.

"Johnny Milano, are you awake enough to hear me?"

"Yeah," Joey said, knowing Milano was one of "the boys" that hung out at Santora's.

"I thought you'd want to know the FBI picked up Carmen a few minutes ago."

"What for?" Joey said quickly.

"You mean you don't know?"

"Know what?"

"Your brother was in the Liberty Bank job."

"What?" Joey cried, praying he hadn't heard correctly.

"Better not say any more. The phone might be tapped."

Joey heard the connection break and slowly replaced the receiver. He took a minute to try to piece things together and then called Mike and told him what had happened.

"I'm sorry, kid. Try to get a couple more hours of sleep, and then we'll go see the sheriff in the morning."

Sheriff Bob Glasser greeted Joey with warmth and sympathy and then brought him into a room where an FBI man was interrogating Carmen.

"Why, Carmen?" Joey asked.

"Kid, I'm sorry. I've ruined everything you've worked for," Carmen said, and he broke down and started crying. He then threw his arms around Joey, hugging him.

"Carmen, forget about me. We're worried about you. Why'd you do it?"

"I didn't tell you because I didn't want you to get involved."

"What happened?"

Carmen looked at the FBI man and asked, "Can we have a few minutes alone?"

"Sure," the man said and left the room.

"Joey, I got back into gambling and got stuck for another five thousand," Carmen said, not able to look at Joey.

"Aww, Carm, you promised you wouldn't gamble like that after I paid off the three grand."

"I know, kid. Anyway, I couldn't figure a way out, so they offered to tear up my marker and give me a cut if I just help scoop up the money. I couldn't say no," Carmen said sitting heavily in a chair.

"Then what?" Joey asked as he sat beside him.

"The day before the robbery, I wanted out, but they wouldn't go for it. They told me it was too late."

"When was this, Carm?" Joey asked.

"Remember when you thought I wasn't going to show up for the Gil Turner fight? I wanted to tell you, but then you'd have been an accessory after the fact."

"Well, I guess the first thing is to get you a lawyer," Joey said already thinking.

"Ah forget it, Joey. I don't want a trial. You're guilty, you're guilty."

"Carmen, that's stupid. Your record's clean. Your army record's clean, and you're not well."

"I'm dead, Joey. Just forget about me. In fact, when people ask, deny I'm your brother."

Joey contacted the best criminal lawyer in Buffalo, Don Lieberman, who knew and liked the Giambra family. He even offered to defend and represent Carmen for nothing, but Carmen just wanted to plead guilty and pay his debt to society. Joey got top billing for Carmen's crime. The next day's front-page headlines in Buffalo read, "Joey Giambra, Leading Middleweight Contender … Brother Arrested for Bank Robbery."

Knowing Shirley would have read about it or at least heard of it, Joey went to see her at the hospital. When he entered her room, hoping he could help her understand what had happened, Shirley shrieked, "You rotten bastard! Your whole family is no damn good! You disgraced my son's name!"

"Shirley, I didn't do anything wrong. My brother made a mistake. Why blame me?"

"I'm changing the baby's name; he's never going to carry the Giambra name!"

"Shirley, don't be foolish."

"I'm foolish? Get out of here! I never want to see you again!"

Shirley flung the morning paper in his face. Joey felt like tearing into her, but he just left steaming instead. Still, the Mob was not going to leave Joey alone. They even found a way to destroy his marriage. Joey was so heartbroken when he found out his wife was seeing a married Mob guy named Nick Saiia.

In 1957, Joey separated from his wife after Joel Anthony was born on January 8, 1957. As always, good news or bad, he went to see Mike.

"It's time we got out of this town, but first, you've got to give the b—, I mean, ex-wife what she wants and get rid of her," was Mike's conclusion.

"All right," Joey finally agreed, knowing they could never get back together.

On January 19, ten days after his son was born, Joey signed the separation papers, and he and Mike packed the Jaguar and headed across the country. Joey moved back to San Francisco with Mike and three of his stablemates, Bobby Scanlan, Richie Todaro, and Rocky Fumerelle, who were Joey's sparring partners. Mike rented a mansion outside San Francisco near the ocean, which was a perfect location. It was expensive, but they sparred often, and the five of them shared the rent. Inside, Joey suffered every day over his failed marriage but buried himself in boxing as much as he could. And every night, he would walk the beach, breathing in the clean salt air. His thoughts were always about his boy, Joel. He also worried about his brother, Carm. By the end of the month, Joey had rented a furnished house on Diamond Street in San Francisco, and Mike had set him up a fight in February. Joey trained long and hard, finding it helped keep his mind off the loneliness he felt for Shirley and his son and the pain he felt when Carmen was sentenced to seventeen years in the federal penitentiary at Atlanta. During the next two months, Joey fought four young guys who were trying to gain reputations, sending them all home, sadder but wiser. By then, Mike figured Joey's mental problems had eased up enough for him to start facing the top competition again and set up a mid-May fight against Chico Vejar.

"Vejar? What does he want to fight me for?" Joey wondered aloud, knowing he was much stronger than the natural welterweight.

"Ah, Steve Ellis, his manager, told me he needs the money," Mike answered.

"He must need it bad. You know I could really hurt him, Mike," Joey said.

"That's what I told Steve, but he said Chico will come in weighing around one fifty," Mike said.

The fight was held in Oakland, California, and a packed house awaited the bell for round one.

"Joey, I want you to go easy on Chico. Carry him," Mike said.

"How come?"

"I kind of promised Steve you would."

"He's worried about him, huh?"

"Sure, he knows you could hurt him."

"Why not? Chico's a nice guy," Joey said confidently.

Both boys put on a beautiful boxing exhibition during the first two rounds, but in the third, Chico tried to butt Joey and hustle him around.

"Something's wrong, Mike. I think I'm being double-crossed," Joey said between two rounds.

"Yeah, it looks that way," Mike agreed.

"Chico's got to be crazy," Joey said.

"Nah, what makes more sense is Steve didn't say a word about us carrying him, and Chico thinks he's in a real fight," Mike said.

"Well, he is now," Joey said ready and bouncing up.

"Go get him, kid," Mike said, and the bell rang for round four.

Joey pounded Chico for the next two rounds and then cut him to pieces and decked him just before the end of round six. Chico had to be helped to his corner, and when he was unable to answer the bell for the seventh round, Joey had a TKO victory.

Mike immediately set up a June fight for Joey against Rory Calhoun. While Joey trained for the fight, Mike went back to Buffalo for two weeks. Joey went to the movies almost every night, but his loneliness, though it had eased, would not leave. One night, he decided to drive to Oakland, have a good dinner at Harry Dellis's, place, and just break the monotony in general. Dellis was always happy to see Joey and had previously expressed his sorrow regarding Carmen. He asked Joey to join him for dinner. As the evening went on, several others joined them, including a lovely young lady who was quite taken by Joey. As bad luck would have it, Herb Caen, the satirical San Francisco columnist, happen to drop by that evening.

Dellis introduced him to Joey, and Dellis answered Herbs' questions. Herb Caen was like paparazzi back in those days Herb would always twist and spin the truth in his columns. Dellis offered other bits of information, and then said good night as the news-gathering Caen went on his searching way.

Shortly thereafter, though he hated to pass up the golden-haired opportunity beside him, Joey's training took him home. The following evening, Joey bought the *Chronicle* and went home. He usually didn't read Herb Caen's column, but he might have mentioned him. And Joey wasn't disappointed; he was infuriated. Caen made it sound as if Joey were a playboy, partying it up, fooling around, and obviously not training properly for the upcoming Calhoun fight. Somehow, Mike found out about the item and called Joey from Buffalo. He chewed him out for ten minutes, not believing a word Joey said.

"If I hear you go out gallivanting again, we're through!" Mike threatened and hung up. Mike returned a few days later, still upset with Joey, and harped about the Caen item right up to fight time. Joey knew he was physically in shape, but Mike's attitude, combined with constantly thinking about Shirley, his son and his brother, all added up to an inability to concentrate for Joey. And this was no novice or little guy; this was an experienced, hard-hitting middleweight.

"Your mind is what beat you," he remembered Johnny Cesario saying.

The bell rang for the first round of the six-to-five pick 'em fight. Both fighters felt each other out in round one, and then in round two, Calhoun caught Joey with an uppercut that almost floored him. Joey recuperated during the rest of the round and all of the third, but every time Calhoun hit him with anything solid in the jaw area, a jolt of pain would immediately blind him. The fourth through the seventh were all Joey's, strictly because of his superior boxing skill, but as the bell ended the seventh and Joey turned away, Calhoun hit him with a roundhouse punch that landed at the base of his spine. Joey shook off the pain of the late blow, but as Mike worked on him, Joey felt his legs getting numb and wondered if his lower lumbar had been hurt again. The bell called the fighters out for round eight, and Joey stood up uncertainly and then hobbled a few steps forward.

Calhoun soon realized Joey was hurt and came in for the kill. Joey spent the majority of the last three rounds leaning against the ropes, unable to move on his all-but-useless legs and taking a brutal beating. Joey staggered to his corner and sank into the stool when the fight ended. Mike didn't say a word as they waited for the decision. He didn't even work on Joey, letting the trainer clean him up as best he could. Despite everything that had happened to him, Joey almost won the fight, barely losing a split decision.

"You looked like a bum, you dumb, stupid Dago! What you do? Screw some broad last night?" were Mike's first words to Joey after chasing everyone out of the dressing room.

When he got back to the dressing room, both of his eyes were puffed and swollen almost shut, his head was throbbing and felt like a balloon, and his sides were alive with pain from the body blows.

"Mike, I'm hurt," Joey said quietly.

"You should be! You deserve everything you got for breaking training," Mike said angrily.

"But I didn't break training," Joey said his frustration mounting.

"Then why did you run out of gas?"

"I didn't. My legs went numb, and they're still numb."

"Bullshit! Caen don't write things he can't back up! You're a phony!" Mike yelled.

Joey couldn't understand. They had all lived together in a big house on a hill, and they always hung out. Joey never had a girl in training, and he rarely took a vacation, even though San Francisco had everything. Joey never really knew what Mike's real dark side was until later. He fought his heart out, even though he was in the depths of despair over losing his wife and the pain he suffered for loving a child he could never be with, yet all Mike could do was say cruel and terrible things that he knew were untrue. It seemed like everything he knew and depended upon had betrayed him in his hour of need. Joey began to cry.

Mike, his "father," was the last person he thought would turn against him.

"Mike, I'm hurt!" Joey pleaded.

212

"Good, maybe it'll teach you a lesson!" Mike said completely unsympathetic.

Joey fell to his knees sobbing bitterly and watched Mike grab his jacket and walk out. Minutes later, Joey's San Francisco attorney, Ed Maley, walked in and found Joey sprawled out on the floor, still crying. He helped Joey up, talked to him a few minutes, and then said, "Why don't you stay at my house tonight?"

Joey agreed, and Ed helped him dress and took him to his rather sumptuous house. He made Joey take a long, hot bath and then put him to bed. When Joey complained about his jaw the next morning, Ed took him to his dentist. X-rays showed the second round uppercut had fractured Joey's jaw, and several hours later, Joey returned with his jaw wired shut for a projected eight weeks. Ed tried to cheer Joey up and take his mind off his troubles. The following morning, when Joey said his back was still bothering him and his legs were still numb, Ed took him to his doctor. After Joey had X-rays and a diathermy treatment, Ed drove him back to his apartment with the knowledge that a nerve had been pinched by the late blow at the end of the seventh round and that he would be fine in a few more days.

Mike had already packed and left, leaving a cursory note stating he had gone to Reno to fish. After the fight, the boxers in Joey's stable all went back to Buffalo. Mike left and gave up the house. For the next week, Joey just lay around not caring about living or fighting, not caring about anything. Thoughts of the wife he couldn't stop loving, the son he couldn't see, the brother who was in prison, and the "father" who wouldn't believe him were all gnawing away at his spirit. Help came to Joey during his second week of torment through a public service announcement imploring veterans to take advantage of the GI Bill and go to school. Joey had already heard about the Elizabeth Holloway School of Theatre, so he called for information and was told they accepted GIs, but that he had to have a high school diploma. Joey went to the local high school, filled out forms, and then took a crash course at a nearby night school.

Mike returned after three weeks, and the first thing he did was apologize for the way he acted. He had read about Joey's broken jaw and pinched nerve that had crippled him for the last three rounds and apologized again after saying he had never seen or heard of anything like it.

"Well, that's water over the damn, but there's a couple of things you should know."

"Like what?" Mike asked.

"Like I'm through with fighting for one, and I want to live alone for two."

"Through fighting?" Mike repeated but couldn't believe it.

"Yeah, I'll have my high school diploma by the end of the summer, and I'm going to drama school on the GI Bill in the fall."

"Drama school?" Mike said again with disbelief. "Joey, you're not even twenty-six yet; you still have a lot of good fighting years ahead of you."

"Look, Mike, I've had it. I'm not going to get killed in the ring, especially when my mind isn't with it."

"Ah, you'll change your mind when you're all healed up, and in the meantime, getting your high school diploma ain't a bad idea at all. How much longer are you gonna be eating through a straw?"

"Five more weeks, but I won't be changing my mind, Mike."

"I might as well go back to Buffalo for a couple of months; this way, you can live alone for a while and you can heal up real good."

Joey turned twenty-six and had his jaw unwired. He received his diploma with very high marks and enrolled at the Elizabeth Holloway School. He soon learned he had talent but needed two solid years of hard work to develop it. He liked his teachers and fellow students, and this prompted him to move to an apartment near the school. Life was gradually becoming a happy experience again, and time was erasing the pain of his broken family.

Mike showed up unexpectedly one day and immediately began his campaign to get his fighter back in the ring. "You're still a good fighter, and I can have you back in shape in no time."

"Mike, I just don't want to fight anymore. I want to be an actor."

"Acting's not for you. It's for fags and degenerates; you're an old-fashioned Italian kid." Mike winced.

"You're wrong about actors, Mike."

"The acting business could ruin you, kid."

"It's not going to ruin me. I've got morals, and I'm going to stick to them."

"Joey, I was wrong. Please forget about what I said. You can still become champion and make a lot of money. Then all those Hollywood studios will want you because you'll have a name; you'll be somebody."

"Mike, I'll be all right. Just leave me alone."

Joey flew home for the holidays. He stayed with his mother, bought her a new fur coat, and spent a lot of money on gifts for his brothers and sisters. He had Sammy call Shirley to let her know he was home, to see how the land lay, but nothing had changed. Shirley was adamant; she didn't want him coming around. Mike came around though, several times, to the point where Joey started to get bugged and was glad to board the plane and return to California. As the plane cut through the night, Joey thought about his almost one-year-old son and how he had quit fighting and gotten rid of Mike, as Shirley wanted. He also thought about her mother and knew Shirley wouldn't have moved to California without her. Joey settled down to care for himself and worked hard at learning his new craft.

Giardello became the number-one contender, and Mike crept back into Joey's life. Without telling Joey, Mike came back to San Francisco from Buffalo. He left messages all over town for Joey. After the hurt he'd caused, Joey really didn't want to talk to him. Secretly, after finding out Joey was in drama school, he came to watch Joey perform. While in the middle of performing his scene, he was interrupted by his theater coach, Elizabeth Halloway, who invited Mike over to talk to Joey. Mike was always a dapper dresser and a charming con man. He charmed Joey's drama coach into interrupting his rehearsal.

Joey said to Mike, "You and I have nothing to talk about."

He said, "Okay, kid, but I thought you'd want to know that Giardello is now ranked number-one contender, and I can get you the fight of your life."

Giardello's manager, Tony Graziano, had called him in Buffalo and asked if his fighter wanted a rematch. The winner of that fight would fight Gene Fullmer, the middleweight champion of the world."

"I won't decide until I see a contract with everything laid out," Joey said.

Mike gave him that crooked, knowing smile of his and said, "Sure, kid."

Even then, Mike knew how to push the right buttons. He knew that Joey was running out of money and also knew he would jump at the chance to have a shot at the middleweight championship of the world. Three weeks later, Giardello, Tony Graziano, and their entourage flew in to San Francisco.

When March arrived, Mike called Joey and told him how rough things were. He also asked Joey if he could lend him some money, because the taxes on his house were due and he didn't have it. Between his monthly payments to Shirley, the money he had spent at Christmas, and the money he loaned Mike, Joey was suddenly faced with the realization that he wouldn't be able to finish two years of schooling without going to work.

April arrived, and Mike arrived with it, but this time, he brought news. "Joey, have you been keeping up with boxing world?"

"A little," Joey responded without much energy.

"Then you know Giardello's won seventeen fights in a row, and they figure he's ready to go after the title."

"Huh?" Joey replied, thinking of the irony.

"So his people came to me, looking for a fight with you. Until he can erase the stigma of those two fights with you, they know he won't be considered a true champ. What do you say, kid? You beat him again, and you're back on top."

"I don't know, Mike. I'll think about it."

Four days later, Joey decided he would fight again. The reason was simple: he needed the money. The fight was tentatively set for late June at the Cow Palace in San Francisco, which gave Joey plenty of time to get in shape. Early in May, Mike had Joey fight a tune-up with a kid named Andy Mayfield from Miami Beach, Florida. Andy was considered a good boxer, good puncher, and all-around tough kid. Before and during the fight with Mayfield, Joey had a gnawing fear that his jaw might break again. In the fifth round, he got careless, and Mayfield hit him with a solid right to the jaw. Joey instinctively countered with a flurry of punches before realizing he was all right. From there on, it was clear sailing to an easy decision. Three weeks before the fight, when Joey and Mike returned to the apartment after dinner, Joey headed for the television set.

"Leave it off a few minutes, Joey. I've got something to tell you."

"Geez, the way you said that, we're going to die at dawn," Joey joked.

"I wasn't goin' to tell you, but, well, I'm not sure that'd be right," Mike said, and Joey knew there was no joke there.

"What is it, Mike?"

"I had to agree to one condition in order to get you the fight with Giardello. You see, his people are afraid he can't beat you."

"Mike, what are you saying?" Joey asked confused.

"You're not supposed to win; that's the condition. You throw the fight."

Joey knew Mike wasn't kidding. He thought for a second before saying, "Well, I can see how that's good for them, but how is that good for us?"

"Ten grand on the side after the fight, if you lose."

"Wow, Mike. You know me. You know I've always been honest about my career. I don't think I could throw a fight, for love or money," Joey said softly shaking his head after thinking for a moment.

"That's why I wasn't even gonna mention it to you. Oh, I told them you would do it, but you won't."

"Mike, these are Mob guys; they'll put cement shoes on both of us and dump us in the ocean."

"Ah, they don't do things like that today. You're still thinking of the old movies."

"They're still playing," Joey said.

"All we got to do is lay low for a while after the fight, so don't worry. I'll take care of everything. You do the fighting, and I'll do the managing."

A week before the fight, Joey Giardello and his crew came to town. Everyone met at Fisherman's Wharf. Even Joe DiMaggio,

Joey's loyal fan and supporter, came. Joe brought his brother and partner, Dominic, along too. They were saying everything they knew he wanted to hear, but by then, Joey was a little wiser than before and he knew they weren't telling it all. Three weeks later, on the eve of the fight—it was June 29, 1958—Mike got a call from Tony Graziano. They met in front of Joe's new restaurant (A chain of Joe's Restaurants, Joe had three of them in San Francisco, this one being the newest. . The official signing of the contract was held at DiMaggio's Restaurant again, and it looked like the all-Italian hour. Johnny Russo, an ex-football player with the Oakland Raiders, had become a trainer. Joey and Mike both liked him and hired him when he asked if the job had been filled. Tony Graziano, Giardello's present manager, called on the fight. He wanted a meeting with both Joey and Mike and said he would be by to get them in an hour. An hour later, Joey climbed into the back of a big limousine and sat next to a husky, cigar-smoking bodyguard. Mike sat in the front with Tony, who immediately drove off in the direction of the ocean.

Joey said, "Who are you?" to the guy next to him.

"Names aren't important. Just do what we say, and drop when we tell you."

(One of his acting scenes was on the waterfront, and Joey played like Marlon Brando.) Joey said in Brooklynese, "Ya might be a cop and if I told you I'd lose, you might arrest me."

"Hey, Joey, you're not punchy. What's the act?" Graziano said.

Joey said, "Tony, does Giardello know I'm supposed to lose?"

"Giardello doesn't know! Besides, you're getting KO'd in the second round. Giardello isn't feeling too good, so we are going to get this over quick!" Graziano said.

"I've not been KO'd before, and I'm not going for it!" Joey said.

Mike then yelled at Joey, "Look, punk, just do what you're told!"

Joey looked at Mike. His face was as white as a sheet, and Joey could see the fear all over him. "Okay, Tony, whatever Mike tells me to do, I'll do."

"You'll get ten thousand dollars in an envelope in your dressing room after the fight before you leave," Tony said.

Joey had no intention of taking that ten grand ever, but he kept his mouth shut so that they could just get out of that car. Tony then turned the car around and drove Joey and Mike back to the apartment. Joey was pacing the dressing room floor just before the fight, and Johnny Russo was sitting quietly, having given up telling Joey to relax. Joey froze at the sound of a knock on the door, and Johnny shook his head as he went to open it. Moments later, Joey warmly greeted his boyhood pal, Johnny Antonucci.

"You're still a camera bug, I see," Joey said noticing the equipment Antonucci was carrying.

"Yeah, I'm going to film the fight. I'll be sitting ringside." Antonucci grinned.

"Hey, that's great," Joey said momentarily forgetting his problems.

"They're betting even money that you won't last ten rounds. How come?" Antonucci said, losing his grin.

"Don't you believe it. If anyone gets knocked out, it's not going to be me," Joey said grimly.

"That's what I wanted to hear. Well, good luck, Joey. I've got to get going," Antonucci said, his grin returning.

Just then, there was another knock at the door. It was the boxing commissioner, the police chief, and the sheriff; they confronted Mike and Joey.

"There are rumors you are going to take a dive?"

Joey then interjected yelling, "I never threw a fight in my life. Unless you have proof, get the f… out of my dressing room. Don't bet against me!"

So they all left the dressing room.

"Mike, I'm sweatin' it. I keep thinking about what those guys are going to do to us after the fight," Joey said nervously.

"I've already taken precautions, so stop worrying. You win the fight, and I'll take care of it from there," Mike said confidently.

"Okay, Mike," Joey said, but he couldn't stop worrying.

Joey got the call, and when he entered the arena, he got a shock. No more than six thousand people had come to the thirty-thousand capacity Cow Palace.

"What's the matter?" Mike asked seeing the look on Joey's face.

"With this kind of gate, we're not even going to make expenses."

"You're bound and determined to worry about something, aren't you?" Mike laughed.

The fighters were introduced and then called to the center of the ring for instructions. The two handsome young men smiled, touched gloves, and returned to their respective corners.

"He doesn't look like he's feeling bad to me," Joey said to Mike through the ropes.

"That was just a con," Mike said as the bell rang.

Both Joeys boxed beautifully during the first round. In the second, Giardello hit Joey with a good right to the jaw and immediately started for a neutral corner. Joey knew that was the punch that was supposed to knock him out, and he loved the expression on Giardello's face when he turned around and saw Joey coming. Joey promptly got in a good right of his own and worked Giardello over to the extent that he almost knocked him out in the second. As Joey looked over to Giardello's corner between rounds, he saw that Tony Graziano had an index finger against his throat, definitely indicating what Joey and Mike could expect.

"Look at that!" Joey exclaimed.

"Forget it," Mike said quickly.

"You can make book that was the round they had their money on," Johnny Russo joined in.

Joey realized at that moment that Johnny knew what was going on.

"You told him?" he asked Mike a bit surprised.

Johnny smiled as Mike said, "He's more than a trainer; he's a great part of my post-fight plans."

The bell for the third round ended the conversation. The fight went as Joey planned through the seventh, with him either winning or getting a draw each round. He figured his superior conditioning would tell the story of the last three rounds, as it had in their previous two meetings. In the eighth, Joey staggered Giardello with a powerful left hook and felt he could put him away. Only once again, Joey's mind got in the way, telling him that things might be worse if he knocked him out.

"You had him. Why did you let him get away?" Mike said after the round ended.

"I know I got the fight. Why take chances?" Joey excused himself.

"Ah, you're getting old, kid, but you're fighting great."

Joey won the ninth round against his tiring counterpart. He cut his eye and had his nose bleeding before the fight ended.

"They can't give him more than three rounds and sleep tonight," Mike said happily, knowing Joey had won it.

When the first judge called it for Giardello, Joey thought, *They're going to give it to him; they've got the judges for insurance. I should have knocked him out.*

The second judge and referee called the fight as it was, giving Joey a split decision win. As he climbed down out of the ring, he saw ten heavyweights moving toward him.

"Don't worry; that's our escort back to the dressing room," Mike said, again reading Joey's face.

"It's that bad, huh?" Joey said out loud.

When he arrived in the dressing room, Joey found the boxing commissioner, two FBI men, the police chief, his lawyer, and a few celebrities, Joe DiMaggio, the San Francisco mayor, and an actor from Hollywood who had come to see Joey fight.

Graziano. Joey wondered surprised.

In the next minute, he found out they were all very proud of him and were there to congratulate him for beating what they called, "the Mob fighter."

DiMaggio said to Joey, "I'm going to give you a big victory party at my restaurant!"

"Okay, boys, you've had it!" Tony said as he burst into the dressing room, flushed with anger.

"What do you mean by that?" the boxing commissioner asked, stopping Giardello's manager in his tracks. Tony struggled through a few sentences about how he didn't feel his boy had gotten a fair shake and he was just blowing off steam because he thought his boy had won and then quickly left the room.

A few minutes later, Mike cleared the room by announcing Joey had to take a shower to cool off properly but told Joey to get dressed the minute he closed the door. Joey and Johnny went out the back way, climbed the fence, Joey getting scratched up pretty good in his male area by the barbed wire on top, climbed into the station wagon Joey had just traded his Jaguar for, and took off.

"How come my car was right there?" Joey asked.

"Mike and I planned lots of things. I also cleaned out your apartment this afternoon and put everything in a U-Haul."

A black limousine with four men in it began following them as they pulled away from the Cow Palace. Johnny spotted them right away and sped into China Town. At Powell and Grant, Johnny was able to zip through a yellow-turning-red light, and the traffic ended the pursuit.

"Boy, can you drive," Joey said with admiration.

"I did some time in a cab in this town." Johnny grinned, having thoroughly enjoyed the challenge.

"Where's the U-Haul?"

"We've got it stashed a few miles from the apartment. When Mike can, he'll be there, and we'll drive straight through to Buffalo nonstop."

"Are you coming with us?"

"Yeah, saves me plane fare. I've been wanting to get back East for a while."

They reached the U-Haul, hooked it to the station wagon, and then settled down to wait for Mike. It was almost one o'clock in the morning before Mike showed up, and just over two days later, they rolled into Buffalo.

They spent the night at Mike's, and then early the next morning, Joey went to see Buck Jones, hoping he'd meant what he said about helping if Joey ever needed anything.

"Is Buck in?" Joey asked when he entered the cigar store. A few questions and a pushed button later, Joey entered the large backroom bookie operation. Buck waved him over to his corner desk as he continued his telephone conversation. He motioned for Joey to sit down and hung up moments later.

"Where's Mike?" Buck asked gravely.

"He's still sleeping," Joey said.

"Call Mike and get him here; tell him to take a cab," Buck said.

So Joey called Mike and said, "Take a cab and get here to Buck's office right away."

When Mike got there, he reached to shake hands with Buck. Buck got up and slapped Mike across the mouth, and his false teeth flew out.

"What did you do that for?" Mike asked ready to hit him back.

Joey jumped in the middle of them and said to Mike, "You don't want to do this!"

"He had no right to hit me!" Mike yelled.

Then Buck explained to them what was going to happen. "The word's out that you pulled a fast one on the boys."

"Let me tell you the whole story," Joey said.

"First, tell me one thing: did they put any money in your hands before the fight?" Buck interrupted.

"Not before or after," Joey answered.

"Now it's important, Joey. Are you sure?"

"Buck, believe me, they said they'd slip me ten grand after I lost the fight, but they never offered anything before the fight."

"Relax," Buck said and then called New Jersey. He talked to a man named Felix Bocchicio, who was the head of the numbers racket there and who also owned Giardello's contract.

"You sure they didn't lay any dough on Mike and Mike held out on you?" Buck asked Joey, covering the mouthpiece.

"I don't think Mike would be that stupid," Joey said.

Then Buck said with authority, "Felix, Joey wouldn't lie to me."

"Okay, we'll wait for your call." Buck hung up.

Before Joey had finished telling Buck the whole story, Felix called back. Buck listened and said, "Thanks." And they hung up. "You're off the hook." He smiled at Joey.

"What happened?" Joey asked with tremendous relief.

"What happened is the money Tony Graziano was supposed to put in your hands before the fight was bet on his fighter. He thought he had a sure thing and figured he could pick up some side money for himself."

"And that gets me off the hook?" Joey questioned.

"We have a rule, a Mob law. If you'd have had the money in your hands before the fight like you were supposed to, that would have been a contract, and there would have been no way out, the end of the road," Buck said.

Then Joey said, "It's GrazianoGraziano who's in trouble."

"Oh yeah, and you get a break, although you are going to have a hell of a time getting any decent fights for a while. We still control the titles, ya know." Buck nodded.

Joey nodded his understanding. "How can I ever thank you, Buck?"

"Forget it. Just don't get yourself in a bind like this again."

"Don't worry. I won't," Joey said.

They went back to Mike's house, and within two hours, they got a call from Buck telling them to fly back to New York City and that Vito Genevese' driver would pick them up at the airport and take them to the meeting place.

When they arrived at the airport, the driver was holding up a sign with Joey's name on it. They got into the limo and went to an Italian restaurant in Brooklyn, which was a known Mob restaurant. When they got into the restaurant, the door was opened for them by one of the boys. Two of them patted Joey and Mike down and then took them into the back room of the restaurant where they were greeted by Don Vito himself and Carbo. They were all smiles, and Joey and Mike were treated to pizza and salad. Joey could barely eat, and finally, Don Vito said, "Joey, I like you, and Buck tells me you're a good paisano. We know you never got the dough in the limo, so the contract on you has been cancelled, but I wanted to look into the eyes of a champ, into your eyes, before you knew that I had your contract cancelled. You got guts, kid. You know I liked you when I first met you in Rochester, when you were just a little kid, and I see you're a fine-looking boy! You got honor and pride, kid. You're a credit to us all. *Bona fortuna* in life. As for you, Scanlan, you don't deserve to be in the same room as this kid; you're lucky to manage him."

He hugged Joey, Italian style, and Genevese' driver took them back to the airport. Mike's attitude changed. Joey's heart was empty for him. He couldn't lie to himself anymore. He was not going to be the father, or even friend, that Joey had hoped for. Joey saw him in his true light, with all of his weaknesses laid bare. He couldn't lie to himself anymore; his hero had feet of clay. Mike and Joey would continue their relationship, though it would never be the same.

1957 Billy Newmans Gym San Francisco.
Giambras training schedule was constant

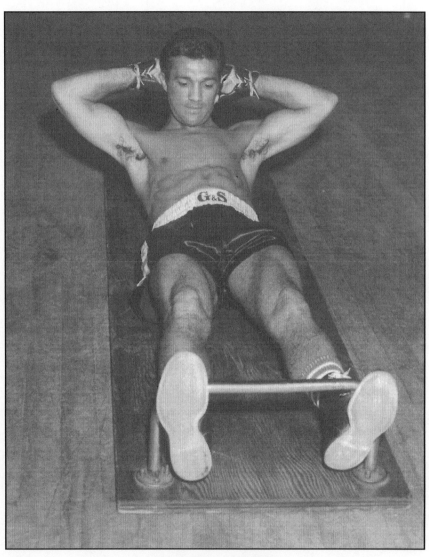

1957 Newmans Gym

Chapter Fifteen

Mike Sells Joey's Contract
(Ages 27–28) 1958–59

Mike was able to get Joey a return match with Rory Calhoun. Joey began training very hard, wanting to square accounts with the guy who had broken his jaw and worked him over after crippling him with that after-the-bell late blow to his back. One day, while working out, Joey began to hurt every time he threw a punch, so Mike took him to the hospital for X-rays. Three bone chips were discovered, and Joey was scheduled to be operated on in two weeks. While he waited for the operation, Joey kept running to stay in good condition, but the extra time on his hands started him brooding over Shirley and his son again.

On his way to the Suburban House, Joey realized it had been over a year and a half since he had been there, since his son had been born, since Carmen had been caught. Joey was a welcomed sight at the Suburban House. He was sitting at the bar having his usual glass of orange juice and talking with the manager, Bob Blair, when two couples came into the bar. Joey's eyes followed one of the most beautiful girls he had ever seen. She reminded him of Anita Ekberg, only younger and with an even better figure. As they sat at the bar, Joey wondered if her long blond hair was real, but as she turned and their eyes met, he didn't wonder about the spark that seemed to fuse them.

"Who's the blonde?" Joey asked Blair.

"I don't know, but the guy she's with is Bob Stranskys. His father owns Beck's Brewery, among other things."

"Rich, huh?"

"The playboy's playboy," Blair answered.

"That means she's either a prostitute or a rich girl," Joey realized.

"It's a shame he's so damn hetero." Blair winked.

Moments later, Stranskys spotted Joey and yelled, "Hey, Joey, when are you going to fight again?"

"It'll be a couple of months; I have to have an operation on my arm."

"You have made a lot of money in the last few years. How about having a drink with us?" Stranskys asked.

Joey gladly accepted the invitation, noticing the smile that came across the lovely blonde's face. Stranskys took care of the introductions quickly and then kept Joey occupied with questions about boxing and fighters. Finally, much to Joey's relief, Stranskys excused himself and went to the men's room.

"Are you Bob's wife?" Joey asked the blonde simply introduced as Ellen. He was grateful for the chance to talk to her.

"No."

"Are you engaged?"

"No."

"Are you going with him?" Joey persisted.

"No, just a date, that's all." Ellen smiled.

"Then you're available?"

"Yes, I guess I am."

Joey learned her name was Ellen Von Holshausen and that she was Miss Frankfurt, Germany, of 1956 and was working as a commercial artist in Buffalo.

"You don't have much of an accent left, but what there is I like, and what I see ... Is there any possibility you and I can get together?" Joey said.

"Thank you, I'd like that very much. You're Italian, aren't you?" She surprised Joey.

"Yeah," Joey said.

"I like Italians," Ellen said and then began speaking the language, telling Joey she spoke five languages which she had learned while attending the finest schools in Europe. Stranskys came back, and he was upset seeing Ellen and Joey obviously enjoying each other's company. No one argued when he "suggested" they leave. As they walked out, Ellen said good night, and Joey wanted to kick himself for not getting her telephone number.

"Well, she knows who you are," Blair rationalized after Joey told him what had happened. "Maybe she'll get in touch with you."

"I hope you're right," Joey said visualizing Ellen's beautiful body walking away.

"She might just call here. I've got your number. If she calls, I'll give it to her," Blair said.

A half an hour later, Joey was ready to leave; he was saying good night to Blair when the phone rang. "Hey, Joey, it's for you!"

"Who knows I'm here?"

"Someone with a slight German accent. Take it on the extension in the hallway."

"Hello?"

"Joey?"

"I'm sure glad you called, Ellen. I've been trying to think how to get a hold of you."

"I am pleased that you wanted to. Joey, do you think I did anything wrong tonight?"

"What are you talking about?"

"Bob was furious with me. He brought me straight home."

"You were a perfect lady as far as I could see. What was he mad about?"

"I'll bet it's because he isn't Italian." Ellen started to laugh again. "He said if I wanted a Dago, I could have him."

"I can't say he was wrong about that," Joey said through his own laugh.

"I had to admit, I wanted to see you again."

"How about right now? It's still early, and I have nothing to do."

"Come on over."

Ellen gave Joey the address of her luxurious apartment off of Elmwood Avenue in one of Buffalo's nicest neighborhoods. She answered the door wearing a beautiful lounging outfit, with a lace collar and an open front, and Joey froze momentarily in the doorway.

"What's the matter?" Ellen asked, knowing she had just knocked him cold.

"I feel like I've just been taken by somebody's best punch." Joey said.

"Clinch and hold on," Joey said, wondering if she knew something about fighting.

"Pretend you're in the ring," Ellen invited and Joey accepted.

"Only thing is, I've never kissed a fighter before," Joey whispered in her ear.

"Would you like some tea?"

"How did you know I like tea?"

"I think I know a lot about you," Ellen said and led him to the sofa.

She poured from a silver tea service already there, and as they talked, Joey felt his heart palpitating, something that hadn't happened since he fell in love with Shirley. Ellen magnified Joey's loneliness, made him more aware of missing love and affection, and responded to his kiss and touch.

"I don't want to do anything that'll get you mad at me, because I am very excited about you," Joey admitted.

"I'm too excited about you to get mad," Ellen said passionately.

They kissed a kiss that took them into the bedroom and into pure rapture. Joey found himself clinging to her after their desire had been momentarily satisfied and felt a tear fall from her face to his.

"Are you crying?"

"A little."

"Why?"

"I have never let a stranger make love to me, and I'm afraid of what you'll think."

Joey really didn't know what to think. He knew she had money and could be telling the truth, but he also knew she could be a call girl like Ruby.

"Have dinner with me tomorrow night?" Joey said.

Ellen kissed him and said, "I like your lips."

"Why?"

"They're like pillows."

"Pillows." Joey laughed.

"Yes, they're soft yet firm, and that's the way they kiss me." Ellen laughed with him.

Joey took Ellen to dinner several nights in a row, and then she invited him for dinner and cooked for him. After dinner, she gave him a key to the apartment and a permanent invitation to dinner. Joey took the key, thinking it was about time he had a girlfriend again, someone he was serious about. After dinner the following evening, Joey told Ellen about Shirley, his marital difficulties, and the separation.

"Why don't you divorce her?" Ellen asked.

"I don't know. I guess I always thought once I got married, that would be it."

"Do you think she would give you a divorce?"

"I never asked her." Joey shrugged.

Ellen didn't push it, but a few days later, Joey called Shirley and said he had something important he wanted to talk to her about. She agreed to meet him for lunch. Joey found it difficult to talk to her, feeling that same coldness that instantly upset him.

"So what's so important that you had to see me?" Shirley asked.

"Well, seeing that we're never going to get back together, I was wondering how you'd feel about getting a divorce."

"You want a divorce?" Shirley asked, not surprised.

"I found someone that I think I'd like to get serious about, and I'd like to feel free to get married again if it works out."

"Who's the girl?"

"What difference does that make?"

"I heard you were going out with some German girl."

"News sure travels fast around here." Joey smiled slightly. He was quiet for a while, merely picking at his food, watching Shirley as she ate. He knew he still felt something for her, but he wasn't sure what it was.

"I'll give you a divorce on one condition," Shirley said, finishing her meal and thinking.

"What's that?"

"You give me ten thousand dollars in cash."

"Ten thousand? I don't have ten thousand dollars." Joey was shocked.

"Five thousand now, and five thousand after the divorce," Shirley bargained.

"Look, Shirley, I'm broke. I've got to have an operation on my elbow, and I don't even know if I'll ever be able to fight again."

Shirley concentrated on her coffee a moment, while Joey was thinking it probably didn't matter anyway. "Well, maybe I'll settle for five thousand," she said.

"I haven't got it, Shirley, and I don't know where I could get it," Joey said all but resigned.

"Save up. You want something, you have to pay for it; five thousand dollars is my price," Shirley said vindictively.

Joey grabbed the check saying, "Drop dead, Shirley," and walked out.

He went to Ellen's apartment, let himself in, and just waited for her to get home from work. Ellen let herself in, saw Joey, and melted into his arms.

"It's nice finding you here like this. Come talk to me while I get out of these things," she cooed.

"Do you want to go out tonight?" Joey asked, following her into the bedroom.

"Not particularly," she said.

Joey sensed she'd had a long day. "I talked to Shirley today."

"Oh?" Ellen brightened.

"She wants five grand for a divorce, and frankly, I don't have it right now."

"What if I give you the money?"

"I don't want your money; besides, you're working hard for it," Joey's pride said.

"Not really, Joey," she said slipping into a light robe. "Sit with me. I need to sit for a few minutes," she said, plopping onto the bed with a pillow.

Joey sat beside her and kissed her tenderly. "Shirley already knew about you. Can you beat that?"

"I'm glad. Joey, money is the least of my worries. My grandfather left me a large trust fund in a Swiss bank; I was the only grandchild, and being a scientist, well, he saw what was coming. The Nazis found out he was working for the British, and he died in a concentration camp. My parents are so very wealthy. They live in Santa Barbara, California, and they send me a thousand dollars a month. And I make over a thousand a month between my job and occasional modeling; so you see, I have plenty of money to help you out." Ellen smiled.

"There's something about taking money from a girl that just eats me up," Joey said shaking his head.

"Think of it as a loan. You can pay me back when you get it."

"I don't like the idea, Ellen, and she doesn't deserve it anyhow. She walked out on me!"

"We'll work something out." Ellen smiled softly, and they both dropped the subject. The following evening, Joey gave Ellen plenty of time before he picked her up for dinner. He let himself in and found Ellen there ready and waiting.

"I've got something for you," she said, picking up an envelope from the coffee table.

"What?" Joey asked, sitting beside her and kissing her lightly.

"It's for your divorce; I had my mother send it to me," she said as Joey took out a cashier's check made for five thousand dollars."

"I thought your mother didn't like the idea of you going out with a fighter?" Joey said staring at the check.

"She doesn't, but I'm over twenty-one, and I'm in love."

Joey looked at her and then back to the check in his hands saying, "This is still your money ..."

"I want you, Joey, and I know that the only thing keeping us from getting married is the divorce," Ellen said simply.

"... And I don't want your money," Joey said finishing his previous sentence. "I love you, and I don't want anyone buying me," Joey said as he tossed the check on the couch beside her and walked out. Joey jumped into his car and drove straight through to Toronto. He went directly to the home of his longtime friend, Joe Natale, where he knew he was always welcome, and for three days, he played the playboy, having a woman on each arm, trying to prove he didn't know what, trying to forget he didn't know what. Joey returned to the general hospital in Buffalo and to the operation on his elbow.

When it was over, he was visited by his family and Ellen. Joey's mother was a bit wary of Ellen at first sight, but when Ellen started speaking to her in Italian, Rosina's attitude changed completely. Before Rosina left Joey and Ellen alone, she made certain Joey knew she approved of this girl.

"I'm sorry about the other day; I couldn't know you would feel so strongly about the money," Ellen apologized, and for the first time since she had arrived, she had a chance to kiss him.

"I know you didn't mean anything by it." Joey smiled.

"I wanted to help you out and at the same time let you know how much I cared about us."

"I guess you chose a way that hurt my pride."

"Forgive me?" Ellen said her lips close to his.

"Sure," Joey said kissing her.

"I'll come and visit every night," she promised.

"I'll only be here a couple of days."

"Where will you stay?"

"I'll stay with my manager and his wife, probably until they take the cast off."

"You could stay with me," Ellen more than offered.

"Would I get the proper bed rest?"

"No." Ellen laughed easily.

Mike didn't like Ellen. She was beautiful, had money, and was a threat to take Joey away from fighting, away from him. Every time she called, Mike told her to leave Joey alone, so only when Joey called her were they able to talk. After a week at Mike's, Joey was ready to get out. He called Ellen at work and asked her to pick him up when she was through.

"Why does Mike dislike me?" Ellen asked Joey as she drove them to her apartment.

"Oh, it's not really that he doesn't like you; it's more like he's afraid of losing me. See, I'm Mike's meal ticket now. He's no kid anymore, and without me, he's got nothing going for him."

"I see," Ellen said.

"Don't let him upset you," Joey said.

"Okay, I won't."

Late that night, Joey held Ellen in his good arm and said, "Do you know how much I love you?"

"How much?" Ellen asked eagerly.

"Do you want to get married?"

"Yes. When?" she said without hesitation.

"When I can work it out, I'll be in the cast for another couple of weeks, and it'll be another month before I get back into shape. The doctors told Mike I should be fighting again in November. Anyway, you said you were thinking of moving to Los Angeles so you could see your folks more often, and I was thinking I could go down to Mexico and get a divorce," Joey said thinking.

"That would solve the money problem."

"Right, and we don't have to be in a hurry either, do we?"

"Not as long as we're together," Ellen said and kissed him.

Joey stayed with Ellen, and she cooked for him, ran his bath, washed his back, and made love to him. Joey began to feel more love for Ellen every day, knowing she really cared for him, as she cared for him. The cast came off, and Joey's training began again. They both found it difficult to cap their sexual desire for each other but looked on it as a good test for the rest of their relationship. Mike told Joey he wanted to take him back to Dallas for a few tune-up fights. Ellen planned to clear up her life in Buffalo, stop off in Dallas, and then spend the holidays in Santa Barbara with her parents. After that, she would get an apartment in Hollywood and have everything ready for Joey when he arrived. Joey drove Mike to Dallas in the station wagon. He was set to test his arm there in December. While training for the fight, Joey met Mike Tedeschi, a big automobile dealer and a big fight fan. Tedeschi was also very Italian and thought the world of Joey. He immediately introduced Joey to the Italian-American Club in Dallas, and Joey was very surprised to learn that there were 16,000 Italian families living in the area. Tedeschi was very proud when Joey won the fight by a knockout. Ellen felt obligated to give her boss ample time to replace her and spent Christmas alone in Buffalo. She and Joey talked quite a bit over the phone, but Christmas was a lonely time for him too. Joey had a good TV fan club, and after a couple of fights, he was ready for the big guys and the title.

Joey had his first fight in Odessa, Texas, against Andy Anderson in 1959. He KO'd him in the second heat (round). The Texans went crazy for Joey and his ability especially after elbow surgery. Joey was a winner, and people knew it. Joey had no trouble getting investors to back him. He met oil millionaires through his friends. Joey met the Campisi Brothers who owned two restaurants. They had oil investments. He also met Benny Binion, who owned a classy club for Western dancing and bull riding. Each of them invested in Joey. So did Jack Ruby who owned two fancy strip clubs and was Mob connected. He was the third investor. Joey was invited to the Campisis' for a fine Italian dinner. The promoters were going to promote their first black-and-white main event at their new arena. Tiger Jones, who had beaten the great Sugar Ray Robinson, was to be Joey's opponent! During the next two months, Joey won two more victories in Dallas, convincing Mike that his arm was as good as new. Mike then went about getting the "iron horse" of the day, Tiger Jones, to fight Joey. Tiger had beaten Sugar Ray Robinson and now wanted to add Giambra to his credentials for his own shot at the title hopes.

The fight was set for early March, and Joey was suddenly made very aware that beating Jones had a twofold importance. Joey knew if he beat Jones, he would once again be in the title picture, but then Mike Tedeschi told him that for a white fighter to lose to a Negro in Texas meant certain disfavor with everyone, everywhere. Jack Ruby, owner of the Theatre Lounge and the Colony Burlesque Club, and Joe Campisi, owner of the Egyptian Lounge, one of the finest Italian

Restaurants in Dallas, promoted the Giambra-Jones fight. Joey had little trouble winning over Tiger Jones, and the promoters of the bout at the Wagon Wheel Arena made a lot of money. Joey suddenly found that he had indeed become a big man in Texas. He began meeting and getting involved with wealthy oil men, contractors, and ranchers, and several of them wanted to buy his contract. Joey, having no thoughts of ever being with anyone but Mike, would always tell the interested party to talk to his manager. One man named Blackwell offered Mike fifty thousand dollars for Joey's contract, but Mike didn't want to sell it all, and Blackwell and most of the Texans wanted all or nothing. Joey was at his gym training for the big fight when Jack Ruby came in to watch his workout. While Joey was finishing his rope skipping and wiping off his sweat, Jack Ruby walked up to him and invited him to have the steak of his choice for five days in a row before the fight.

Joey said, "I didn't know strip clubs served food?"

"We don't. I only like to cook for my visiting friends from New York and Chicago. I have a nice kitchen, and I only gourmet cook. And after you eat, you can sit in my first-class booth and watch the show. I know when you see my girls, you'll be turned on, but only after you beat this Negro will I get you a date with my number-one girl, Candy Barr."

On his fifth and final day of eating the best steak and baked potatoes, Candy Barr danced especially for Joey. Joey dreamed about her every night after that. In Joey's dreams, he was her knight and she was his lady. He would vanquish all opponents for her. When the fight came, he actually had this image in his mind when he went out to fight; he was a knight doing battle for his lady. Joey won the fight big-time at the arena, which was standing room only. It was a huge success. The next day, Joey got his reward from Candy Barr. (We won't discuss what happened, but it was all good!) Jack Ruby, the Campisi brothers, Benny Binion, and two oil tycoons offered Mike $100,000 for Joey's entire contract. Mike decided it was time to go back to Buffalo. Joey had only thirty days left before his contract with Mike would run out.

Soon, Ellen called, and she had finally cleared up everything and was on her way.

"Don't get in too deep," Mike warned after Joey hung up. "You're better off forgetting about that girl; she's not for you."

"She's on her way, Mike. I care about her," Joey said, and his smile stayed.

"You're over twenty-one. I've told you that you were doing the wrong thing. I'm not going to tell you again." Mike surrendered.

Joey had met the manager of the Statler Hilton, who happened to be Italian, through Joe Campisi. He went to see him, and the man was so proud of Joey for beating Tiger Jones, he set Ellen up with the honeymoon suite and made arrangements for everything to be complimentary. The following afternoon, Joey and Ellen greeted each other at the airport as reunited lovers. He drove her to the hotel and brought her to the honeymoon suite, and for the next three hours, they utilized the place as it was meant to be utilized. Joey had Mike join them for dinner in the hotel, and then they all joined Tony Bennett, who was appearing there. Later, Joey took Ellen carbureting (dancing at a bar), and everywhere they went, Ellen found that people either knew Joey or wanted to—especially the young women.

"What's wrong?" Joey asked, watching Ellen take out her hankie and dab gently at her tear-filled eyes.

"It's all these women making eyes over you," Ellen said, her jealousy showing itself.

"You think every guy around here doesn't look at you wishing they had x-ray eyes?" Joey countered.

"I have been true to you for over four months, but I'm beginning to think you haven't been true to me."

Joey's sensitive nature came to the fore again, and he thought of the times he had been falsely accused before. "Whether you believe it or not, I have been true to you, but I'm not going to try and defend myself. I believe you, and you believe me."

"I'm sorry, Joey. It has been on my mind, I suppose."

"Tell me, is there anything else bugging you?"

"Frankly, yes. Mike is no good for you. You know he's just using you. He doesn't care about you, Joey, just the money," Ellen said putting away her hankie.

"He doesn't think a hell of a lot of you either, and I'm getting to the point where I don't know what to think anymore."

Joey took her back to the hotel, and although they spent the night together, he found himself acting differently, feeling differently. In the morning, he suggested she leave for California right away and forget about him. Ellen cried and apologized, but Joey simply told her he didn't think they could make it together anymore. He took her to the airport and kissed her tear-stained face good-bye. As he drove back, Joey felt that he didn't even want to see her again.

Joey was given an offer: the honor to become the godfather of Mike Tedeschi's daughter, Rhonda Elaine, which he gladly accepted. But after two months had passed, he and Mike decided they were too limited and they should drive back to Buffalo, tie up a few loose ends, and then move back to California. While Mike took care of business, Joey saw his family again and said good-bye again, and they began the long drive to the West Coast in the new Ford Joey had bought for the trip. A month after arriving in California, Joey and Mike had to face reality. It wasn't that they were limited in Dallas; they were still being blacklisted by the Mob. The Sunday *Los Angeles Times* printed a nice article about Joey's living in Los Angeles and questioning why the top middleweights, including the champion, were ducking him. Before Joey finished the thick Sunday edition, the phone rang.

"Joey?"

"Ellen?"

Forty-five minutes later, Joey parked in front of Ellen's apartment building off of Sunset Boulevard in Hollywood. She asked if he would like to come over for breakfast, and he thought it would be nice if they could be friends. He entered a luxurious penthouse and thought, *Someday, when I become champion, I'll be able to live like this.* After a polite greeting and a friendly hug, Ellen served them breakfast. She insisted Joey fill her in on what he had been up to and asked him many questions about his present problems. Finally, she asked, "Do you still want to be an actor, Joey?"

"Yeah, someday … Why?"

"I'm with Columbia Pictures. I have what they call a 'starlet' contract. They signed me strictly because of the way I look, and now, they're giving me all sorts of lessons."

"Hey, that's great!" Joey said happy for her.

"I had a 'get-acquainted' session with Jerry Wald, one of the top producers in the business, and I happened to mention that we were good friends. Well, one thing led to another, and he said he would like to meet you the next time you were in town."

"No kidding?" Joey said happily surprised.

"I can set it up for you, if you'd like?" Ellen offered.

"Sure. Anytime."

By the time Joey left Ellen that afternoon, he felt he had a good friend, someone he really cared for and someone who really cared for him. On the following Wednesday, he met Ellen and a friend of hers, Jack Peluso, at Nickodell's, a popular lunch spot near Columbia. Jack was a film editor at Columbia. He was a soft-spoken, mild-mannered gentleman, and it was obvious to Joey he was very much in love with Ellen. After lunch, Ellen took Joey to Wald's office at Columbia and waited in the outer office with him.

"Are you and Jack going together?" Joey asked.

"No, not really. He's been very sweet, takes me everywhere, but nothing more."

"It looks to me like he's nuts about you."

"I think he's hoping I'll grow to love him, but I'm afraid I don't love easily."

Joey was wondering if she was trying to tell him something when he was summoned into Wald's office.

"You sure you can't wait?" Joey asked feeling nervous.

"I am going to be late now as it is. Call me tonight and let me know what happens," Ellen said almost apologetically.

"Okay," Joey said and went in to meet Jerry Wald.

Joey's meeting with Wald was very pleasant. They seemed to talk about everything except motion pictures, but when Joey left the office, he had a good feeling. Early that evening, he called Ellen and told her what had happened and what he had felt. Two days later, Ellen told Joey that she heard that the studio was contemplating giving him a one-year contract with an option!

"Fighting's your game, kid; you've only got a few more years to become champion. After that, you can play around with acting for the rest of your life if you want," Mike said in response to Joey's sudden excitement.

August came and went, and Joey stopped waiting for Columbia pictures to call. He saw Ellen quite often but strictly on a friendship basis, and he and Jack were also becoming good friends. Mike still hadn't been able to get Joey a worthwhile opponent and began thinking of moving to San Francisco or even back to Buffalo again. Joey was having lunch with Jack one afternoon after spending an hour watching him edit film. When Joey finished asking all the questions he could think of, Jack changed the subject.

"Joey, are you aware that Ellen still loves you?"

"Oh, I don't know, Jack; it's been a long time."

"Just between you and me, how do you feel about her?"

"Well, you know I care for her, but I think I'm afraid to get involved again; I still think about my wife and kid a lot. Besides, I know how much you love her, and you'd be good to her. I've been hoping you two would get together," Joey said thoughtfully.

"So have I, but she doesn't want me," Jack said wistfully.

"Hang in there. I'm usually not in one place too long," Joey said, patting him on his shoulder.

Jack heard what Joey said and was grateful for the hope. September came and went with Joey staying in training for the fight that never seemed to come. Joey, Ellen, and Jack decided to have dinner at Chasen's in Beverly Hills one night. After a truly delicious dinner with the elite, Jack excused himself and went to the men's room. Ellen took the opportunity to say, "Joey, I want you to come back tonight after Jack leaves. I want to talk to you."

Ellen's request was unusual enough for Joey to immediately say, "All right," without a question.

Joey said good night and then drove away. He pulled around the corner and waited until he saw Jack come out and drive off. Ellen had already changed into a beautiful negligee by the time Joey arrived.

"This reminds me of the first time we met." Joey smiled.

"That was the most beautiful night of my life," Ellen said remembering.

Joey swallowed twice before saying, "I won't be able to stay long, Ellen. You know I'm training."

"For something that might never happen …oh, Joey!" Ellen pressed against him from her thighs to her lips.

His mind wanted to fight off the kiss, but his body couldn't. "I thought you wanted to talk to me?" Joey said when she finally took her mouth from his.

"And I do," she said, touching the pillows she felt his lips to be.

"I know how wrong I was before. I know when you're training, you abstain, and I want you to know that you were the last man to make love to me. I want you to know since the first time we met, I haven't been with another man."

"Ellen, I know you were hurt when we broke up, and I don't want to hurt you again," Joey said painfully.

"They want you to sign a contract at Columbia," Ellen said quickly.

"What?"

"There's a catch though; they don't want you to fight anymore."

Joey was stunned. For the first time since entering the apartment, he moved away from the door and sat heavily in an easy chair nearby. Ellen followed and curled down to the floor at his feet.

"I've been fighting all of my life," Joey said thinking about it.

"That's the only way they'll sign you, and acting doesn't require celibacy," she went on.

"I don't know," Joey said shaking beneath her touch.

"Break training, Joey. Break it with me, and never put it together again," Ellen enticed.

"But I've come such a long way, and I am so close," Joey said softly screaming inside.

"And I am so close," Ellen tempted, and Joey had to kiss her.

"You could get pregnant this way," Joey said as they moved into the bedroom.

"I just finished my period," she said unwilling to let anything interfere with the moment that night.

When calm settled and breathing became quiet, Joey held the clinging Ellen in his arms. Guilt filled him, and he had to tell her what he felt and didn't feel. "It's all right," she assured him.

"But I don't know if I love you, and I should love you," Joey said almost angrily.

"As long as I have you once in a while, I'll be happy."

"You deserve more than that."

"I think you're worth the gamble," she said and kissed him lightly, then fully, and then passionately.

Joey stayed with Ellen that night, and she didn't mention the contract again until he was ready to leave.

"Do you think you'll sign with Columbia?"

"I don't think I'll quit fighting yet, but I'll kick the idea around."

"It may be a once-in-a-lifetime opportunity."

"So is being champion."

Jack saw a vacancy sign in front of Ellen's building near the end of the month and decided to move in. It was a two-bedroom apartment, and he thought he could use the second bedroom as a den, but suddenly, Joey came to mind. Jack asked Ellen how she would feel if he asked Joey to move in with him, and she expressed her delight. Jack called Joey at his hotel. Joey thought it was great idea. Mike had gone back to Buffalo to see if he could straighten some things out, and Joey hated being so alone. On the first of November, the boys moved in and then went up to Ellen's for dinner. Mike returned before the end of the month and moved to a nearby hotel. He had managed to put some irons on the fire but hadn't been able to set anything definite.

Along with December came an unexpected phone call for Joey. The William Morris Agency wanted to see him. The first thing that impressed Joey was that they didn't have an office; they had a building. Several men talked to him about a television series called *The Untouchables*. They were looking for an ex-fighter to play one of

Elliot Ness's untouchable cops. Joey left the building, again knowing he would have to give up fighting if they offered him the part. The money the Columbia contract paid wasn't very much and made it fairly easy to pass up, but the money he would get for doing the series was another story.

Mike laughed when Joey told him about the interview and the series. "That would be something; you breaking the same Mob in the twenties on TV that's breaking you for real in the fifties, but, kid, you'll make more money in one fight than in playing cops and robbers all year," he said.

Joey kept training and wondering what he would do if they offered him the *The Untouchables* part. Ellen told him he'd be a fool if he turned it down, and Jack told him never to let anyone make his mistakes for him.

"Joey, could you come up for a while?" Ellen asked over the phone.

"Sure, I was waiting for you to get home. There's something I want to ask you. I'll be right up!" Joey never used the elevator, knowing the stairs were good for his legs.

When Ellen let him in, he didn't notice the melancholy look on her face, being too consumed with the question. "It's been a week since the *Untouchables* interview; does that mean I didn't get it?"

"No, sometimes those things take months; they'll probably call you in to read first and then give you sort of a screen test."

"Oh, I seem to be spending a lot of my time waiting for things to happen," Joey said feeling somewhat let down.

"Something has already happened, Joey," Ellen said, as he then noticed her somber look and tone.

"Hey, you don't look so good. What's the matter?"

"I'm pregnant," she said, turning away and moving toward the sofa.

"Who did it?" Joey callously asked.

There was a wounded look on Ellen's face for a fleeting moment before she said, "You're the only man I've been with in over a year, Joey."

Again, Joey's mind tripped back to Shirley. He couldn't help thinking how beautiful Ellen was, how many men had tried to make her, and how he was going to get the blame.

"What are you going to do? Have the baby?"

"Yes," she answered simply.

"Don't you think that's kind of foolish? I mean, you have a career, a contract. Why have a baby?"

"Because I'm pregnant."

"Yeah, but you're single, and it's going to be embarrassing to you and your family. Are you sure there couldn't be a mistake?" Joey said thinking about himself and the consequences.

"My doctor's sure."

"Ellen, you know I'm still married. If this comes out, I'll get it for adultery. The best thing for both of us is for you to get an abortion."

"I know," her logic admitted. "But that would be murder," her emotions said.

"Well, I suppose I could run down to Mexico and get a divorce; we could even get married down there."

"I do love you, Joey, and I do want to marry you, but not like this."

Joey thought for a minute and shook his head. "I don't know what else to say, Ellen."

"You don't have to say anything, Joey, and you don't have to feel guilty either. I'm more to blame than you are. I lied to you about just finishing my period, and now I'll have to pay for it."

Joey was really tearing into the heavy bag the next day, trying to release some of the unbearable frustration consuming him.

"Lay off awhile, kid. We can't afford to replace that bag," Mike said grabbing one of Joey's arms.

Joey gave the bag a final punch and then spun away saying, "Mike, guess who's knocked up?"

"Oh no, we can't handle the problems we've got." Mike groaned.

"There's no problem, Mike," Joey began and then told him the story and Ellen's intentions.

"Pack up your stuff; we're getting out of this town," was Mike's reaction.

Joey was packed by the time Jack got home from work. Jack already knew about Ellen's pregnancy and was very much the understanding friend. "Frankly, Joey, I'm glad to see you go. With you out of the picture, maybe I'll have a chance with Ellen."

"Why didn't she fall in love with you?" Joey said.

"Most people fall in love with the wrong people, it seems."

"Yeah, me too." Joey thought of Shirley.

"Whenever you get to town …" Jack said offering his hand.

"Thanks, Jack. I'll send you my address. Maybe Ellen isn't pregnant, but if she is, let me know," Joey said, shaking his hand.

"Don't worry about her, Joey. I'll take care of her."

Joey spent another lonely Christmas and then welcomed in 1960 by walking across the Golden Gate Bridge. January passed, and still there were no fights for Joey. He read that Abel Fernandez had been signed for the part in *The Untouchables* he had been up for, and he felt he had really blown the Hollywood opportunities that presented themselves. And then he got a letter from Jack. Ellen was four months pregnant. They had spent a weekend with her parents in Santa Barbara. Her parents wanted to get a paternity suit going. But Ellen said that if they did anything to hurt Joey, she would deny he was the father. Ellen continually insisted that her getting pregnant was more her fault than Joey's.

"Anything for me?" Mike asked pouring himself a cup of coffee.

"Yeah, here's a Valentine card for you," Joey said putting the letter from Jack away.

"Who the hell would be sending me a Valentine?" Mike said as he tore it open.

"Who is it from?" Joey asked the snickering Mike.

"Ah, a guy named Dominic Stillian. I met him up here when you fought Bo Bo, and he's one of the owners of the Golden Hotel and Casino in Reno. That's where I stayed for the three weeks after the Calhoun fight."

"So what's he sending you a Valentine for?"

"It's an invitation. He wants us to come there, be his guests for a while, and stay with him and his wife at their ranch house."

"Gee, that sounds great," Joey said enthused.

"Yeah, it'd be a nice change of pace; I can do business out of Reno just as I can here."

Joey and Mike took Stillian up on his offer, and through him, Joey met the owner of the classy Riverside Hotel. The man was a fan and asked Joey to be his guest whenever he wished. He told him everything would be complimentary. Joey took advantage of the Riverside Hotel swimming pool quite often, and one day, a cute sixteen-year-old introduced herself.

"Hi, I'm Maureen Mitchell. You're Joey Giambra, aren't you?"

"Yeah, are you a fight fan?"

"Well, sort of. My dad's the real fight fan, and a lot of it's rubbed off, I guess."

"I look forward to meeting your dad. Are you here on vacation?" Joey said enjoying her bubbly attitude.

"I am, but Daddy's working. He's the sound guy for *The Misfits*."

"You mean the movie with Clark Gable and Marilyn Monroe?" Joey asked.

"You must be a movie fan."

"Are they here in Reno?"

"Sure, Mr. Gable and his wife are staying at the Mapes Hotel, and Miss Monroe and her husband are staying in one of those fancy mobile homes."

"Where are they shooting the picture?" Joey asked enthusiastically.

"Oh, twenty miles or so from here. Hey, would you like to go on location one day?"

"I sure would." Joey beamed.

Early the next morning, Joey and Maureen were a part of the caravan that drove to the location site; he met Maureen's father, Phil Mitchell, and after they talked for a while, Phil introduced Joey to another great fight fan.

"Clark, I'd like you to meet Joey Giambra," Phil said, and Joey felt awed at meeting Clark Gable.

For almost an hour, Joey and Gable sat under a shade tree and talked. Joey thought Gable was just being kind when he told him that he was one of the best all-around fighters he'd ever seen and there was no doubt in his mind that Joey could become champion, but when Gable started talking about specific rounds in some of Joey's fights, he knew he meant everything he said. And they talked about Joey's son and the son Gable hoped his wife Kay would soon have. Just before Gable had to return to work, he called the still photographer over saying he wanted a shot of him and Joey together, and after the photo, as he watched Gable walk away, Joey knew he would never meet a classier guy.

After Clark walked away, Marilyn Monroe shouted, "I would like to take a picture with you, Joey."

Joey beamed. The set photographer took two pictures of Marilyn and Joey. Marilyn wanted one more shot flirting with him, but her husband, Arthur Miller, walked up to her and pulled her away from Joey's arms, and a drinking Montgomery Cliff shouted, "Man, look at that erection!"

Joey was wearing tight jeans at the time and really was turned on by how Mrs. Monroe was rubbing up against him. He was excited in the male kind of way, but smiled with embarrassment. Arthur Miller wanted Joey off the set, though he was already on his way off still smiling. Joey saw Miller taking the camera from the photographer and tearing up the film. Joey knew he might have made a wrong impression, though the cast and crew were all clapping their hands as Joey walked off the set. Marilyn was also at the fight in Reno, Nevada, at the Ballpark; Joey KO'd his opponent in the second round. Clark Gable and all the actors in *The Misfits* movie were all sitting ringside. Joey was very pleased to see them there. The Ballpark was sold out that night.

Moving forward … Joey truly liked Dominic Stilliano (Stillian) and his wife, who were very gracious to him and Mike, but fishing, swimming, and training were far from fulfilling. A month had passed and still no fight loomed on the horizon, and when months had passed, Joey became more and more discouraged. Joey was climbing to the high board at the Riverside pool one afternoon when he saw an exceptionally beautiful young girl toss her robe on a lounge chair and then gingerly descend into the shallow end of the pool. As Joey walked to the end of the diving board, he couldn't take his eyes off the glow of her reddish-black hair. He knew she had just come from a beauty parlor. Joey's swan took off and his eyes met those of the beautiful young girl, but the swan crashed into the water sending a spray all over her. A contrite Joey swam over to the laughing girl and apologized profusely. After she assured him it was all right and that no harm had been done, Joey introduced himself and the effervescent young girl told him she was Ann Margaret Olson and that she was appearing in the hotel lounge.

That night, Joey heard her sing and watched her dance. He told her after the show that he thought she was great. They met again the following day, and Joey was pleased when she eagerly accepted his invitation to dinner. He was also pleased that her night off coincided with the Silver Spurs Award dinner, where he was to be the guest presenter. Joey felt like a million bucks having the beautiful Ann Margaret as his date for the award dinner, which honored the top Western television actor of the year, and when Joey returned to her after presenting the Silver Spurs to Jim Arness, he could tell she was impressed. That night, as he drove back to the ranch house, he thought how nice it would be to get something going with her, but he knew she would soon be off on the next rung to the ladder of success, and only God knew what was in store for him.

"How'd it go?" Mike asked as he turned off the motor.

"Fine."

"What are you doing out here?"

"Thinking," Mike said.

"About what?" Joey asked getting out of the car.

"That we can't straighten things out from here and that maybe we ought to pack up and go home."

"Buffalo?"

"Yeah, maybe our luck will change."

"Why not? There's nothing to hold us here," Joey said.

The next day, Joey went to the hotel Ann Margaret was staying at and asked if she was still staying there. After Joey had given the man at the desk his name, he said, "She left a letter here for you. It read, "Joey, I have a contract with MGM pictures, and if you ever come to Hollywood, please call the studio for my phone number. I'm really happy that we had met and would like to continue our relationship." Joey was pleased; he put the letter in his pocket, thanked the clerk, and left the hotel with a cheese smile on his face knowing he'd have something to look forward to when he got to Hollywood.

*1958 Another devastating body punch Giambra
inflicts on future champion Joey Giardello*

1958 Giambra taking fencing lessons for drama school.

1958 Giambra leaving drama class in San Francisco

1958 Giambra training for a new career. ACTING!

1959 Giambra vs. Calhoun

1960 Giambra and friend and fan the legendary Clark Gable

Chapter Sixteen

Life with Paul Mitrano and Car Accident
(Ages 32–35) 1963–66

While the telephone poles were passing by in rhythm and Buffalo was getting closer, Joey decided he would call Shirley and try once more to save their marriage from the throes of death. The saintly, most understanding woman, aptly named Mary, welcomed her wayward boys home yet again. Joey called Shirley the next morning, brighter and warmer than the June sun, but there was no sun in her voice, only the lingering chill of a remembered winter.

Joey kept training. Mike kept trying, and Joey had to take back his vow never to fight in Canada again. Mike got him a match with Andy Watkins in Fort Erie, Ontario. July 12 came and saw Joey knock out Watkins in the second round. One week later, Joey received a letter from Jack Peluso. Ellen had given birth to an eight-pound baby girl in Los Angeles on July 8. Jack had enclosed a picture of Ellen and the baby. On the back of the picture, she had written, "Mother—Ellen Von Holshausen, Father—Joey Giambra, Daughter—Linda Angelica."

Tiger Jones wanted a return match with Joey in order to blot that stigma from his record, but in August, Joey beat him again, showing him it was no fluke the first time. Two weeks after the fight, Joey resolved his thoughts about the situation with Shirley, packed a bag, and flew to Reno. Dominic Stilliano put Joey in a lovely room at the Golden Hotel and Casino, and the same day Joey arrived, he filed for a divorce. For the first three weeks of the required six weeks residency to obtain a divorce, Joey trained, but several women seeking their divorces made it difficult for heavy training. Mike called as Joey's fourth week in Reno began.

"I've got you set up for a November go here in Buffalo with Rory Calhoun, so just keep up the light workouts until you get back here."

"Okay, Mike, and don't worry; you know how much I want to square things with Calhoun," Joey said.

At the end of the fourth week, Joey got another telephone call, this time from Shirley. "Joey, Joel has been asking for you. He's over three and a half years old now, and he's starting to miss not having a father," Shirley said and the trace of a whine was there.

"Well, what do you want me to do about it? You're the one who kept me from him," Joey said irritably.

"I know, and I'm sorry. Should we try to get back together and make a life for little Joel?" Shirley said, letting Joey hear her tears.

Maybe Joey wanted to hear a ring of truth in her voice, for that's what he heard. Joey flew back to Buffalo, automatically ending the divorce action and took Shirley out to dinner. They talked about many things, but mostly about their son. Gradually, they agreed upon the near future. Joey would stay at Mike's and visit his son and Shirley every evening after his workout. He would bank the money from the two or three fights, and then they would move to California and start all over again. Two weeks before the fight with Calhoun, Joey came down with strep throat. Mike wanted to postpone the fight when he heard Joey had to spend a few days in bed, but Joey figured he could make it and he needed the money. So the doctor filled him with penicillin and vitamins, and though he was weakened, Joey met and defeated Calhoun. Joey went to bed after the fight and stayed in or around it for a week, regaining his health and strength.

A phone call came from Mr. Saiia's wife. She didn't bother to go into her reasons but wanted Joey to know that the night of the Calhoun fight, Nick and Shirley were shacking up in Niagara Falls. Joey thought, *Here I am fighting sick, just to get things going again, and she's cheating.*

He didn't want to believe it, but an hour later, he confronted Shirley with what he had heard.

"It's true. Nick promised me he was going to divorce his wife and marry me, but I finally got wise. After I told him I was going back to you and then you came around, he came around, and he started getting his divorce. That's why I went to Niagara Falls with him," Shirley said, and the way she said it, Joey knew she had used him.

There wasn't anything to say. Joey got up and started for the door.

"He's got money, a house, and a Cadillac," Shirley spewed in Joey's direction.

Joey opened the front door, saying to himself, "Thou shalt not kill."

"I'd rather go with a guy that's got it, than with a guy who's still struggling!"

"Vengeance is mine sayeth the Lord." Joey went to a private detective agency and had Shirley followed. Three weeks later, he had all the evidence he needed to get a divorce in New York, on the grounds of adultery. He paid extra to have the papers served to her on Christmas Eve, wanting it that way. On January 5, 1961, Joey won his divorce by default when Shirley didn't show up. Joey was also awarded custody of his son, a rarity in New York. Two weeks before he was supposed to take custody of his son, Joel, Joey decided he wanted to see him. He had been told not to go around the house until he received all the necessary papers, so he took a friend with him to act as more of a witness than anything else. Lonny Allison was an ex-fighter and an ex-con on parole. Joey had helped him get a job when he got out, and Lonny felt grateful for any chance to show his appreciation. Joey parked in front of the house, right behind Nick's El Dorado. Lonny stood off to the side as Joey rang the doorbell.

"What do you want?" she said, her hatred boiling. "He's not your son. He never was."

"That won't fly with me, baby. He looks too much like me." Joey smiled.

"Damn you!" Shirley screeched and wanted to scream.

"Look, I know you're occupied, so just send him out here."

"If you don't get away from here, I'll call Nick," Shirley threatened.

"So call. What, do you think I'm afraid of him?"

"Okay, punchy, get out of here," Nick said filling the doorway.

"Not until I see my son."

"Get going, buster, back to the arena where all you punch-drunk pugs belong."

"I don't care if you're Mafia or not. I came here to see if my kid's okay, and that's what I'm going to do," Joey said knowing Nick was baiting him to fight.

"You don't belong here, and you're never going to get that kid," Nick said slowly reaching into his jacket.

"Pull out a gun, and I'll shove it down your throat. It's people like you who are destroying my life, in the ring and out. Why don't you go home to your wife, ya bum, before I really do something stupid?" Joey said tense and ready.

"It looks like you need convincing," Nick said, his hand starting out of his jacket. Joey was waiting to see something in Nick's hand before releasing his own weapons, but Lonny came out of the shadows, threw Nick to the ground, and started to pummel him mercilessly. Joey had to drag Lonny off of Nick before he killed him. He pulled Lonny into the car and told him to take the car to Canada and stay at the cottage and to call him at midnight at the poolroom. When the police came, Shirley yelled at the police that Joey had beat Nick up. Joey explained that he didn't touch the man and that he was a deputy sheriff of New York State.

They said, "You know Saiia's Mafia, and you have to know he carries a gun."

"Believe me, he started to pull it out after threatening me, and that's when my friend jumped in. The guy was protecting me; that's all. And I'd hate to see him get in trouble for it."

And then the neighbor across from Shirley, who liked Joey, ran over and told the police, in her Italian accent, that she had seen everything. She told them a man got out of a car, beat up Nick, and pulled off. The police officer was going to put the cuffs on, but Joey explained that wasn't necessary and he offered to go down to the police station with them to see the sheriff.

After Joey explained it all to the sheriff, he said, "Joey, all I want is the gun."

Joey told them Lonny grabbed the gun and threw it in the bushes at Shirley's house.

The sheriff said, "I want that gun, and if Lonny's got it, tell him to bring it back to me, and I won't press charges 'cause I know he was protecting you."

Both officers and the sheriff shook Joey's hand and expressed their pleasure at meeting him. This was important because at that time, there had been several murders in Buffalo and they needed the gun for ballistics. Later that evening, Joey went to the pool hall and waited for Lonny's call. While Joey was waiting, he looked out the front window and saw a black sedan parked in front of the pool hall with the engine running. Joey unlocked the back door of the pool hall to let Lonny in. He asked Lonny, "Where's the gun?"

Lonny explained, "I threw the gun in Lake Erie off the Peace Bridge and went back to the cottage waiting to call you."

"If you have the gun, I need to get it to the sheriff; if you don't have the gun, then I will tell the sheriff that. You know there's a suspicious car outside that has been parked there since I got here." Joey's assumption was that there were Mob guys waiting for Lonny to show up. Joey went to the floor safe and pulled out a grand and the ownership of the car Joey gave Lonny to drive.

"I don't want to know where you're going, but call me when you get to your destination," Joey said.

Lonny nodded. They embraced as friends, and he left. Meanwhile, Joey called Mike Scanlan to pick him up and explained everything to him. Joey got a call from his lawyer asking him to drop by the office. Joey assumed that he was going to get the papers that would allow him to go and get his son.

"Sit down, Joey," his attorney said.

During the next five minutes, Joey learned that Nick and his high-priced lawyers had the divorce put aside on appeal and that Shirley was insisting on having her day in court. With money and power against him, Joey was advised to give her what she wanted. She wanted to keep her son and a clean out-of-state divorce, and for that, she agreed to waive alimony. As he waited for the divorce action, which would take place in Birmingham, Alabama, Joey had two quick fights. He won the first over a Buenos Aires Italian but lost the second to the Bimini Islands' Yama Bahama, again feeling he was robbed. While still brooding over the bum decision and depressed by his general circumstances, Joey received an emergency call at the gym informing him that Mike had suffered a heart attack. Joey celebrated his thirtieth birthday before he was even able to see Mike.

"The doctor told me he's going to keep you a few more weeks, but you look like you're ready to go home now," Joey said cheerfully.

"Yeah, but I'm going to have to take it easy for a long time. Joey, you like Bernie Blacher, don't you?" Mike said, still unable to pull out of his own depression.

"Yeah, he's a nice guy. Why?"

"I've known him for over twenty years, and he's always been aces with me, and he thinks the world of you."

"What's on your mind?" Joey asked knowing Mike was leading up to something.

"I gotta get out of the game, kid. Doc wants me to retire; you know I'm damn near broke, and Bernie offered me fifteen grand for your contract, so if it's okay with you …?"

"Sure, Mike," Joey said, with tears rushing to his eyes. "Sure isn't going to be the same without you."

"Poor Mary, she's always had her hands full with me. Now she's gonna have to take care of me."

"Well, we can make it a little easier on her. I'll move back over to my mother's."

"Yeah, just come and see the old man every once in a while." Mike smiled at his thoughtful kid.

"You know it," Joey said, squeezing Mike's hand.

"And never forget I'm you're number-one fan," Mike said fighting tears of his own.

Joey had to float a loan from Bernie to finance his trip to Birmingham, and the chapter in his life titled "Shirley" was finally over. Bernie booked Joey a late November fight in Philadelphia against a black kid name Ike White. Even though it was supposed to be nothing more than a tune-up, Joey trained hard thinking of the last fight he had lost, and it was a good thing he did. Joey ended up determining White one of the roughest fights of his career. After the fight, Joey spent a week thinking about his situation in life, what had happened, and what he wanted to happen. He got together with Bernie and told him he wanted to go back to California, get his own fights, and gradually buy back his contract. Bernie agreed to everything, wanting nothing more than for Joey to be happy. That same night, Joey wrote Ellen a beautiful letter, telling her he would have his divorce papers in a few days and that he was returning to California and he wanted to marry her. As usual, Christmas was quite slow, and Joey's letter was delayed. Ellen didn't receive it until she and Jack returned from a weekend in Las Vegas, where they had just been married. Joey received a telegram from Ellen and Jack just before Christmas telling him of their marriage, their desire to retain his friendship, and that he would always be welcome in their home. Joey felt disheartened at first, before philosophically accepting that things were undoubtedly as they were meant to be. He spent the holidays with his family and friends and Mike saying good-bye all the while. And with the New Year, he filled his car with almost everything he owned and began his journey west, alone.

Joey checked into an apartment hotel in Hollywood, and the following evening, he had dinner with Ellen and Jack and Linda Angelica. They were beautiful people; he loved them all, and that was why he knew he couldn't see them very often. That same week, Joey went to see a well-known boxing figure named Willie Ketchum. For 15 percent of Joey's purses, Willie would act as Joey's agent and book fights for him all over the country. Joey felt good about the arrangement because Ketchum had the same deal going with a couple of other champions, and he knew all the right people. Joey's first fight for Ketchum was in Las Vegas at the Convention Center.

One night, prior to the fight, Joey was having his orange juice and watching Don Rickles's lounge act.

"Hey, Joey, remember the Alamo!" Rickles yelled from the stage.

The crowd roared; everyone was aware that Joey's opponent was Aurilio Armenta, the Mexican middleweight champion. Joey beat him by a decision. Ketchum then had Joey set to fight in Oakland for promoter Jimmy Cosenza, when the opportunity arose for Joey to fight Florentino Fernandez in Florida. Fernandez was ranked the number-one middleweight contender in the world, and Joey, because of his inactivity, was no longer ranked at all. Naturally, the Fernandez fight was desired. Ketchum called Teddy Brenner, the matchmaker for Madison Square Garden, and made arrangements for Cosenza to be paid a thousand dollars to let Joey out of the Oakland fight. Joey was in Florida preparing for the fight with Fernandez when he learned that Cosenza had reported him to the California Boxing Commission for not honoring the Oakland contract, even though he had already cashed his thousand-dollar check.

"Ah, he's just trying to hold us up for more money; we'll fix it up when we go back there," Ketchum said, when Joey asked him what was going on.

Joey found out Cosenza did want more money and he had tried to stop the bout with Fernandez. He also learned that Cosenza had his license to box in California suspended when no payoff money was forthcoming. Joey was ready and waiting and feeling a little more nervous than usual. He knew this was a big fight for him, his chance to prove that despite the inactivity, he was still a contender for the title. He also knew that at his age, pushing thirty-three, if he got beat, he could forget about ever becoming the champion.

"What's the matter, Willy?" Joey asked, seeing that Ketchum was more nervous than he was.

"Ah, it's going to be a tough fight, Joey."

"Did the odds come down?"

"Nah! Four to one he beats ya; even money if he knocks you out!"

"Don't worry. He ain't going to knock me out, but it's his hometown, so if it goes to a decision … well, they gave me the shaft here before when I fought Bobby Dykes."

"Ah, I don't understand those odds. It's like somebody knows something I don't know," Ketchum said.

When he was called to the center for instruction, Joey got his first good look at one of the roughest guys he had ever seen. Fernandez had a black five-o'clock shadow, a big parrot-like nose, and scar tissue over both eyes. Minutes later, Joey saw that face coming toward him with fists cocked beside it. Fernandez started throwing heavy punches right away but couldn't connect with the quick-moving target before him. Joey ran like a deer and didn't stop well into the third round, when with a sustained flurry, he put bad cuts under both of Fernandez's eyes. After bleeding profusely throughout the fourth and fifth rounds, in the sixth, Fernandez tried to butt Joey, who then began to slash at his bleeding eyes. Between rounds, Fernandez's corner threw in the towel.

A jubilant Joey rushed back to the dressing room, because many different people lost a lot of money that night. So picture this, Joey was in the shower and the trainers and the manager were guarding the door, and there was a knock at the door. His manager and trainers were telling him that Cassius Clay (Muhammad Ali) was there and wanted to see him. So they let him in, and when Joey got out, Cassius said, "I liked all of your moves tonight and especially the one move you showed me in the gym. I'm calling it the 'Rope-A-Dope'!"

Joey and Cassius smiled and shook hands, and Cassius said, "So long, Champ!"

Joey felt proud because he believed Cassius was speaking the truth, because he knew he had all the good moves like Joey had. Joey knew he was going to be a great fighter. It was a camaraderie and respect they had for each other. The next day, Joey found that his expenses, especially those charged to him by Willie, were way out of line. Of his seven-thousand-dollar purse, Joey walked away with only two grand. He knew he wasn't getting a fair shake. On the way back to California, Joey began thinking about how to get away from Willy Ketchum. Ralph Gambino was a boxing trainer, and his timing was perfect. Two days after Joey got back into town, Gambino approached him, saying that Frank Sinatra and Hank Sanicola, who was from Frank Sinatra's label, Reprise, wanted to buy his contract. Joey couldn't help but be excited, knowing Sinatra was a fight fan and a nice guy. He also knew that Sinatra had the money to back him in a title fight and he could help him in the acting field when his boxing days were over. That night, Joey had dinner with Gambino and Sanicola at the Plymouth House on Sunset Boulevard, in the heart of the "Strip." Joey told Sanicola he wanted fifteen thousand dollars for his contract, ten thousand of which he still owed Bernie Blacher, and he also told him about the suspension in California. They shook hands on the deal.

"When am I going to meet Frank?" Joey asked as they were leaving the place.

"We'll have a meeting as soon as he gets through singing in Lake Tahoe," Sanicola said.

Sanicola brought a friend in from Boston named Nuno Cam and gave him a piece of Joey's contract, because Cam said he could get Joey a title shot in Boston against the reigning champ, Paul Pender. "How much of my contract does Frank own?" Joey asked his new manager, Carlo Gambino.

"Frank owns half the action," Gambino replied.

Joey went before the California Boxing Commission with an attorney friend of Nuno Cam. During the next five months of hearings, Joey put the down payment on a house in Laurel Canyon and then borrowed twenty-five hundred dollars from Sanicola to furnish it. Joey became so disgusted with all the legal delays that he decided to do the talking at the next hearing before the commission. Meanwhile, Joey met John Wayne's sons, Michael and Patrick. They liked Joey, and their father was a fight fan, so they had no trouble getting him a part in Wayne's upcoming picture, *McClintock*. They signed Joey for a small part, which enabled him to join the Screen Actors Guild and to get his union card. Since the picture wasn't scheduled to begin production for a month, Joey wasn't given any specific notice as to when he would work.

Another hearing before the California Boxing Commission was held, and Joey's eloquent, impassioned plea brought a sympathetic vote to restore his license on the condition he would now honor the Oakland contract. Joey agreed, but after what he had done to Florentino Fernandez, the original opponent no longer wanted to fight. But Joey had his license back again. Paul Pender wanted eighty thousand dollars to put his title on the line against Joey, and being the champion, that wasn't an exorbitant amount to ask for. Sanicola tried to get Pender to agree to accept fifty thousand dollars, but Pender's price was fixed. Joey couldn't understand why they weren't just putting up the money, until Sanicola admitted Sinatra had nothing to do with Joey's contract and that he and Cam couldn't raise more than fifty thousand. Joey was sick about it, angry about it, but he had signed a contract and couldn't do anything about it. Sanicola set Joey to fight Denny Moyer for a new 154-pound title, the junior middleweight championship. Joey knew that Moyer was a good, sharp little fighter, and when he heard the fight was to be held in Moyer's hometown, Joey said, "Listen, I've never fought fifteen rounds before, and I haven't had a fight for five months. Can I get a tune-up fight first?"

"Don't worry, Joey. You can beat Moyer. You can punch harder and box better."

So Joey was signed to the fight, which guaranteed him six thousand dollars. He flew to Portland, Oregon. While he was training a week before the fight, he learned that Sonny Liston the Heavyweight Champion of the world, was to be the guest referee. During the week, it was apparent to Joey that Sanicola and Gambino were interested in one thing: money. His welfare meant nothing to them; he was just a piece of meat. Joey was nervous as he waited for the fight to begin and kept thinking, *Mike wouldn't have gotten me into this kind of fight without a tune-up, not after a five-month layoff.* The bell rang, and the first round featured boxing with both fighters feeling each other out. In the second round, Joey busted Moyer in the nose and had him bleeding badly. When the bell ended the fifteenth round, Joey returned to his corner without a mark on him. He moved over to the nearby Sonny Liston while waiting for his decision, shook his hand, and said, "Sonny, you did a good job refereeing."

"You won it, baby," Sonny told him.

"I hope you're right," Joey said wishing the fight had been held on neutral ground.

"The way I got it figured out, you won it," Sonny said.

The judges gave Moyer the fight by a single point. Joey returned to his dressing room wondering why he kept beating his head against the wall of the fight game. Back in the dressing room, Sanicola and Gambino started yelling about this and that until Joey finally blew his top. "Get out of here, and leave me alone! All you care about is money! You don't give a damn about me! Well, forget it! I'm through with both of you!"

By the time he got back to Hollywood, he found out he was too late for the part he was to play in *McClintock* and the company had already gone on location. Then the check he received from the Moyer fight bounced, which really put him in a bind. After a lot of arguing, Sanicola made the check good and Joey agreed to continue fighting. Emile Griffith had become the middleweight champion. Luis Rodriguez was in for the title shot, but Griffith's people didn't want him to fight Rodriguez. So they were trying to make a deal with Sanicola to have Joey fight Rodriguez first, figuring Joey could be a spoiler and stop Rodriguez.

"I hate those hit-and-run-type fighters. I'd have to knock him out if the fight's going to be in Florida."

"So knock him out," Sanicola said.

"Let's put it this way, I'll fight him, but I want a twenty-thousand-dollar guarantee," Joey said sarcastically.

Joey knew they wouldn't give him anywhere near twenty grand, but when Teddy Brenner called from New York and offered him a seventy-five-hundred-dollar guarantee and five grand under the table if he won the fight, Joey accepted. Joey flew to Florida and had the same feeling about Sanicola and Gambino as before. He knew they didn't give a damn about him, the fight, or anything; money was their god. In the first round, Joey hit Rodriguez with a left hook and right hand and almost knocked him out. After that, Joey never got near him. Rodriguez ran his legs off and just jabbed at Joey, and when the decision went to Rodriguez, Joey just couldn't complain. On the flight back to California, Joey's depression brought him into deep thought. He wanted to get into the acting field, but he knew that was another rat race and it wasn't likely he would make a living at it. By the time he landed, he had made his mind up to keep fighting, save money, and then go into business for himself.

The holidays came and went once more, and Joey prayed he would never have another year like 1962. The first thing Joey did was work out another deal with Sanicola. He walked away from his long, bitter deal with 50 percent of their gross, and Sanicola was to pay all expenses. Joey took a little time off before going back into training for a fight against an upcoming kid, Bill Miller, which was to be held in Reno, Nevada. As the fight neared, Sanicola got a call from back East. Joey Archer had hurt his ribs and had to pull out of a big fight with Joe Dinucci, and they wanted Giambra on a three-day notice. Miller's people agreed to let Joey out of their contract if he was to fight Miller next, and the following day, Joey was on a flight to Boston. He was three pounds over contracted limit, so he just stopped eating. During the flight, he got the dry heaves and was so sick, the stewardess had the pilot call ahead for an ambulance. When Joey heard about it, he thought, *Oh fine! That's all I need: reporters taking pictures of me being loaded into an ambulance a day before the fight.*

"Forget the ambulance; I'll fake it for the photographer. Just see that you and Carlo hold me up," Joey said to Sanicola.

"You look green," Gambino said.

"Thanks a lot," Joey replied sarcastically.

When he got to the hotel, Joey lay down and slowly began to shake the nausea. An hour later, he telephoned Mike in Buffalo and couldn't stop talking for twenty minutes.

"The dirty bastards. I wish I could help you out, kid," Mike kept saying.

"You can, Mike. Fly over here and stay with me, and then be in my corner tomorrow night."

"Gees, I'd love to, Joey."

"Good, I'll take care of everything; at least with you in my corner, I know I won't get killed."

Mike flew in immediately, spent the night with Joey, and then accompanied him to the weigh-in the next morning. Still not having eaten, Joey came in at 159 pounds. And when Dinucci tipped the scale at 164 pounds, Joey burned. When Gambino didn't even say anything about it, Joey looked helplessly at Mike and said, "You see what I mean?"

"When we leave here, you're gonna eat like a king," Mike said.

The doctor began to check Joey over, and when he got to his heart, he stopped. "I'm picking up a slight murmur, Joey. Have you had it long?"

"There's never been anything wrong with my heart," Joey said instantly concerned.

"This is a big one, Doc, you know, television and everything," Sam Silverman, the promoter, said.

"Yes, I'm going to pass you, Joey, but I'd get it checked out after the fight if I were you," the doctor said completely intimidated.

Joey and Mike spent the day together, talking, eating, and resting. Just before leaving the dressing room, Mike said, "If you're not right, kid, you shouldn't fight."

"I know, Mike, but I really need the money."

"Okay, kid, but if anything goes wrong, I'm gonna stop the fight." Mike nodded.

"That's why I wanted you here." Joey smiled.

For the first three rounds, Joey was not only boxing masterfully, he was in control and was able to do anything he wanted with Dinucci. In the fourth round, he hit Dinucci with a left hook that almost knocked him out. *Ah, I'm Italian; he's Italian. I'll just go ten rounds. I need the workout anyway,* Joey thought. The fifth and sixth were all Joey's, and in the eighth, he staggered Dinucci again. During the opening seconds of the ninth, Dinucci tried to butt Joey, so Joey grabbed him and whispered in his ear, "Cool it, or I'll open up on you." The tenth round went the way the whole fight had gone, and Joey returned to his happy corner.

"It was beautiful watching you work again," Mike said remembering some great moments.

Dinucci was gifted the win with a one-point split decision, and Joey began to laugh. Sanicola and Gambino swore a few times and then started back to the dressing room. "Come on, kid," Mike said.

Joey laughed all the way back to the dressing room. He and Mike were both laughing when they entered, and Sanicola and Gambino looked at them as if they were both nuts. "What the hell's so funny?"

"Ah, I was just thinking, I get no breaks … I must have had a half a dozen called like this against me, but nobody ever gave me one," Joey said through his laughter.

"Don't regret it; the price is too high for those kind of connections," Mike said.

The following morning, Joey read the accounts and the opinions in the papers. Everyone knew he had won and Dinucci had been given the fight. Joey and Mike said good-bye at the airport and flew their separate ways. During the flight, the more Joey thought about it, the more disgusted he became. Then he thought about what had happened to him since Mike retired and said, "I've had it."

"What?" Sanicola asked not hearing the unexpected words.

"Boxing is just not for me. I'm going to quit fighting."

"You can't quit; you've got a contract." Sanicola laughed.

"You just try and stop me," Joey said quietly and returned to his pensive state.

Joey had a cousin named Carl, who had recently transferred from San Jose to Los Angeles. Carl was an executive for the Executive Car Leasing Corporation, but being family oriented, soon found he didn't like living alone. Joey immediately had Carl move into the house with him on Laurel Canyon. When Joey told him he was quitting the fight game, Carl offered Joey a job as a fleet manager. Joey soon learned that being a fleet manager meant he was a glorified car salesman, but he enjoyed the work, and he and Carl got along great. Joey didn't train at all for a month, but he missed working out and decided to join the Beverly Hills Health Club. While working out a couple hours a day, Joey met a lot of actors and soon became friends with Ricky Nelson, John Saxon, and Tony Franciosa. Once again, Joey's mind became set on acting, and he enrolled at James Best Acting Studio in North Hollywood. The next month went by with Joey working, going to the health club, and going to acting classes. He had momentarily settled into a place between happy and unhappy, when he received a phone call from Ralph Gambino saying, "Joey, I want to see you."

"Oh yeah, what about?"

"To see how you're doing and talk a while."

"Well, you caught me on a good night. My cousin and I are just sitting around watching television. Do you remember where I live?"

"Sure, I'll be over in a half hour," Gambino said.

Half an hour later, Gambino arrived, and he wasn't alone.

"Come in," Joey said and watched a big, heavyset arm breaker follow Gambino. Polite introductions were followed by a few minutes of general conversation before Gambino got down to cases.

"Joey, Hank and I want you to start fighting again."

"Look, I won't say no chance, but you have to give me a hell of a good reason why I should," Joey said after a moment of thought.

"Oh, I could give you a lot of good reasons, but I'll give you a couple of the happier ones. First of all, you're too young to quit. You've got a few years of big money ahead, and second of all, Hank and I are sitting on a piece of paper. If you don't fight, you're leaving us holding the bag."

"Excuse me," Carl said and left the room, seemingly disinterested in what was going on.

"Now, we've left you alone. You needed a vacation. The rest has done you good, but now Hank and I figure it's time to take some money off of your investment."

"Money, money, money," Joey repeated.

"Lemmie tell you something. If you don't fight, you won't be able to do anything," Gambino said, coming to the edge of his chair.

"Just what does that mean?" Joey asked, feeling the hairs on the back of his neck stand up.

"You know what it means, but come on, let's not talk about that. Sure we want to make money, but what's the matter? You don't?"

"No, I … I want to make money. Tell you what, Ralph, I'll fight on one condition: you guys let me buy back my contract."

"There's no way in the world you can buy it back," Gambino said firmly.

"Then there's no way in the world you're going to get me to fight," Joey said just as firmly. "And besides, you lied about Sinatra to get me to sign that contract in the first place, so you've really got no beef coming!"

"Joey, don't make me get back to things we could do to you," Gambino said with no veil over the threat. The arm breaker took it upon himself to stand up and stretch, and then Carl took it upon himself to come back into the room carrying an Italian Beretta.

"I think it's about time you gentleman be on your way," Carl said.

Gambino looked from the gun to Joey. "That's not going to be easy to forget."

"Neither is he," Joey said gesturing to the arm breaker.

After they left, Carl sat down. "That wasn't any fun at all," he said rubbing his stomach.

"I'm sorry it happened."

"Joey, forget about fighting again. You're not a kid anymore, and I don't want to see you get hurt."

"What am I going to do, Carl? These are bad guys."

"They're not going to do anything to you, not if they want you to fight."

"I hope you're right, Carl. Anyway, we'll wait and see."

Joey continued his routine while waiting for something to happen, and something did happen. First John F. Kennedy was assassinated, and then Joey watched Jack Ruby, who had co promoted the fight with Joey against Tiger Jones in Dallas almost five years earlier, kill Lee Harvey Oswald on national television. But the rest of 1963 passed by with no further word from Sanicola or Gambino.

One night as he returned home from his acting class, Carl came out before he finished parking. "Joey, let's go down to the Body Shop. You know, Herb's been there a week, and we promised we'd stop and see him."

"Why not?" Joey said, and Carl got into the car.

Less than a mile from the house, on Sunset Boulevard, was a strip joint called, the Body Shop. Herb Eden, a comedian and a good acquaintance of theirs, was working as the master of ceremonies. Joey ordered an orange juice, while Carl ordered a drink, and they sat through several girls waiting for Herb to do more than just introductions.

"… And the star of our review is, Miss Angel Carter!" Herb said before darting into the shadows.

The other girls were okay, but when Joey saw Angel Carter, he sat up. Angel was dark and beautiful and the possessor of a fantastic body. She not only moved as she stripped, she danced, and Joey thought, *That's class.* As Angel paraded out onto the ramp that split a third of the audience, wearing only a black sequined G-string, Joey smiled his biggest smile. Angel hovered over Joey's table, and he wished the smile she had returned had really been for him instead of just another customer. Joey clapped his hands red after Angel finished, and then Herb joined them for a drink during intermission.

"Hey, Herb, can you introduce me to Angel?" Joey asked hopefully.

"Sure, you like that, huh?" Herb said.

"Just tell me she isn't married."

"She isn't married, at least not that I know of." Herb laughed.

A few minutes later, Angel appeared wearing a red jersey dress that fit her like another layer of skin. She spotted Herb's signal, smiled in Joey's direction, and started their way. Joey stood up when Angel was still two tables away, and she liked that. She stayed with Joey and Carl while Herb went through a ten-minute routine, and then she gave Joey her phone number and told him she was off on Mondays. When Monday rolled around, Joey took Angel to dinner and a show. They hit it off beautifully, and so Angel invited him to dinner at her place the next evening, before she had to go to work. Joey couldn't help being surprised when he found out Angel was a cook. Joey picked her up after work, took her home, and stayed with her that night. The next day, Angel cooked dinner for Carl and Joey at their place.

"Would you like to live with me?" Joey asked simply.

And Angel's simple reply was, "Sure, I'd like to live with you. Before the weekend arrived, Joey had Angel moved in completely, and Carl felt like a third thumb, despite Joey telling him he wanted him to stay. Joey got together with Ralph Gambino and told him he wanted to give Sanicola part of every purse until he bought his contract back. They agreed, figuring it was better than nothing, convinced that Joey wouldn't fight any other way. Joey then went back into training. Out of the blue, Joey Bishop contacted him and asked him if he would like to be on his show.

"I'd love it!" Joey said.

"Okay! In about two weeks, we'll get a script together and do a thing together," Bishop said.

Joey was excited about getting his first acting job, and when he made his debut on television, he was good and he was happy. Joey kept training, kept his job, and really started to pursue other parts as an actor.

"When do you want to fight?" Gambino asked Joey when he would be ready.

"Don't push it; I'm making arrangements with Dewey Fregetta in New York," Joey said.

"The European agent?"

"Yeah, I figure I'll tour through Europe for six months to a year and come back with a bundle."

Joey kept working himself back into shape, and then he got a call from Fragetta.(a fight promoter) "Get your passport, get your shots, and be ready to leave in a couple of weeks."

Joey went to Hank Sanicola's office to get their deal in writing. They talked for a while, and then Sanicola said, "Okay, I'll have my lawyers draw up the papers."

A week later, Joey was working out when Billy Stephen, a heavyweight contender approached him. "Joey, do me a favor. I'm fighting Ski Goldstein in New York in a couple of weeks, and I'd like you to go a few rounds with me just for speed."

"Sure, just as long as you don't throw any bombs at me," Joey said, knowing and liking Billy. Joey made Billy chase him around the ring for three minutes, and then between rounds, he saw Gambino come into the gym. Again, Joey started dancing around the ring, and again, Billy chased him. As they neared the end of the second round, Billy caught Joey with a left hook that really stung him, and Joey instinctively lashed out with a right that caught Billy flush and knocked him down. Billy jumped up quickly, and Joey yelled, "Remember, I'm doing you a favor!"

Billy started to laugh, and that ended their workout.

"Hey, Ralph, when am I going to get the papers Sanicola promised me?" Joey said, climbing out of the ring.

"Look, Joey, stick with us. I think we can still win the championship."

"We made a deal, Ralph."

"Hank and I think you look too good. We don't want to sell you back your contract."

"Either you stick to the deal, or I don't fight," Joey said flatly.

"You have to fight; you're in too good of shape." Gambino laughed.

"We've been down this path before," Joey said walking away.

"You're biting off your nose to spite your face!" Gambino yelled after him.

Joey collected all his gear and went home. Angel had already left for work, but Carl was there for Joey to use as a sounding board.

When Joey finished his tale of woe, Carl said, "Joey, I've told you, the best thing for you to do is to forget about boxing completely."

"Sometimes, I think you're right. I'm so confused, Carl," Joey said and began to relax.

"Stay with acting and forget about fighting. Meanwhile, the car business will pay the bills."

"Yeah, I guess you're right."

"Now for my news, I'm going home. I don't like Los Angeles very much. It's just too crowded and too fast. I'm transferring back to San Jose." Carl grinned.

"Aww, Carl, you sure you're not leaving because of Angel moving in?"

"Believe me." Carl smiled.

After Carl left, Joey and Angel enjoyed their privacy, and the months began to roll by. Joey became disenchanted with his job at Executive Car Leasing shortly after Carl left. It just wasn't the same around there without him, Carl Maggio, Joey's nephew. And when people kept promising him acting jobs that never came through, Joey again became disenchanted.

"How would you like to live in Vegas?" Joey shocked Angel by asking.

"I'd love it," she said excited.

"I was thinking I'd lease the house and we'd get a nice big apartment in Vegas, and if you don't mind, I'll have my sister Lena come stay with us."

"I don't mind, but do you think she'd want to?"

"Yeah, the last letter, she wanted to know if I had room here."

"Then we'll get settled and send for her," the agreeable Angel said.

Joey immediately contacted some people he knew in Las Vegas and was suddenly working for a liquor company during the day and campaigning at night for Burt Leavitt, who was running for city commissioner. Soon, Lena arrived. She was an attractive, five-foot-three-inch girl, with reddish-brown hair and hazel eyes. But her slim figure was now thin, and it was apparent to Joey she needed a good rest. He had never seen her so nervous before, so unsure of herself, and he was glad he had sent for her.

Angel was enjoying a vacation, but finally, Joey lined her up an audition. He lined her up several auditions before it dawned on him that Angel didn't want to work; she wanted to play housewife. After a while, Joey decided it was time to get both girls back on their feet. He lined up another audition for Angel and told her if she didn't get a job, he was going to send her back to Hollywood. Then through friends, he got Lena into the culinary union and a hostess job at the Sahara Hotel. Barry Ashton auditioned Angel, and though he couldn't place her in Las Vegas at the time, he did offer her a good job in Reno.

"I don't want to go, Joey," Angel pleaded.

"It's best for you right now, Angel. I think we both have to find out if it's 'absence that makes the heart grow fonder' or if it's 'out of sight, out of mind.'"

Joey drove a protesting and crying Angel to the airport. She said good-bye, wondering if they would ever see each other again, and he said good-bye, wondering if he meant it. Several months came and went, during which Burt Leavitt lost the election for city commissioner, and Joey found that he just wasn't happy with his job at the liquor company. Every Wednesday night, the Silver Slipper held fights, and Joey became a regular at ringside. He would be introduced, jump up into the ring, take a bow, and then settle down to enjoy the action. One night after the last bout ended, a man introduced himself as Paul Mitrano, a wealthy businessman from North Easton, Massachusetts, just outside of Boston.

"Joey, would you like to fight again?" he asked.

"Once in a while, I think about it," Joey answered.

"Well, you're still young enough, and you still look good. I could do a lot for you," Mitrano went on.

"Yeah, I've heard that before." Joey chuckled.

"I'm serious, Joey. I've been involved with a couple of fighters, but I've always wanted a guy with your talent to fight for me," Mitrano said in a tone that made Joey listen.

"Look, I wouldn't mind getting back into the ring, but I've had too many problems with the people who own my contract. I won't fight for them anymore, and they won't let me buy back my contract."

"Who are they?" Mitrano wanted to know.

"Hank Sanicola, Ralph Gambino, and Nuno Cam."

"I know Nuno from Boston, and I'll bet I can work something out with him." Mitrano brightened.

"If you can do that, you got a deal. One thing I've got to tell you, I haven't been doing too well here financially, and I've got a few bills I'd like to pay before I leave town."

"How much are we talking about?" Mitrano asked.

"About a thousand dollars."

"All right, I'll send you a check and an airline ticket in about a week if I can make the arrangements with your contract. I'll pick you up from the airport, and we'll go from there." Mitrano nodded.

Joey gave Mitrano his address and phone number, but deep down, he thought the guy was just blowing smoke and he would probably never see him again. The next day, Mitrano called Joey and said, "Can you join my wife and I and a few friends for dinner tonight?"

"Sure," Joey said starting to believe the man might be on the level.

That night, Paul Mitrano introduced Joey to his wife and friends, one of whom was Arty Stroll, the vice president of Soundex Radio Company in Brockton, Massachusetts, Rocky Marciano's hometown. After a while, Stroll said, "You speak very well, Joey. I might have a job for you if you come up to Boston."

Before the evening ended, Mitrano slipped Joey two hundred dollars. "This should tide you over until you hear from me."

"Thanks, Paul," Joey said, wanting to refuse, but needing the money too much.

Joey waited anxiously for Mitrano's call, but when a full week passed, he began to think the guy had just felt sorry for him and had fed him and slipped him some money just to give him a lift. Two days later, Joey got a long-distance call from Boston.

"Did you get the check and ticket yet?" Mitrano asked.

"What are you talking about?"

"I sent you a check and ticket; it should be there by now," Mitrano said.

"Maybe it is. I haven't checked the mailbox in a couple of days."

"Go see. I'll hang on," Mitrano ordered.

Joey dashed downstairs, and sure enough, there it was. He ran back up.

"I got it, Paul."

"Good! When can you leave?"

"In a few days. I want to pay my bills, and I'll have to get my sister set up so she can stay here."

"Okay, so call me when you're ready, so I can pick you up at the airport," Mitrano said.

"Right. By the way, what kind of deal did my ex-managers ask for?" Joey said, finally feeling that his luck had changed.

"Double what they paid, thirty grand," he said matter-of-factly. "And, Joey, from my point of view, I got a good deal."

"Thanks, Paul. You won't regret it."

Joey moved Lena in with a girlfriend he had been seeing once in a while and then put his furniture in storage. He squared away his accounts and then called Angel in Reno, just before he left. "I'm going back East again, Angel. I don't know what's going to happen, and I don't think it's fair for me to tie you down."

"You've found somebody else," Angel said flatly.

"Believe me, Angel, there's no one else. I'm going back into training. I've got to fight; all I've ever really wanted was to be champion of the world. I am a darn classy fighter, and I can make some money and then go into business for myself. I'm sick and tired of working for other people and having them tell me what to do all the time."

"Let me wait for you, Joey," Angel pleaded.

"Aww, come on. You're young and beautiful. There's no sense waiting for something that might never happen."

"Please, Joey, I'll wait!"

"Forget about me, Angel, and have a good life," Joey said and hung up.

Paul Mitrano, his wife, and Arty Stroll were waiting for Joey when his plane landed in Boston. On the thirty-mile drive to North Easton, Joey became aware of how much he had missed the beauty of New England. It was September 1965. It was Indian summer weather, and though he was going to a strange town, he felt like he was going home. Joey quickly realized that Paul Mitrano hadn't boasted. He had a beautiful home, two Cadillac's, and two Chevrolets and owned two Chevrolet agencies, a piece of a bank, and a dog track. He also owned a lot of real estate, property in Puerto Rico, and a summer home in Cape Cod. Joey spent the first week at the summer home, fishing, swimming, and running his thirty-four-year-old legs back into shape. After that, it was back to North Easton and his regular training routine. Mitrano had adopted his wife's son from a former marriage but never had any children of his own, so when he began calling Joey "son," Joey began thinking of him as another father figure in his life; it was all very natural. Mitrano put Joey on the payroll for two hundred and fifty dollars a week, so Joey could feel independent, and shortly thereafter, Arty Stroll had Joey join Rocky Marciano and Willy Pep in public relations for the Soundex Radio Company. They would go out, shake hands, sign autographs, and entertain distributors in general. For this, Joey received another two hundred and fifty dollars a week. Suddenly, making five hundred dollars a week with no expenses since Mitrano was taking care of everything, Joey was getting flush. Near the end of October, Mitrano threw a big party for Joey in North Easton. Over two hundred people, employees of the bank, car agencies, and friends, showed up. Joey felt very proud, being treated the way he was and not even having fought yet.

"Even if you don't become champion, you're such a good, clean-living young man, I'm proud to have you live with us."

"Thanks, Paul. I can only promise you I will do my best."

Joey began talking to the photographer who had been taking pictures all evening. The man turned out to be a postman and introduced Joey to his beautiful wife and very cute daughter. Joey took the daughter out a couple of times during the weeks, and when Joey asked to skip going to Cape Cod one weekend, Mitrano was very understanding. That day, an hour later, Joey got a call from Al Siciliano, a distant cousin of his from Boston. He was home on a four-week vacation from the Los Angeles Police Department. Al had been a boxer for a while, and when Joey was in LA, they would often get together and work out.

"I thought maybe you could use a sparring partner for a few weeks," Al said hopefully.

"What's the matter? A week with the family all you can handle?" Joey laughed.

"You know it." Al laughed with him.

Joey had Al stay with him at the house, knowing Mitrano wouldn't mind, and Joey's girl brought a girlfriend along for Al. The four of them spent a marvelous weekend together, and when the Mitranos returned, they were delighted to have Al stay there to spend the remainder of his vacation. Joey and Al worked out and sparred every day together, and Joey started looking really sharp. November ended, and no sooner had Al left for California than Mitrano brought home the word that Joey was set to fight Nino Benvenuto in Milan, Italy, in January 1966. Joey was again ecstatic, because Benvenuto was ranked the number-two middleweight contender in the world, and Mitrano assured him if he beat Benvenuto, he would get a shot at the title. Joey automatically increased his training to the maximum and was bringing his body to the absolute peak of condition when he received a call from the postman's daughter.

"I missed my period, and I think I'm pregnant," she said calmly.

"You've got to be kidding," Joey said, panic sounding through his voice.

"It's okay. I know a doctor who will give me the abortion, but it'll cost five hundred dollars and I don't have it," she said quickly.

"I'll get back to you," Jocy said and hung up. Joey had the money but decided he should talk to Mitrano about it first.

"Tell her I want my doctor to see her, and if she's pregnant, we'll take care of her."

When Joey told her what Mitrano said, she refused, and Joey realized she was just trying to shake him down.

"She probably just wanted some extra money for Christmas," Joey concluded when he told Mitrano her reaction.

"What's the world coming to? Incidentally, about Christmas, how would you like to spend the holidays at your folks'?" Mitrano said shaking his head.

"Gee, I'd like to Paul," Joey stated.

"Sure, then after the first of the year, you just come back here and we'll take off for Italy. Joey made plans to go home, and two days before he was to leave, Mitrano said, "Joey, come down to the agency with me. I've got a little Christmas present I want to give you."

"Gee, Paul, you don't have to; you've been so good to me as it is."

"Just come with me, okay?" Paul smiled.

"Okay," Joey said grinning like a kid.

On the way to the agency, Joey was thinking about the money he had put away, the presents he would be able to buy, and the things he would be able to do for his family. When he arrived at the Chevrolet agency, wondering what his Christmas present would be, Mitrano took him over to the service area and pointed to a brand-new Chevrolet Caprice worth over five thousand dollars.

"I hope you like it, son," Mitrano said, and Joey put his arms around him and began to cry.

"Nobody ever gave me anything like this before; you've been more of a father to me than I've ever dreamed of having, even as a kid," Joey sputtered.

"And you're the son I've always wanted," Mitrano said with his own voice cracking.

"Now come in the office and sign a few papers, and then you can drive it home."

The next day was Sunday, and Joey was anxious to begin the drive home, but not so anxious as to miss church Mass. It was raining as he drove the new car to church, and he thought, *What a lousy day to go on a trip!* But after Mass, the sun came out, and as he drove back to the Mitranos for breakfast, he thought, *It's going to be a nice day after all.*

Before leaving, he called his mother and told her he was on his way. "Be careful. The weather's bad out here," Rosina cautioned.

"Okay, Ma, I'll be careful." Joey wished the Mitranos, "Merry Christmas and a Happy New Year," and then packed up the car and headed for the Massachusetts Turnpike. He had no sooner reached the turnpike, than the weather began to change. It started to get dull and gray as it did often in the East during the winter. Joey was driving from Boston to Becket, Massachusetts, the first leg of the trip. As he approached the highest point of the turnpike, he could feel it getting colder, and when the car began to fishtail, he knew the morning rain had turned to ice. Joey immediately slowed down, but suddenly, he drove into a snow flurry. Within a few minutes, the flurry became a blizzard, and Joey could barely see in front of him. Since the traffic was light, he decided to pull over to the side of the road and put on his safety belt. He hit a sheet of hidden ice under the snow on the right side of the highway, and the car shot into a skid with the nose pointing to the center of the guardrail. Joey's previously fifty-mile-an-hour speed instantly registered eighty on the speedometer, and the guardrail was coming closer. Joey kept playing the brakes and started to pull the wheel to the right when the engine cut out. Without the motor running, he lost the power steering and power brakes, and he began to panic, knowing if he went through the guardrail, he would fall onto another highway a long way beneath the one he was on. He turned the wheel with all his might, and finally, the car began to straighten out but then continued past the center going into another sideways spin. Joey looked past the nose to the side of the mountain which was beginning to come at him.

It'll be better to hit the mountain than go through that guardrail, Joey thought as he again tried to straighten out the car. Suddenly, a three-foot drainage gully appeared at the base of the mountain. "Oh my God!" Joey screamed aloud and thought, *If I hit that ditch, I'll turn over.* The brand-new Chevrolet Caprice bounced through the gully and crashed into the mountainside. Joey's back hit the back of the seat, and then his chest was crushed against the steering wheel. His face skidded over the dashboard, and his head went through the windshield. The car ended up half in the gully and half on the highway, and sparks and smoke were coming from the engine which had made its way under the dashboard. Joey slowly straightened up and shook his head from the blow that reminded him of someone's best right punch to his forehead. He shook his head again trying to bring clarity to his thinking and his eyes, and he began to feel a warm wetness running freely down his face. He raised his hands to his head and gingerly touched himself. He knew his head had been split wide open.

"Jesus!" he called, as he began struggling to get out of the smoking, sparking car fearing it might blow up.

The door was jammed, and Joey's pain came alive as he jiggled the handle and pushed against the door. The door finally popped open, and Joey was propelled out into the gully, landing on all fours. Blood was raining down his face and splattering the snow before his eyes, and Joey knew if he didn't get help, he would bleed to death.

Still on his knees, he scooped up a pile of snow and placed it high on his forehead in an attempt to at least stop the bleeding. Joey learned in the Military this knowledge to stop bleeding and military instinct kicked in. The shock of the cold stung for an instant, but the hot blood in the cold snow quickly turned the snow in his hands to red slush. Joey crawled up the embankment and knelt at the edge of the highway. In the distance, he could see headlights which were growing larger. He tried to get to his feet but couldn't make it, so he settled on his knees and began to wave his arms. The car stopped, and a man got out. He took one look at Joey and then went quickly back to his car. He opened the passenger door, took the baby from his wife, and told her to slide behind the wheel. He secured the baby in the car crib and told his wife to drive carefully to the highway patrol station a few miles ahead. He grabbed several diapers and then closed the door saying, "Have them send an ambulance!"

"Can you hold this?" the man asked, after placing a diaper on Joey's head.

"Yeah," Joey said, his hand replacing the man's hand.

"I want to take a look at your car," the Good Samaritan said already on his way.

A few moments later, he returned, and Joey said to him, "It was smoking before."

"Looks okay now. Let's use it for shelter," the man helped Joey down the slight embankment, sat him sideways on the driver's seat, and then replaced the already blood-soaked diaper with a fresh one.

"How bad is it?" Joey asked.

"I don't know. It looks pretty bad, but these things usually look worse than they are. Don't worry; we'll get you to a hospital." Joey saw the accident-curious people slowing down, and by the time the ambulance arrived, three other cars had smashed into each other, and the light traffic was quickly backing up. Joey had already begun to slip in and out of consciousness, but he knew he was on a stretcher being put into more of a station wagon than an ambulance. As a patrolman began driving him away from the scene, Joey saw a couple of tow trucks and hoped no one else had gotten hurt.

"Hey, fella, keep talkin' to me!" the driver shouted.

"What for?" Joey asked.

"As long as you're talking, I know you're all right!"

"Okay, how bad am I?" Joey said adjusting the diaper that didn't seem to be doing much good.

"All I know is it's a head injury, and you've lost a lot of blood, so you'd better keep talkin'!"

Joey couldn't remember if he had said thanks to the man who had stopped and helped him. He hoped he had. He hoped the guy would come in and see him, so he could thank him properly.

"Hey! You're not talking! Hey!" the driver called out.

The patrolman muttered something under his breath, but Joey's semiconscious state wouldn't allow him to speak. He felt the ambulance station wagon speed up a bit and knew the driver was going faster than he wanted to, but Joey didn't have any idea how long it took to reach Saint Luke's Hospital in Becket, Massachusetts.

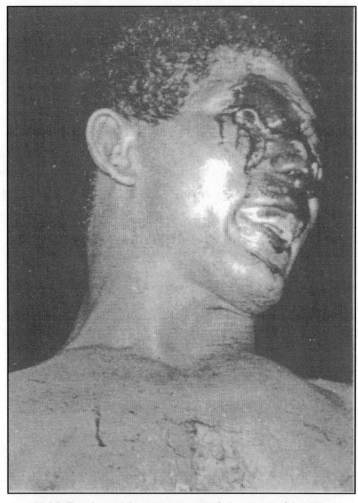

*1962 Boxings biggest upset of the year Giambra
destroyed Fernandez despite being a 5-1 underdog*

who never was...

IMPRESSIVE: He tears Fiorentino Fernandez to shreds

The two judges were Mob judges so every one was booing and screaming, 'It's a fix, it's a fix'. The commission found that when they collected the [score]cards they'd been tampered with.

"They'd erased and changed the numbers."

Giambra, left the ring to a defiant standing ovation and there had to be a rematch. The New

knocked out Jimmy Herring in four. "Frank Sinatra was in attendance when I knocked out Jimmy Herring. They called it the 'Battle of the Beauties'.

"The old garden held 14,000," Joey recalled, "but when I fought him there was standing-room only and a crowd of 15,500. And it was all

was just a little guy. They came at me and worked me over [in sparring]. I weighed in at 157 1/2lbs so had to drink beer and whisky to put on the weight.

"But I came into the ring that night with great determination, especially after those liberties in sparring. Bobo was a good inside

despite a string of great wins he still get a title opportunity. He notched solid victories over Al Andrews and Ch and fought a draw with heavy-hitti Calhoun, but still no nearer.

He beat Jimmy Welch and lost to C an upset. He faced some heavy bang time and ranks Calhoun up there with of them.

"Rory Calhoun, he broke my jaw second round [of the first fight]. It's a between him and Kid Portuguez [whi the hardest].

Far from allowing defeat to discour he came back to beat Giardello in which launched a two-fight rivalry wit mean machine, Ralph "Tiger" Jones.

"I beat Tiger Jones twice. I knocked on his feet. Oh, he was tough. He wa fighter, though – he didn't fight dirty. gentleman.

"I thought I beat him decisively bo The promoter was a man called Ja [who would later gain all-time not gunning down supposed President assassin Lee Harvey Oswald].

"Jack was also a fantastic cook – h us steak every night."

However, Giambra also highligh shocking side of Ruby. "He was a k conceded.

The second win over Tiger Jo preceded by revenge over Calhoun. losses to Yama Bahama and Farid S him once more on the outside looking

A eighth-round knockout victory ov puncher and No. 1 middleweight c Florentino Fernandez pulled him b contention, however.

Ring magazine reported: "The features were smeared with blood. Th refused to let him go out when the be the eighth."

iambra was finally rewarde

1962 Giambra lands a solid right hand to Fernandez face

1962 Giambra with one of his best friends Frank Godfriend

1962 VICTORY party at Caesars Palace
Las Vegas after the Fernandez fight

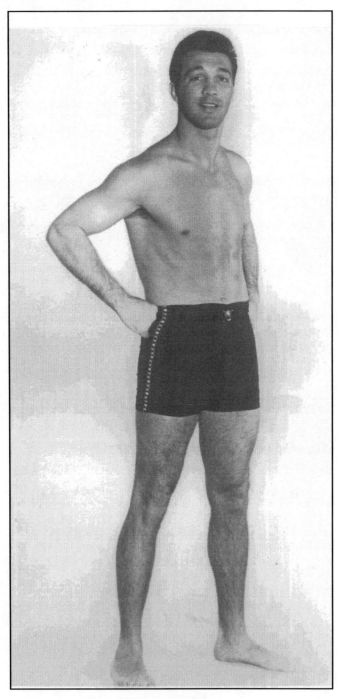

1964 photo shoot

Chapter Seventeen

After the car accident that nearly killed Joey (Age 35) 1966

Joey regained consciousness as he was being shifted from the operating table back onto the gurney. *I know my life passed before my eyes, but I'm alive,* he thought. They wheeled him into the X-ray room, and after concentrating on his head, they x-rayed every part of his body. He remembered being shifted into a bed and a nurse giving him a pill, and he knew the pain in his head was what woke him up.

Joey's pain came quietly from the corners of his eyes, which were looking at the needles in his arms and the bottles hanging alongside him. At around six in the morning, the priest Joey remembered receiving the last rites from the priest and he came into his room with a nun walking beside him, and the priest asked, "Mr. Giambra, would you like Communion?" the priest asked.

"I haven't had Communion for a long time, Father. I'm divorced," Joey admitted softly.

"Have you married again?" the priest asked.

"No," Joey said.

"Then you may receive the Sacraments."

The nun left the room, and the priest heard Joey's confession, allowed him to say his penance, and then gave him his Communion. When the priest left, Joey's tears came faster, not from the pain, but from fear. *I'm going to die. That's why he gave me Communion. I'm never going to be champion,* he thought.

Joey began feeling sorry for himself. He wasn't leaving anything behind to be remembered by; he wasn't leaving anything to his son, to his family, to anybody. A short time later, a doctor came in to see him and said, "How do you feel, Champ?"

"You know who I am?"

"Certainly, I know who you are. You are Joey Giambra, the fighter. Your face is very famous, and I myself have seen you fight many times on television."

Joey heard a distinct Jewish accent and knew this man had to be a good doctor to be working in a Catholic hospital. "Tell me the truth, Doc. How long have I got?" Joey said in no mood for chitchat.

"What sort of Italian are you?" the doctor chided.

"I'm Sicilian. Why?"

"I thought you might be Calabrese. I understand they are supposed to be very hardheaded, and you have a very hard head," the doctor said, his smile broadening.

"What does that mean?"

"You are a very fortunate young man. I have seen pictures a state trooper took of your automobile. It's a miracle you weren't killed."

"What's the verdict?" Joey asked tentatively, beginning to think he was going to die.

"Your head was badly cut, you lost a great deal of blood, and you have a fractured rib."

"Is that why I hurt when I breathe?"

"That's why. I will tape it up for you if it's too uncomfortable," the doctor offered.

"No, it's all right."

"You won't be able to fight for three or four months, but if you take care of yourself, you will be as good as new."

"Are you sure I will be able to fight again?" Joey asked, thinking it'd be impossible the way he felt.

"I see no reason why not," the doctor assured him.

"When can I go home?"

"In about ten days, we must keep you under observation, build you up a bit, and make certain no blood clots form. It is nothing for you to be concerned about."

"Thanks, Doc." Joey sighed with relief, and the doctor left the room.

Later that day, Joey made up his mind and called Paul Mitrano. He told him what had happened. Mitrano was very upset and said he would be there in the morning. He, his wife, and the driver all came into the room, and Mitrano was sick seeing Joey in such a condition. He blamed himself and felt responsible for everything.

"Paul, it wasn't nobody's fault. It was the weather and an accident. Anyways, I've got good news. The doctor said I can fight again in about three months."

Mitrano looked at Joey, shaking his head slowly. "Joey, as far as I'm concerned, you are not going to fight again, ever," Mitrano said.

"What?" Joey said, his head turning and eyes opening widely like a small boy being told he could never eat candy again.

"I think all of this has been kind of an omen. I think it means you're not supposed to fight again," Mitrano said slowly but firmly.

"An omen?"

"Look, Joey, you're all right now, but if you were to get hit in the head or something else was to happen … No! I will not be responsible. You must forget about fighting," Mitrano said laying his hand on Joey's. He shook his head again.

"But look, Paul, you put so much money into me, the contract, the car, putting me on the payroll. I can't pay you back for all that unless I fight."

"Forget it, Joey. You pay me back by getting well, and that's final."

Joey stared without speaking for a long time and then breathed deeply and slowly shrugged. "Well, you're my manager, and whatever you say is okay, I guess," Joey said.

"You can still spend the holidays with your folks, and when you're ready, we'll take you to the airport. Okay, Champ?"

"Yeah, I guess so," Joey said turning his head to face the blank wall.

"Don't worry about the car, Joey. It was in your name, and it was insured. Consider the insurance money as a Christmas present," Mitrano said unclasping Joey's hand.

295

"Yeah, Paul, thanks." Joey never looked away from the wall and didn't know when Paul left the room. Soon, Joey drifted into sleep. The first few days in the hospital went by slowly, but as the bandage on his head grew smaller and his strength returned, he became anxious to leave, to get away from the antiseptic smell of the hospital, to get away from the knowledge he would never fight again. Joey clasped Paul in a hug of heartfelt gratitude when they said good-bye at the airport. Tears began to form in Joey's eyes, but he quickly shook them away, smiled, and strode toward the plane. He walked firmly as a major contender should, even though he knew he was beginning a new, strange journey away from a world where all he had ever done was seek the championship of the world and into a world that to him was unknown and for which he was completely unprepared. The Mitranos stood where Joey had left them. They watched him wave a last wave and then disappear into the airplane.

"Here, what's that all about?" Paul asked as he brushed a tear from his wife's cheek.

"Oh, Paul, it's so sad. His dream to become a champion ... he worked so long, so hard. His dream is dead ... and he could've been champion, except that wasn't his fate, and now he'll never fight again."

Paul put his arm around his wife and pulled her close to him. "Maybe he won't fight in the square circle, honey, but he's still a fighter, a champion," he said looking up at the plane. "He didn't get the crown he went after in boxing, and God knows, the outside world is a much bigger ring than any he has ever fought in, but you can bet Joey Giambra will fight, because that's his nature." He turned back to his wife. "Don't worry about him, and don't count him out. Just when you think he's down for the count, he's up and swinging again. I know his heart."

They turned and walked away slowly from the terminal as Joey's plane climbed away from Boston toward an uncertain future which would include a move west to Vegas. It was a future which would hold more pain, sorrow, and heartbreak.

The plane Joey was on was a gambling charter plane for the Sands Hotel and Casino. Joey had a beautiful suite and all the complimentary privileges. Paul had two other partners who owned three charter planes. Paul's partner, Arte Straul with Soundex Radio hired Rocky Marciano, Willie Pep (all-time featherweight champion), and Joey as goodwill ambassadors for Soundex auto radio (as stated before). They worked two days a month, but got $5,000 for Rocky, $3,500 for Pep, and $2,500 for Giambra. All of Joey's checks from Soundex and the car agency were deposited in Paul's small bank. In less than a year, Joey had accumulated $50,000.

When the plane took off, it veered to the right. Joey had a window seat, and the sun came through the window. He blinked a couple of times and thought, *Hey, I'm still alive. I'm holding $55,000, and I'm still sharp, so even if I am unable to fight anymore, I have people talent!*

When some of the wise guys on the plane recognized Joey (Boston fans), they invited him to dinner and to maybe do a little gambling. Joey had gotten their names and called them after two days. He wanted to be alone, to gather himself, and planned to not gamble too much.

From the car crash, just before the surgery, they shaved his head near the hairline. This was a month earlier. A month later, Joey was able to comb over his hair, where it looked like Julius Caesar, covering his ten-inch scar. Joey was people-watching and walking around the casino. The craps tables were screaming; the twenty-one tables were packed. Joey went to get a massage, and he was completely relaxed. He wouldn't gamble until the third day.

The third day came, and Joey was ready. He called the Italians he had met on the plane and told them he was ready for craps. They met at a craps table. It was four deep at this table, and the dice finally came to Joey. Joey had taken $500 from his stash and took out $10,000 in markers. He was running scared, having only $45,000 left. He took a break from the tables and ate a hearty meal. Joey went back to chase after his losses (as many gamblers do). He had gotten another $10,000 marker, leaving him $35,000. It was now 12:00 AM, midnight, and Joey caught up with his two Italian friends. They said, "Let's go to a private table with a $200 minimum."

Joey agreed to lose $10,000 more. He felt if he had half his money, he was still good. So they went to a private table, and Joey got the dice. And what a streak Joey had! He held on to the dice for thirty-five minutes, had accumulated $40,000, and was still rollin'! Joey figured he was $10,000 ahead and would quit after his roll. Joey's two Italian friends said, "Let's go for broke!"

It was now Sunday morning, 1:00 AM. Joey grabbed the dice. He had $500 on the come out, and $100 on the seven and eleven. Joey made three passes, and on every pass, he doubled the bets. On his near-last roll, he had covered on the table $2,000 on the come-out line. Joey doubled his bet to $4,000 on the come-out line, $200 on the seven and eleven. Incidentally, each made the seven! The two Italians were throwing chips every pass. Joey put their tips on his second rack. Now came the big one. He bet $5,000 on the come-out line and $1,000 on seven and eleven. Joey made the seven again. He didn't know how much he had won so far and was getting exhausted, so he put $200 on the come out, $100 on the seven and eleven, and rolled a four. He then placed $15,000 on the hard four. He held the dice with his thumb, index finger, and forefinger; he put a twist on the toss, and in slow motion, one die was two. The second die twirled into a spin and landed on a two! Hard way four! If you know gambling, then you know it pays nine to one. The table went completely wild. There was a huge crowd watching and screaming as the two Italians kept saying, "The uncrowned champion, Joey Giambra! Joey, Joey, Joey!"

The stickman counted his chips to over $250,000 plus $30,000 in markers paid off. The table had lost $1,000,000 on Joey's roll. He tipped the dealers $1,000 a piece. Believe it or not, Joey was, and still is, the uncrowned champion after all!

This unknown future Joey would face, not confident he would win, but sure in the knowledge that he would fight the fight. In his mind, he would always be a fighter, able to shake off stunning blows and come back still fighting. In his mind, Joey was still the uncrowned champion of the world.

I dedicate this poem to Paul Mitrano, who died of cancer before this book was published.

The Honest Man
By Joey Giambra

I will not cry; I will but speak.
I will but tell of what I seek.
A friend I need, he will not come.
To your demand, I will succumb.
The time grows near to what I ask.
It seems to be a burdensome task.
Yet in my mind, I know it well,
Far down below, it cast its spell.
Why must it be?
I ask the sea.
As waves come crashing over me.
My life will end,
I won't pretend.
I need the word of thee to send.
Should I live and stay alive;
Perhaps it's best to just survive;
And then somehow I'm sure I can …
Solve the puzzle of finding,   The Honest Man

This poem won the National Library of Poetry Award.

"Beautiful, touching, inspiring," Julio Iglesias.

"Blockbuster," Don Diguilio, *Review Journal*

"A sizzler," Jerry Vale

"Joey's fighting back again," Matt Hamilton, The *Sun*

"Close second to The Great Sugar Ray," Ralph Pearl, *Las Vegas Sun* and TV Host

Deserted by his father as a young child and raised in utter poverty, the young Joey Giambra decided to become the middleweight boxing champion of the world.

He almost made it. Almost.

This is his story. It's the story of a naive young man who always expected the best from people, but who invariably received less. It's the story of his women; the story of his fights with Bo Bo Olson, Tiger Jones, Joey Giardello, Jimmy Herring, Tony Amato, Rocky Castellani, Andy Anderson, and many, many others; and the story of his dreams, his heartaches, his frustration, continuous run-ins with the Mob, the stars who knew and loved him, and the accident which would forever deny him the final fight to victory.

This is the story of Joey Giambra, the uncrowned champion of the world.

It's the best human interest story regarding boxing, the Mafia's control of fighters and their futures, and the hardships of the golden era of boxing. But it's also a story of a man who didn't play by the rules, a human interest story of family, love, integrity, and the Mafia, through the eyes of an uncrowned champion—the uncrowned champion, Joey Giambra.

Some of the many great "hooks" (pun intended) that *The Uncrowned Champion* has in its amazing story are:

A large Italian family and their struggles during the golden era in New York …

Famous and infamous Italian Mafia members trying to kill and then saving the young Giambra, despite him not joining the Mafia or playing hardball with them.

Mobsters, such as Vito Genevese, Carlo Gambino, Frankie Carbo, and Jack Ruby were all key figures in Giambra's career.

He had real friendships with major sports figures such as heavyweight champions Rocky Marciano and Cassius Clay (Muhammad Ali), who was taught the "Rope-A-Dope" by the young Giambra. A middleweight champion, Sugar Ray Robinson, openly stated he would not fight Giambra for the title when he was champ! Lightweight champion Willie Pep and baseball legend Joe DiMaggio were two of Giambra's biggest fans!

And being in Hollywood during the romantic era of the 60s, he acted in movies, such as *The Misfits*, and the television series, *Mission Impossible* and *The Joey Bishop Show, a* comedy series, and had friendships with Ann Margaret, Marilyn Monroe, Clark Gable, and Joey Bishop.

The original self-published book, *The Uncrowned Champion*, has sold over 100,000 copies since its release in 1980, despite not being marketed. A lot of material was left out of the original book due to sensitivity to subject matter, people, and many situations. This *is the new book* and is a *tell-all*. These "hooks" are some of the many people and situations that play a significant role in the adaptation of Giambra's life story and make it a *best-selling book and motion picture*!

1968 Beverly Hills charity event

1968 Beverly Hills

1968 Photo shoot Giambra enters Hollywood

1968 Photo shoot in Hollywood

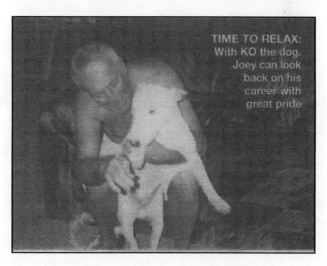

2005 Giambra with his loving dog Kayo

JOEY GIAMBRA
Middleweight contender
Buffalo, New York

1949

Jun 28	Lee Phillips	W KO 2	Fort Erie, New York
Sep 27	Jesse Bradshaw	Draw 4	Buffalo, New York
Nov 7	Manuel Gonzalez	W KO 2	Buffalo, New York
Nov 15	Danny Junior	W KO 2	Buffalo, New York
Nov 29	Henry Powell	W KO 1	Rochester, New York

1950

Jan 10	Johnny Miller	W KO 1	Buffalo, New York
Feb 7	Leroy Nolan.	W KO 2	Buffalo, New York
May 2	Sammy Daniels	W KO 3	Buffalo, New York
May 16	Rolly Johns	W PTS 6	Buffalo, New York
Aug 15	Gordon Hunt	W KO 2	Buffalo, New York
Sep 16	George Warren	W KO 2	Buffalo, New York
Sep 25	Pete Pauline	W KO 1	Buffalo, New York
Oct 30	George Andrews	W KO 1	Rochester, New York
Nov 14	Jesse Bradshaw	W PTS 8	Buffalo, New York

1951

Feb 20	Eddie Grambell	W KO 1	Buffalo, New York
Mar 7	Kid Bartley	W KO 3	Detroit, Michigan
Mar 28	Mel Reed.	W KO 1	Detroit, Michigan
May 22	Johnny Cesario.	L PTS 8	Buffalo, New York
Jun 6	Albert Adams	W PTS 6	Detroit, Michigan
Sep 5	Herbie Phillips	W KO 3	Detroit, Michigan
Oct 11	Maurice Jenkins	W KO 1	Long Island, New York
Oct 18	Hurley Sanders	W PTS 8	Long Island, New York
Nov 3	Charley Early	W KO 7	Brooklyn, New York
Nov 24	Gus Rubicini.	W PTS 8	Brooklyn, New York

1952

Jan 12	Mario Moreno	W PTS 8	Brooklyn, New York
Feb 22	Sal DiMartino	W PTS 8	New York, New York
Jun 6	Tony Amato	W RSF 8	New York, New York
Sep 15	Billy Whye	W PTS 6	Syracuse, New York
Oct 13	Joey GiardelloL	PTS 10	Brooklyn, New York
Nov 11	Joey Giardello.	W PTS 10	Buffalo, New York

1953

Jan 26	Danny Womber	W PTS 10	Brooklyn, New York
Feb 24	Bernard Docusen	W RSF 7	Buffalo, New York
Mar 10	Otis Graham	W PTS 10	Brooklyn, New York
Apr 18	Danny Womber	W PTS 10	Buffalo, New York
Apr 27	Otis Graham	W PTS 10	Toronto, Ontario
Jun 20	Tuzo Portuguez	W PTS 10	Buffalo, New York
Sep 28	Tuzo Portuguez	W PTS 10	Buffalo, New York
Oct 28	Don Oates	W RSF 1	Cleveland, Ohio
Dec 4	Jimmy Herring	W KO 4	New York, New York

1954

Jan 6	Bobby Dykes	L PTS 10	Miami Beach, Florida
Feb 12	Italo Scorticini	W PTS 10	New York, New York

1955

Apr 5	Andy Anderson	W KO 7	Galveston, Texas
Apr 26	Jimmy Welch	W PTS 10	Houston, Texas
May 5	Sherman Williams.	W KO 6	Austin, Texas
Jun 11	Jimmy Watkins	W KO 2	Killeen, Texas
Aug 26	Carl (Bobo) Olsen	L PTS 10	San Francisco, California

1956

Jan 25	Al Andrews	W PTS 10	Norfolk, Virginia
Apr 6	Johnny Sullivan	W PTS 10	Syracuse, New York
Jun 13	Johnny Sullivan	W PTS 10	Syracuse, New York
Aug 3	Rocky Castellani	W PTS 10	New York, New York
Oct 19	Gil Turner	W PTS 10	New York, New York
Nov 27	Sammy Walker	W PTS 10	Buffalo, New York
Dec 10	Rocky Castellani	W PTS 10	San Francisco, California

1957

Mar 19	Al Andrews	W KO 6	Oakland, California
May 14	Chico Vejar	W RSF 7	Oakland, California
Jun 21	Rory Calhoun	Draw 10	Syracuse, New York
Aug 6	Jimmy Welch	W KO 6	Reno, Nevada
Aug 26	Rory Calhoun	L PTS 10	San Francisco, California

1958

Apr 14	Andy Mayfield	W PTS 10	Oakland, California
Jun 30	Joey Giardello	W PTS 10	San Francisco, California

1959

Mar 19	Andy Anderson	W KO 2	Odessa, Texas
Apr 1	Al Andrews	W PTS 10	Dallas, Texas
May 18	Ralph Jones	W PTS 10	Dallas, Texas
Nov 30	Orlando DiPietro	W PTS 10	Long Beach, California

1960

Jan 19	Woody Winslow	W PTS 10	Fresno, California
Apr 21	Pal Lowry	W KO 2	Reno, Nevada
Jun 11	Kid Alfonso	W KO 2	Ft. Erie, Ontario
Nov 15	Rory Calhoun	W PTS 10	Buffalo, New York
Dec 6	Ralph Jones	W PTS 10	Buffalo, New York

1961

May 6	Yama Bahama	L PTS 10	New York, New York
Nov 23	Ike Whito	W PTS 10	Philadelphia, Pennsylvania

1962

Mar 10	Farid Salim	L PTS 10	New York, New York
Apr 2	Everardo Armenia	W PTS 10	Las Vegas, Nevada
Apr 28	Florentino Fernandez	W RSF 8	Miami, Florida
Oct 20	Denny Moyer	L PTS 15	Portland, Oregon
	(Vacant W.B.A. Light-Middleweight Title)		

1963

Jan 19	Luis Rodriguez	L PTS 10	Miami Beach, Florida
Apr 6	Joe De Nucci.	L PTS 10	Boston, Massachusetts

77 fights - 65 wins -10 (many controversial) loses - 2 draws - 31 knockouts
Giambra was NEVER knocked out or stopped in his entire career!

Manufactured By: RR Donnelley
                    Momence, IL USA
                    May, 2010